GW00459141

THE
FASHION
BUSINESS

Also by Sidney Packard

The Fashion Markets: Case Studies
Strategies and Tactics in Fashion Marketing
The Buying Game: Fashion Buying and Merchandising
(with Miriam Guerreiro)
Concepts and Cases in Fashion Buying and Merchandising
(with Nathan Axelrod)
Consumer Behavior and Fashion Marketing
(with Abraham Raine)
Fashion Buying and Merchandising
(with Arthur A. Winters and Nathan Axelrod)
Readings in Consumer Motivation in Fashion
(with members of the F.I.T. faculty)
Start Your Own Store
(with Alan J. Carron)

THE FASHION BUSINESS

DYNAMICS AND CAREERS

SIDNEY PACKARD

Florida Atlantic University, Boca Raton

HOLT, RINEHART AND WINSTON

New York   Chicago   San Francisco   Philadelphia
Montreal   Toronto   London   Sydney   Tokyo

Book production by Annette Mayeski
Jacket and book design by Gloria Gentile
Photo research by Marion Geisinger

Library of Congress Cataloging in Publication Data

Packard, Sidney.
    The fashion business.

Bibliography: p.
    Includes index.
    1. Clothing trade.   2. Fashion.   I. Title.
TT497.P25   1983   687'.0973   82–12154

ISBN 0-03-054026-7

9 0 038 9 8 7 6 5 4 3

Holt, Rinehart and Winston
The Dryden Press
Saunders College Publishing

To the women in my life,
Beverly, Lauren, Margery,
Roslyn, Samantha, Vanessa

PREFACE

A logical approach to a decision to seek a career in fashion marketing is to study the manner in which fashion products are conceived, produced, and finally sold to ultimate consumers. *The Fashion Business: Dynamics and Careers* is intended to make just such a study possible.

After reading this text, a student should be able to:

- correlate current fashion industry practices with past events
- list the leading functions of major fashion and fashion-related jobs
- describe each fashion sector's dimension of importance to the total industry
- relate the process by which fashion apparel is conceived and placed in the hands of ultimate consumers
- show knowledge of the fashion industry's importance to our economy
- identify and realistically evaluate fashion marketing as a career opportunity

The text is organized in five parts:

I. Fashion Marketing (Chapters 1–2)
II. Sources of the Materials of Fashion (Chapters 3–6)
III. The Manufacturers of Fashion Apparel (Chapters 7–9)
IV. The Retailers of Fashion Apparel (Chapters 10–12)
V. The Auxiliaries of Fashion Merchandising (Chapters 13–16)

Each part progresses from the broadest aspect, background, and/or conceptual meaning to specifics. This system gives the reader a solid foundation in understanding how and why fashion marketing and production are unique. This comprehensive treatment in each part also offers students the opportunity to participate in action-based classroom sessions. For example, after all have read Part III, an instructor and students can hold a seminar to develop conclusions about the future of domestic apparel producers, the importance of apparel imports, and what stand our representatives should take in negotiating international trade agreements. This type of classroom activity leads to relating the material to other disciplines and, above all, produces stimulating sessions enjoyed equally by instructor and students—sessions that create the best atmosphere for learning.

A considerable part of the text (four chapters and two appendixes, plus shorter sections elsewhere) is specifically devoted to areas of employment (geographic and business organizations), how and where to apply for a job, job specifications, and job descriptions. This information is as practical as it can be made.

Although some texts on fashion include readings from other sources, I have deliberately avoided them in this book. The reasons are: (1) to present the material in one writing style for easiest comprehension; (2) to concentrate on my own experience in the fields of textiles, retailing, manufacturing, and resident buying. Actually, the text closely follows the way I present the course to students.

Entry into the world of fashion can be a very fulfilling choice. A fashion career can offer professional status; personal growth; the opportunity to express creativity; career maneuverability, with experience leading to options in related specializations; foreign travel (buyers); often, the ability to be mobile, work in a selected region; better than average level of pay, consistent with responsibility and performance.

If this text explains clearly how fashion products flow and the competencies required of fashion professionals, it will have fulfilled its purpose: to help readers make wise career decisions.

I gratefully acknowledge the help of the organizations that permitted the inclusion of their ideas or materials. I also express my gratitude to my students, past and present, whose interest and curiosity were the motivation for this text.

I extend particular appreciation to the following, who were most generous with their advice or material: American Apparel Manufacturers' Association; Frederick Atkins, Inc.; Sam Bleiweiss, EMBA Mink Growers Association; Joseph Brodie, Loomskill, Inc.; Henrietta Dabney, American Clothing & Textile Workers Union; Judy Feller, Independent Retailers Syndicate, Inc.; Shelly Foote, Smithsonian Institution; Jim Gordon, United Merchants & Manufacturers, Inc.; Michael Kemp, Textile Economics Bureau; Walter Mankoff, International Ladies' Garment Workers' Union; Herbert Miller, Tanners' Council; Carl Priestland, Priestland Associates; Will Rapp, Tanners' Council; William Rosenthal, Business International Asia/Pacific, Ltd.; Tom Slasinski, Celanese Fiber Marketing Company; Sweetland Smith, Fashion Institute of Technology; George Wind, American Textile Manufacturers Institute, Inc.; Dr. Arthur A. Winters, Fashion Institute of Technology.

ix

I am grateful to the following, who read the manuscript at various stages and made constructive suggestions: Mary Anderton, Memphis State University; Gregory Arend, Nassau Community College; Alfred Berkowitz, C.U.N.Y. Kingsborough Community College; Barbara A. Buchner, Daytona Beach Community College; Karen J. Covington; Sara Cox, University of Wisconsin–Stout; Roberta J. Fedorko, Prospect Hall College; Newton Godnick, Fashion Institute of Technology; Fred P. Green, Broward Community College; Rosalyn Halperin, Miami Dade Community College; Marvin Hirshfeld, Temple University; Cheryl L. Jordan, Oregon State University; Charlene Parsons, International Fine Arts College; Nancy Ann Rudd, Ohio State University at Columbus; Bob Salem, Associated Merchandising Corporation; Barbara Schlinkert, Purdue University; Sylvia Sheppard, Fashion Institute of Design and Merchandising; Linda Stone, Bauder College Specializing in Career Education; Shirley Stretch, Texas Technical University; Harriet Lagrange Swedlund, Oregon State University; Arthur A. Winters, Fashion Institute of Technology; Margaret A. Zelinko, Marshall University.

I also express my thanks to Robert Rainier, H. L. Kirk, and Pamela Forcey of Holt, Rinehart and Winston.

S.P.

CONTENTS

Contents

Contents

Contents

11   Fashion Retailing   196

12   Career Opportunities in Fashion Retailing   205

Contents

DIAGRAMS AND CHARTS

THE
FASHION
BUSINESS

Fashion is an indispensable ingredient of the industry of the United States, one of the main reasons for the movement of tremendous amounts of goods from producers to ultimate consumers. Our 1982 Gross National Product was more than $3 trillion—and no small part of this huge sum came from our desire to be in fashion, a desire that affects us all.

The term *fashion* is often restricted to clothing, but it has a more comprehensive meaning. For example, before the energy crisis, at least, trading in an automobile with 35,000 miles—when it is just broken in—for a newer model was succumbing to the attraction of being fashionable.

Fashion in economic terms is defined by some as a luxury on the theory that product purchase decisions should be made only on the basis of intrinsic value. This theory presupposes rational purchase motivation to replace products that are worn out or inoperable. But people do not live by logic alone. The human psyche seeks values that express more than the level of

PART I

FASHION MARKETING

utility—more than mere maintenance. How else can one explain the frequent replacement of still serviceable apparel or the widespread purchases of products that are used as symbols of social and financial status?

To discuss fashion comprehensively, we first consider its broadest aspects, then the subject of our narrower focus—fashion apparel. Our major topics are the movement of apparel, the channels of distribution, the procedures and practices of purveyors, and, finally, fashion as a career.

Part I is an overview of the importance of fashion to the economy and a basis for the discussions in the chapters that follow. The objectives of this part are to show the following:

1. The importance of fashion to the economy
2. The meaning and diffusion of fashion and fashion apparel to consumers
3. The marketing structure of the fashion apparel business

Photo Salvatore Ferragamo, Inc.

1

FASHION AND FASHION APPAREL

The word *fashion* is a good example of a word with various meanings; it can be an encompassing term as well as a specific reference. For our purpose, we choose the definition that puts it into truest perspective: that which is *accepted* by a substantial group of *people* at a given *time* and *place*.

The reader can properly respond to this definition by saying that fashion is no more than the current culture. What people believe in, what they practice, what they accept adds up to the culture of the time, the fashion of the age. Culture and fashion can indeed be synonymous, but what consumers accept is influenced both by the availability of technically feasible products and by the broad influences in the environment that affect consumer attitude about those products. The broad influences on consumer selection are technology, economic conditions, social values, current cultural attitudes, and political climate—conditions that marketers do not create. The marketer must nevertheless employ strategies that respond to these conditions by offering products with the features consumers want.

INFLUENCES ON FASHION ACCEPTANCE

Technology

Every period of culture is influenced by forces that create a unique environment. Norms or standards of taste, need, beauty, and manners vary with time and to a large extent depend on what is available. People now over sixty could not enjoy television, fly in jet airplanes, wear clothing of man-made fibers, or purchase TV dinners when they were of college age. In fact, more than 90 percent of the products now in supermarkets have been developed during the past twenty-five years.

Technology constantly broadens our knowledge as well as controlling the nature and assortment of market offerings. Science has advanced so rapidly in recent years that the variety and abundance of new products are staggering. Space technology alone has helped create over two thousand new consumer items that range from medicine to apparel.

Product availability is only one important aspect of this scientific era. The successful marketing of goods also depends upon the means of educating potential customers and establishing the place where products can be purchased. Therefore, of no small consequence are the achievements that produced modern systems of communication and transportation.

Communication in the last quarter of the twentieth century is instantaneous and includes the use of satellites that offer the opportunity to speak to any part of the world without the use of cables. Dissemination of information about new products is no longer limited by distance.

Transportation affects both the availability of desired products and the place at which they can be purchased. Multitudes of United States citizens traveling in Europe since the development of the jet airplane, for example, help condition tastes to accept the products of foreign lands, and the means of rapid transportation make the products of other countries almost immediately available to us.

Technology is thus a strong fashion influence because it determines what, when, and how fashion material is available. Money can only buy what is technically possible, and fashion can only be exercised when ideas and products are physically within our grasp.

Economics

Income and fashion are intertwined tightly; each supports the other. The importance of fashion in any country is dependent upon its economic health. Where money is tight and incomes are low, the practice is to make things do, and the main concentration is on utilitarian values. In countries that enjoy a high standard of living, fashion becomes more important and is constantly changing. It takes more than a subsistence standard of living to practice fashion within the context of our definition, which incorporates the *elements of change*. In countries of generally low family incomes, fashion is decreed by custom and reflects fashion stagnation: a limited number of manufacturers and product sameness to a point of monotony.

4 The population of the United States enjoys an annual per capita income of approximately $9500, an economic state that permits most people to exercise varying degrees of discretionary power and, above all, to discard usable possessions (the factor of **consumer obsolescence**—rejection of presently owned goods in favor of something newer, even though the old still has utility value) in favor of the newer and more fashionable. An economy characterized by the capacity of many people to spend money for preferences encourages a life style in which the assortment of needs is often motivated by whim, attraction, and, not infrequently, impulse.

The definition of *need* is certainly debatable. Classically, a need is a necessity. But need can also be an urgency to

- Fit into a peer mold
- Enhance sexual desirability
- Show social position
- Achieve a state of betterment

What is certain is that more purchasing power broadens needs. When one has the ability to spend, mobility becomes greater, and the resulting exposures nourish appreciation and acceptance of a more comprehensive list of needs.

The products and practices of the nation reflect our economic status; in fact, they are unique to this society. Witness the following:

- Although we are one-fifteenth of the population of the earth, we consume one-half of its total product.
- Our homes have more telephones than bathtubs (nearly one-third of the telephones of the world are in the United States—95 for every 100 households).
- Ninety percent of our homes have television sets.
- The average U.S. citizen uses 21,000 gallons of gasoline and $6300 worth of clothing in a lifetime.
- There are more than 120 million cars on the highways, with a million discarded yearly.
- Well over 60 percent of families have a yearly income of over $15,000.

Engels' law that as income rises the proportion spent on necessities declines and the proportion spent on luxuries rises applies to the pattern of our daily life. Most of the people of the world cannot practice fashion to the same degree.

Another consideration is that it takes the spending concentration of many people to total our current yearly rate of retail sales of over $1 trillion! But this achievement demands many product variations to negate usable product ownership for newer versions; that is the foundation of fashion—and a necessity for the economic health of the United States.

Social values

Within each society there are standards of behavior and social levels based on a system of rating people in some order of superiority or inferiority. Although this is not the place to discuss the justice or equity of social ratings, we are interested in interpersonal relations insofar as they relate to fashion. Extremes of social relations can be illustrated by the dominance of men over women in many Far Eastern countries compared with the roles of women in the United States. One can observe that where there is a strong imbalance of the role of   **5** one sex over the other, particularly when women are confined to housewifery, fashion does not flourish.

Surveys have shown that in the United States married women strongly influence the final selection of many different kinds of items when they and their husbands are making buying decisions. These items include cars, cameras, television sets, and other major purchases. In other words, women are important decision-makers in our society, in contrast to many cultures, where they are limited to influencing decisions for those products that are eaten, worn by themselves and their children, or related to some aspect of the welfare of the children.

In United States society, despite continuing disparities of economic and other rewards, the social balance between the sexes is sufficient to permit wide latitude of choice by either, or both, about almost every aspect of life. In this environment, fashion feeds on the number of people who can express freedom of action.

In our social relationships we tend to conform to the manners and dress of our peer groups, as well as to those groups in which we aspire to membership. This is a force natural to all groups, from junior high school to senior-citizen clubs. Standards, measurements, constraints, practices, and values are all part of our interactions with others. Few are sufficiently individualistic to go down the road alone and opt for products or behavior that deviate from accepted norms.

Every consumer act is influenced by other people. No one ever makes a purchase in isolation; decisions are affected by social interactions. Human beings are part of a social structure, and everyone, in varying degree, wants to live up to the expectations of society and to compare favorably with others. Fashion, therefore, has a strong relationship to our social values and practices.

These are some examples of fashions that are group standards:

- Shiny and beaded fabrics for disco wear
- Three-piece suits for business wear
- Shorts, pleated skirts, short-sleeve and sleeveless shirts for tennis wear
- Blazers
- "Alligator" Izod–Lacoste four-button knitted shirts for casual and playwear

These items by no means reflect the choices of all consumers, but they have relevance to peer-group standards. Not all businessmen wear three-piece suits, but there are sufficient numbers who do accept them as most appropriate for occasions that "demand" conformity of dress to be considered a group.

Culture

Long-held values, attitudes, and symbols or artifacts handed down from generation to generation are components of culture. All countries, and even

different regions of the United States, practice particular customs or use products that have some historic special characteristics; one can think of any country
6 of the world and list at least one unique fashion; for example,

- Greece: skirts for men
- Scotland: tartan plaid kilts for men
- India: saris for women
- Japan: kimonos for men and women
- Mexico: ponchos for men
- England: umbrellas as part of male attire

The architecture of each country also retains some lines, shapes, details, or colors indicative of the long-term fashion or culture of that country:

- England: the thatched cottage
- France: the provincial cottage
- Japan: the country cottage with rice-paper screens

In the United States, by reason of its size and population diversity, there are groups that have characteristic preferences. Consider these examples:

- Amish: wear black appropriate to the nineteenth century
- Texans: wear cowboy clothing (ten-gallon hats and string ties)
- Californians: wear cardigan sweaters like capes and prefer casual clothing
- Hawaiians: prefer colorful prints

These values or practices can be traced to regional availability, climatic conditions, economic necessity, pride, or ethnic origin. Whatever the reason, groups often have some common-denominator values that they cultivate and retain and hand down to succeeding generations. (It is true, however, that over a period of time there has been a lessening of ethnic-origin loyalty in favor of current American standards.)

In a world of instant communication and high-speed transportation there is a marked tendency toward sameness—or, put another way, for the world to become "smaller." In fact, the one-world concept, the theory that people tend towards homogenization, enhances the internationalization of current ideas and acceptance. Marshall McLuhan, in *Understanding Media*, suggests that "Modern living is turning the globe into a village, and catapulting man back to the life of a tribe."

Although there is a trend toward the internationalization of fashion, some people of particular countries, or regions within countries, continue to accept the values of their predecessors. In order for fashion as we understand it— change and the ability to apply obsolescence—to be practiced, there must be an environment with favorable conditions of economy, social values, available technology, and political attitudes.

Political climate

The economy of the United States is based on a capitalistic structure, and business operates within a marketing system where all efforts are focused on

These Chinese children are wearing clothes unique to their culture. (Photo Marc Riboud/Magnum)

the production of goods and services for a profit, as long as they are within the guidelines of the law. At the same time, regulations restrict or prohibit the manufacture of certain products. In effect, the government is a partner in every firm since it can be involved in what is to be sold, when, where, and at what price. It also shares in profits through tax laws.

Since legislation, judicial interpretations, and regulatory agencies place a wide variety of pressures and mandates on marketing efforts, there are limitations on what is produced and distributed. In turn, consumers can only purchase what manufacturers are able to produce.

8 In an example of governmental restriction, during World War II certain details of apparel were prescribed by the government for the purpose of restricting civilian commodities that might interfere with the needs of the armed forces. Dresses were limited to specific yardage. Skirts were held to 72 inches around, ruffles were banned, coat cuffs were eliminated, hems confined to a maximum of two inches, and pockets restricted to one patch-type per blouse. Men's suits had to be made without the traditional vest, and cuffs on trousers were eliminated. (Also during that period, automobiles for civilian use were not produced.) What was in fashion was obviously determined by the government. In fact, fashion was stagnant.

A current government concern is the import problem. With recent trade imbalances that have been averaging about $26 billion a year, unions and manufacturers are lobbying for stricter import limitations. Such products as automobiles, steel, television sets, textiles, shoes, and apparel are cited as those that give ultimate consumers wider choices and cheaper prices to the detriment of domestic workers and manufacturers. It is within the power of the government to eliminate or lessen this flow of products and restrict the marketplace to domestically manufactured merchandise. The Orderly Market Agreements of the 1970s restrict the units of certain products of particular countries that can be exported to us. Actually, the import problem has much broader implications than is generally realized. We do not have self-sufficiency in all the products required by our economy. Our need for oil alone can cause us to think twice before taking the stand that importation is necessarily an unfair practice. The present discussion nevertheless focuses on the power of government to affect what can be fashion. A greater variety of merchandise at wider price ranges makes for broader consumer choices, which in turn make for more widespread fashion possibilities. Too, imports of lower-priced goods widen choices for those with limited incomes. The subject of imports will be discussed in detail in Chapter 8.

Government can restrict or prohibit the marketing of products. Examples include the engine size of automobiles; cyclamates; certain fire-retardants used in children's wear; liquor sold only in state-owned stores (21 states).

Political, legal, and regulatory forces create an environment that plays a strong role in the buying and selling of products. What we accept, the most important condition of fashion, must be available. What is available can be a governmental decision.

FASHION APPAREL ACCEPTANCE

If we accept the definition of fashion as what is accepted by a substantial group of people at a given place and time, we have all the elements of the meaning of fashion apparel. What clothing we wear and why we wear it is an intriguing subject.

Clothing is a necessity. From a general point of view, Abraham Maslow's classification of basic needs could be applied as motivation for apparel purchases. According to Maslow, an individual normally satisfies the most basic needs first and is then free to devote his or her efforts to the next one in the sequence:

1. Physiological requirements
2. Safety
3. Love
4. Esteem
5. Self-actualization

Similarly, clothing is tangible evidence of self-concept:

- This is who I am.
- This is what I would like to be.
- This is how I would like people to think of me.
- This is how I think people think of me.

The most fundamental use of clothing is protection from the elements. Therefore silhouette, fabric, color, and details can vary with climatic conditions, the extremes of which are garments for the tropic and arctic regions. Five broad areas have been detailed as influences on fashion. Within those areas are more specific factors or needs that affect our fashion apparel purchases.

Social position

Despite the democratization of fashion brought about by the world of technology, man-made fibers, and easy availability, there are opportunities to express social position by what is worn. Clothing can reflect country club or college fraternity membership, suburban life, or a coal-mine job, to mention a few possibilities. Social groups tend to have standards for the apparel worn by their members. There are rebels who defy the dicta of their groups, but they are in the minority.

Authority or achievement

Police officers, military personnel, firefighters, and some religious are among those who wear apparel that distinguishes position. And even within those groups, details indicate the rank of an individual within the hierarchy. The list can be extended to include college graduation robes (again with the addition of features that show degree of achievement) and such career-related uniforms as those of airline pilots, stewards, and ground personnel. We can supply many other articles of apparel that reflect the wearer's profession or position.

Wealth

Clothing as conspicuous purchase goods is obviously a way to express the possession of money—or enjoy the luxury of quality, frequency of purchase, and satisfaction of wearing what is in short supply, newest, and beyond the means of others. An ocelot coat at $15,000 retail tells a story, as does a mink coat, especially when it is high-styled. **High style,** fashions accepted by only a few, suggest rather obviously that the wearers probably have other precious furs in their closets.

Dignity or occasion

One reason for wearing specific garb is to fit an occasion, to dress up, or to look well.

College seniors may first wear suits in the last days of their college life: They are going to job interviews and are dressed to suit the occasion. Whether we like it or not, we are all involved in role-playing and to some extent conforming to the expectations of others. And graduation robes, of course, reflect both the achievement of the graduate and the solemnity of the occasion.

The other extreme is the use of clothing to express opposition or disagreement. In the days of widespread student dissension during the 1960s, apparel often became work clothing, and in some instances graffiti (the American flag sewn on the seat of a pair of jeans, for example) were superimposed to symbolize disrespect for authority.

Improvement

We all seek to improve ourselves, to appear in the best possible light for ourselves and others. Clothing as an extension of our bodies can be modified (to a degree) to make us appear taller, shorter, more robust, leaner, or sexier, among other desired conditions. People who are heavy often wear clothing with vertical lines, thin people may favor horizontal details, short people can add height with platform shoes. It is not difficult to think of improvements for every part of the body, from head to toenails, among them false eyelashes, padded bras, and corsets.

What is considered a state of improvement depends upon an individual's taste and is subjective. The emotional value, a principle understood by marketers of fashion, plays a most important role. Fashion as we practice it has an acceptance based largely on emotional decision. One can say that fashion apparel is an economic waste, but the psychology of what satisfies a consumer—what an individual's assortments of needs are—is more often than not the realization that a new apparel purchase soothes tensions and gives emotional uplift.

Conformity

The vast majority of us are followers. We all tend to conform to the dictates of what peer groups set up as the norm, an accommodation to role expectancy that starts very early in our lives. Think back to the days when you were twelve or thirteen years old. What the group wore you wanted badly, whether sneakers, sailor blouses—or jeans. Peer-group approval is one of the strongest motivators of fashion acceptance.

Sexual desirability

This evident motivation of sexual enhancement is a fashion constant so common that there is hardly any need to discuss it in detail. Nevertheless, a related and significant marketing subject concerns the part of the body that clothing highlights to feature what is currently considered most attractive. Bosom, derrière, stomach (for men in the nineteenth century), ankles, and legs

In some areas, a hat is one way to peer-group approval. (Photo Dominique Vergos/Sygma)

have varying degrees of importance depending upon the era. In 1979 the leg came into focus with high-slit skirts and dresses. The "uncovering" of the body, in whatever way, has a relationship to the sexuality of apparel.

Esthetic values

It would be difficult to find an individual who would admit not having good taste or the sensitivity to what is right in clothing compatibility. There are indeed many who recognize and buy clothing that enhances their appearance: outfits that harmonize with their natural endowments in shape and color. The agreement on what constitutes good taste depends on many variables.

Fashion is an art form, however, and there are inherent esthetic values that are timeless. A visit to a museum will prove that even though garments of the past are outdated, many could be construed as true art pieces. What is a timeless fashion, what is representative of the art of fashion design, we leave to the experts of art history and design.

Events or personalities and fashion

Current events and prominent people have an effect on fashion apparel. We have already mentioned the influence on apparel caused by specific restrictions during World War II. Some other events and the resulting fashions are these:

Tennis craze   Clothing suitable for the game, après-game, or for spectator wear has become popular (the same applies to golf).

12

Man-made fiber developments   Synthetics have come into wide use, particularly since 1968. Chemical-based fibers helped democratize fashion by making available fabrics for garments that could be produced for mass acceptance.

Pop-art importance   Pop-art designs and slogans have appeared on many items of clothing.

Personalities in the news, past and present, have had an immediate impact on fashion:

- Jacqueline Kennedy popularized the A-line skirt and the pillbox hat when she was First Lady.
- General Eisenhower inspired the Eisenhower jacket and helped the single-breasted suit gain acceptance.
- Barbra Streisand gave prominence to thrift-shop clothing.
- Diane Keaton personified the "Annie Hall" look.
- Diana Ross, Lauren Bacall, Princess Caroline of Monaco, Catherine Deneuve, Melba Moore appear on television and in motion pictures in both formal and casual clothes. Viewers emulate these styles.
- Nancy Reagan is popularizing elegant classic styles.
- Cheryl Tiegs has encouraged the popularity of sportswear.
- John Travolta's roles influenced the urban cowboy and disco costumes (*Saturday Night Fever, Urban Cowboy*).

Emulation of admired figures, particularly motion picture, sports, and television stars, is a most significant motivator of customer fashion acceptance. The following are well-documented examples of personality or media influence:

- Cher and roller-skating outfits
- *The Great Gatsby* and the full-cut men's white suit
- *Bonnie and Clyde* and the look of the 1930s for men and women
- The Beatles and clothing that suggested irreverence for the establishment

Specific events and how they affect clothing could be treated very seriously in a book of encyclopedic size. Almost anything or anyone of importance, from prominent personalities to national and international events, can have some effect on the fashion of the times.

ENVIRONMENT AND FASHION APPAREL ACCEPTANCE

What comes into substantial fashion acceptance is the result of one influence or a combination of influences. A cursory examination of the periods within the history of modern ready-to-wear clothing indicates the effects of the environment on fashion apparel. During the period of modern ready-to-wear in the United States, there have been eras of distinctive fashion characteristics. Here

Two pages from the fall 1900 Sears, Roebuck catalogue. (Sears, Roebuck and Co.)

we are interested in the environmental factors of those eras, starting with the nineteenth century, and how they were expressed in fashion apparel.

Before World War I

From 1850 to 1900, the country embraced the Puritan ethic: work was the imperative activity for cleansing the soul. Business achievement held a high status level. We were deep in the age of development of mass production, with work clothing a necessity for most people. Sunday dress was a standard, a

14 costume for church and limited social occasions. Children's clothing styles were dictated by the woman because the man no longer dominated the household during the day. He was at work in the plant.

The examples on page 13 from a Sears, Roebuck catalogue of 1900 represent clothes of the era. (The wide lapels on the men's coats and suits are also good examples of the **cyclical nature of fashion**—the return of a fashion of an earlier era, with some difference in detailing.) Women are covered from shoe tip to just under the chin, a fairly easy way to hide natural endowments. The Puritan value system is evident. The nipped waist, however, accentuates the bosom; hats are decorative. These women's fashions are certainly not geared for fast physical activity, driving a car, or using an escalator. It took a later influence, when women entered the mainstream of life, to bring women's clothing closer to functionalism. Children's clothes were versions of adult apparel.

The 1920s

The Roaring Twenties was the age of the flapper, prohibition, wild stock market investments, and frivolity. Much of the United States went on a binge after the somber years of World War I. Puritanical views were cast aside by many: liquor, the Charleston, Hollywood romances, land speculations, "Buy today and worry tomorrow" are characteristic of the age that brought about a radical fashion change.

Women's clothing became revealing. Legs were exposed with the shortening of the hemline to just below the knee—and the hosiery business as we know it today was born. Men's clothes were more functional, not too far removed from those of today. Pants were baggy, jackets double-breasted and with wide lapels. Economics, social values, and a new morality were evidenced by the clothing of the times.

Bathing suits, however, still featured cover-up styles, and some women still wore stockings when swimming; men wore two-piece swim suits. From this point on the trend was toward the more undressed styles.

The 1930s

The stock market crash of 1929 put an end to the spree of the twenties. The thirties was a time of national stress that strained the very institution of government. Breadlines; "Brother, can you spare a dime?"; collapse of the banking systems of England and Germany; 13 million people jobless; the breakthrough of sound movies; and the Golden Age of Radio were distinctive events and conditions of the decade. Socioeconomic events caused a desire for more classic clothing, types that did not connote frivolity. It was the era when women's sportswear was born, since women became more active in sports. The movies were in their sparkling days; an escape from the realities of life became one of the prime motivators for fashion apparel. The movie stars included Joan Crawford, Marlene Dietrich, Bette Davis, Jean Harlow, Edward G. Robinson, Cary Grant, Paul Muni, Clark Gable. Hollywood was in its greatest glory.

When European fashions were cut off late in the decade because of the war,

Bathing suits in the late 1920s. (Brown Brothers)

Over the years bathing suits have steadily diminished in coverage. The contemporary bikini has almost reached the minimum. (Photo Georges Tirfoin/Sygma)

American designers came into their own. Such names as Sophie of Saks Fifth Avenue, Gilbert Adrian, Adele Simpson, Claire Potter, and Sally Victor were in the vanguard of the movement to establish the importance of the American designer.

Indeed, the events of the thirties were a strong stimulant to the furtherance of fashion apparel on the American scene. Every broad and specific influence that causes changes in fashion was important in this period: economics, social values, culture, technology, and political climate.

Apparel of the 1930s featured:

1. A hemline well below the calf (hemlines go up and down as a reflection of the national economy)
2. Bathing suits in the process of becoming more revealing
3. The introduction of the jump suit; its silhouette was baggy, but the idea of the modern version was there
4. Men's suits rather stagnant in fashion development and usually double-breasted (men's suit designers did not exist at the time)

The 1940s

From a fashion point of view, the two highlights of the forties were World War II and the New Look by Christian Dior, a change from wartime severity marked by natural shoulders, cinched waist, and full, long skirt.

During World War II women played a greater role than at any earlier time in our history; many were members of the armed forces. Naturally, uniforms were a fashion of the times for millions of men and women. The economic importance of the war to fashion was the need for mass production of uniforms, which laid the groundwork for the capacity to make garments in greater quantities for wider consumption. Included in this economic scene was the new technology that came out of the war. The 1940s responded to a great degree to politics (war), economic conditions (caused by war), and technology (speeded up by war).

The 1950s

Television came of age in the 1950s. In 1950, 3 million sets were owned. During the next five years, annual sales averaged 5 million. In 1956, $15.6 billion was spent on sets and repairs. By 1954 the average family was watching television between four and five hours a day. The medium became a tremendous influence in molding opinions as never before, including attitudes about fashion. Elvis Presley, for example, a product of television, sparked the leather-jacket fashion among his followers.

The economy was on the upbeat; annual per capita income went from $2941 in 1950 to $3505 in 1960. Americans were enjoying postwar prosperity, and apparel marketers were having unprecedented success. The average consumer was in the best economic circumstances in history and was trading up—buying higher-priced apparel.

As part of the postwar events, large segments of the population moved to

Christian Dior
La ligne corolle
Jaquette cintrée en shantung,
jupe longue finement plissée.

Christian Dior introduced the New Look in 1947. The artist included the House of Dior in the sketch. *La ligne corolle* is the special name Dior gave to that year's collection. The costume is described as a cinched shantung tunic and a finely pleated long skirt. (Sketch by Bérard/*Vogue* France)

the suburbs for a new life style. This had three major effects of importance here:

1. The establishment of branch stores by retailers who followed their customers
2. An environment that led to the development of modern discount stores (mass merchandisers)
3. The trend to more casual clothing

The national mood of the era was relatively calm, a period when America was back to "normal," concentrating on establishing new roots in a period of prosperity.

Fashion apparel's responses to the environment were

- Continued high popularity of Dior's New Look
- Hemlines below the knee to midcalf
- Sportswear's growing importance: Bermuda shorts, pedal-pushers, halter dresses and tops
- Sport jackets
- Ivy League suits with vests and slim tapered pants

The 1960s

The sixties began on a most optimistic note: the economy was still rising, a new young president, John F. Kennedy, projected the spirit of youth and talked of a new frontier; and all signs pointed to a period of high technology, high wages, and high expectations. But the era turned out to be one of disenchantment and strife.

The discontent of young blacks, liberals, consumer advocates, hippies, and the poor is best explained by historians. Nevertheless, we are interested in the broad issues and how they affected fashion apparel. Some of the issues were these:

- The Vietnam War (political)
- Sexual inequality (social, cultural, and political)
- Civil rights (social and political)
- Consumerism (economic, social, and political)
- Poverty (economic)
- Technology (dehumanization factor and unemployment)

Many young (and some older) people challenged the establishment and questioned the values of our political and economic system.

Clothing was a means of expressing attitudes; since the attitudes were often revolutionary, clothing was used to display opposition to long-held social and cultural customs. Those whose views were most deeply opposed to the "system" veered as far as possible from the old standards. Hippies wore work clothing and long hair, students took to denim and emulated the hippies, and soon the fashions influenced the establishment itself. If clothing ever changed in a revolutionary manner (the principle is that it does so in an evolutionary process), this would be the period. Denim became the fashion in jackets, pants, dresses, handbags, and hats. With the acceptance of denim, the trend to the most casual became the main fashion thrust. Clothing was more democratized than ever before in the history of the world. Clothing as a symbol of social status became less important, and the ability to determine a person's role in life, social position, and wealth by apparel alone was almost lost. (The irony of the movement to new forms of apparel and hair styles was its later embrace by the establishment, including those who had sometimes violently expressed strong distaste for the dissident groups.)

Other fashions that reflected an environment that challenged long-held values were these highlights:

- The bra-less look

- Topless bathing suits
- See-through blouses
- Costume jewelry, bracelets, and necklaces for men
- Boots
- Discarding of hats
- Cowboy and Indian styles
- Unisex clothing
- Thrift-shop clothing
- Afro styles
- Above-the-knee hemlines

Different fashions for different people is a fashion principle. Therefore, despite a fashion's importance, there are fashion directions for those who choose to wear the opposite of what is popularly accepted. As an example, if a coat fashion has surface interest, bouclé, there could be a fashion of lesser importance in smooth broadcloth. Hence, while discontent with traditional styles and a shift to proletariat costume were characteristic of the 1960s, there were people who sought refuge in clothing styles that were elegant and symbolic of status. In fact, designer names began to blossom in both men's wear and women's attire. Although some of these designers had been in the field for years, it was in the 1960s that they became household names, among them Pauline Trigère, Bill Blass, Donald Brooks, Oscar de la Renta, and Norman Norell.

The 1970s

The unrest of the sixties was followed by the calm of the 1970s. The Vietnam War, one of the main causes of dissension, was concluded; the economy was beset by inflation and recession; and youth realized the need to join the mainstream of society. America entered a more sober period and apparel accommodated the mood by becoming more conservative. By the end of the decade there were signs of a trend toward traditional and more elegant clothing.

Although there were some spillover values from the 1960s expressed by hot pants and printed T-shirts (1971), these were the dominant fashion elements:

- The greater importance of the dress, with the hemline below the knee
- Men's greater interest in business suits, ties, and button-down shirts
- Three-piece corduroy suits, manufactured by jean makers
- Classic, wearable clothes

The so-called **Peacock Revolution,** men's heightened interest in fashion, brought an abundance of new style ideas. The young and antifashion group became more interested in dressing up, wearing apparel to befit occasions in the traditional manner.

The advertisement on page 20, selected from 1979 fashion supplements of *The New York Times*, illustrates how apparel reflected the greater calmness of the era.

The 1980s

The new decade began with most consumers still beset by the effects of recurring recession, relentless inflation, and continued increases of energy costs.

The average American was forced to spend 90 percent of disposable income
on the necessities of food, housing, energy, transportation, and medical costs.
Taxes, how to husband savings when available, and the ability to maintain a
standard of living were critical concerns. College students, for the most part,
equated the purpose of education in pragmatic terms with a means of earning
a living.

Consumer purchase behavior was concentrated largely on seeking value. This attitude was expressed by following one of two directions: to seek lowest prices or to buy quality, classic merchandise to last longer in service or style.

The fashion trend of the 1970s for classic wearable fashion apparel continued into the eighties. Designer name clothing accommodated the mood of the times. Consumers maintained considerable independence by their refusal to follow designers or manufacturers. The result was a multiplicity of fashions that ranged from the very dressy to the very casual. Women's dress and pant suits were important in silk and satin, not infrequently accessorized by "bronze" shoes and handbags. Blouses and skirts (with variation, of course) could have been appropriate in the 1950s. Sweaters shared the fashion limelight, but at retail prices that would have been outlandish a few years previously. They were featured in lacy types, leno stitches, and other styles that "dressed up" an ensemble. The return to importance of sweaters, skirts, and blouses in times of economic downturns is predictable. Wardrobe components always become wardrobe essentials when consumers are under economic stress.

Men's clothing lost the flared pant bottom, and jackets no longer featured exaggeratedly wide lapels. The three-piece suit retained its popularity for business wear, for men and women.

The casual trend was expressed by the continued importance of slacks and jackets. The new fashion interest, however, was the wide acceptance of Western apparel and accessories in the form of blue jeans, denim shirts and jackets, Stetson-type hats, tooled boots, silver belt buckles. Blue jeans continued to feature such design names as Calvin Klein, Pierre Cardin, Sasson, and Gloria Vanderbilt. The high fashion of the Western trend was worn by urban cowhands whose outfits included $700 boots, $400 animal-skin shirts, $500 silver buckle belts, $200 Stetson hats, and, of course, blue jeans that were drycleaned and pressed, never washed!

Apparel and accessories to suit an occasion and/or to give an opportunity for exaggerated self-expression included jogging outfits, tennis costumes, T-shirts and sweatshirts with slogans, sneakers of every type, and "uniforms" for almost every sport or exercise activity.

The major fashion apparel trends of the early 1980s can be characterized as predominantly classic, but with minor trends that responded to those who desired to evidence off-beat forms of self-expression or levity, or to be appropriately dressed to suit the occasion.

READY-TO-WEAR

Our subject is primarily the American fashion business, so our focus is on the production and distribution of clothing made to fit the body of the average customer. Our industry is best known as one that mass-produces for mass acceptance. Ready-to-wear is factory-made apparel produced with a group of customers in mind. Before mass production, clothing was made in the home, at a dressmaker's, or in a tailor shop. Modern ready-to-wear blossomed fully in 1920, although it began in the early seventeenth century. Its history is interesting, and the influences that caused its birth and growth are all related to the five broad influences we have already discussed.

The earliest ready-to-wear was suits for men sold in London; by the latter part of the seventeenth century additional men's ready-to-wear establishments could be found in Liverpool and Dublin. There was strong opposition from the members of the tailors' guild, who did everything they could to impede the progress of ready-to-wear, including unsuccessful attempts to set up legal barriers. Despite their fears, ready-made clothing did not catch on in England or Ireland. By the end of the eighteenth century, however, some firms in Paris and Hamburg were featuring ready-to-wear. The evolution continued, but its pace was very slow. The nineteenth century was the period of gestation, during which early ready-to-wear became established. Its success was the result of three developments, two of them an outgrowth of the industrial revolution in England.

England is the country that developed the factory method of producing the materials of fashion as well as the means of combining them into a finished garment. Historically, there are several reasons why this country was able to change the world with technological advances. England was wealthy; it was unified into a single strong state as a result of long continuity of government; it was a center of enthusiasm for science and engineering; and energetic Englishmen sought money and glory.

Although we tend to consider the industrial revolution to have started around the mid-nineteenth century, it was already a fact of life in England in the eighteenth.

Starting in the latter part of the eighteenth century, English inventors turned out a series of inventions that made possible, among other innovations, the mass production of iron, practical steam engines, and—best of all for our purposes—the spinning frame and the power loom. Two Englishmen's contributions to the ready-to-wear story should be noted. Richard Arkwright, the father of the factory system, erected the first practical cotton mill in the world and invented the Arkwright spinning jenny. Edmund Cartwright also played a major part in working out the necessary steps for the improvement of the spinning machinery. Arkwright established a mill in 1771; by 1779 it had several thousand spindles, more than three hundred workmen, and operated day and night. The eighteenth century had seen the founding of the first requirement for mass clothing production, machinery that could produce fabric in quantity.

The second crucial event in the history of ready-to-wear was the invention of the sewing machine. From the middle of the eighteenth century, inventors in many countries had been aware of the need for such an item, but no one was able to make a workable model. Finally, in 1830 Barthelemy Thimonnier of France patented a chain-stitch, one-thread machine that was immediately purchased by two Parisian manufacturers of uniforms. The enraged tailors of Paris considered the invention a means to displace them and united to take action. They ransacked the firms and tried to destroy the machines. One firm

The first Singer sewing machine, 1851. (Photo Ralph Stein)

hid its machines and saved them for the future, but the inventor was attacked and almost lost his life.

Between 1832 and 1834 Walter Hunt, an American, invented a two-thread machine; Elias Howe, another American, made improvements and secured patent rights in 1846. No one was really interested in using the invention, although William F. Thomas of London bought the English patent and hired Howe to come to England to adapt the machine for making corsets. This arrangement did not work out, and Howe was discharged. When Howe returned to the United States, he sued three American firms—Singer, Wheeler and Wilson, and Graver and Baker—who had started successfully to sell his machine. Howe was awarded a royalty of five dollars for each machine sold by his competitors.

The U.S. market was now ready for the sewing machine, even though its unit cost was extremely high. Home seamstresses were at first more eager than manufacturers to purchase these early models, and it was not until 1860 that manufacturers first used them for the production of clothing. The machine was still expensive, and it remained so until 1876, when the patent expired and competition proved a price leveler.

The third and final important early development in the history of ready-to-wear was the sized or graded paper pattern introduced in 1863 by Mr. and Mrs. Ebenezer Butterick. Up to that time, clothes had been cut from a muslin copy that was perfected before making a garment in the intended fabric, a time-consuming and expensive process. The Buttericks and a business rival, Ellen Demorest, known as Madame Demorest, published fashion magazines in which they advertised their patterns. The Butterick magazine was called *Metro-*

politan and later *The Delineator*. The paper pattern had tremendous success from the beginning, and by 1870 the Buttericks and Madame Demorest were selling 10 million patterns a year throughout America and Europe. The original idea was to supply patterns for individual homemakers, but clothing manufacturers soon began to use them.

But the cycle was not yet complete. Up to this point the elements for manufacturing were fabrics, machines, and patterns. Several additional elements were necessary, of which the most important was need. Ready-to-wear is basically a response to a group need. Ready-to-wear clothes were always a need for those who lacked the ability to make them or did not have the time or money to purchase individually tailored garments. Soldiers, for example, required mass-produced apparel, a condition that necessitated some type of factory method system. As early as 1648, European soldiers were supplied uniforms made by army tailors in prisons or commercial factories.

In an expanding America there were also groups that needed help to obtain clothing. The Gold Rush of 1849, for example, created a need for sturdy pants for those who had neither time nor tailoring skills to make them. A prospector named Levi Strauss went to California to seek gold and found an imaginative

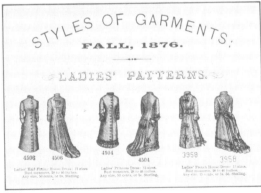

Butterick pattern advertisements, 1876. (Butterick archives)

way to acquire it. He produced pants made of sailcloth, reinforced seams with top stitching, and provided pockets that resisted the strain of gold nuggets stored in them. The most popular fashion in the world had been created.

Other groups required ready-made apparel. The slaves, particularly men, needed clothing, and factories were started in Chicago, St. Louis, and other metropolitan centers to make it. Another group with a clothing need that could be filled by ready-to-wear was sailors who did not have either wives or sufficient time in port to have their clothing made. New Bedford, Massachusetts, was a thriving port city and was a most likely place for the manufacturing and selling of factory-made clothing. In 1818, Henry Brooks started a men's clothing business in that area; it became Brooks Brothers in 1850 and finally a chain-store operation with a headquarters store in New York City and twenty-seven other stores in thirteen states, the District of Columbia, and Japan.

The Civil War, from 1861 to 1865, stimulated the mass production of apparel. Army uniforms had to be made in great numbers, which was an additional impetus to the founding of clothing factories. As part of this Civil War mass production, specifications for the standardization of sizes were adopted and later carried over to the manufacturing of civilian garments. This sizing procedure was confined to men's attire, however; women do not appear in the ready-to-wear picture until World War I.

The term *factory* suggests the concentration of machines and people under one roof, but at first each manufacturer depended to a great degree on the cottage industry process. Fabric was cut in a plant; women, usually housewives, came to the plant, carried the cut components home, and sewed the garments there.

Ready-made clothing up to the end of the nineteenth century was largely confined to clothing for men and children. The Sears, Roebuck catalogue of 1900 still shows women's apparel in terms of cloaks, capes, skirts, and shirtwaists.

There was much to be desired in the factory system of the late nineteenth century. The women workers had to travel to and from the factories, which was time-consuming and resulted in a slow production rate. The workers were an unhappy lot; the pay was poor, and they had to use their own machines, or needles required for hand sewing, and pay for any trimmings required for garments.

During the twenty years from the last decade of the nineteenth century through the first decade of the twentieth, the United States had an influx of immigrants from Europe. These people had known hardship and persecution and were willing to accept low wages just to stay alive. Many had tailoring skills. They were willing to work in the factories; factories as we know them today really began and the factory method of clothing manufacture was under way. Until the entry of foreign labor a complete garment had been made by one worker.

In order to speed up the production process, a new system was introduced in England around 1880 that provided for a division of labor, a process whereby each worker was assigned a segment of a garment. This system was brought to the United States by some immigrants who had worked in England and landed in Boston. It was initially called the "Boston system," and is known today as **section work.** Under this method, workers work on one segment of a garment, are paid for piecework, and are able to mass-produce. This system is still used today.

With the advent of the assembly line came the sweatshops and a series of abuses that affected women, men, and children. The workers were captives who toiled for wages that ranged from $3.50 to $7 a week. In 1900 a union called the International Ladies' Garment Workers' Union was founded. This organization was remarkable in that its strength came from 2000 ill-educated immigrants, mostly women, who were so unified and so determined that they were able to resist the entrepreneurs. Their success had a signal effect not only in their own industry but also on working arrangements between employers and employees in other industries. Their cause for reform was given public support following a catastrophe in New York in 1911. This was the Triangle Fire, in which 156 young women workers at a shirtwaist factory lost their lives from burns or from having jumped from windows. Despite the inhumane factory conditions, the owners were able to collect a $200,000 damage settlement from the insurance company. Public clamor gave force to the importance of the union's demands, and eventually the ILGWU was able to effect changes

A sweatshop in the 1890s. (Brown Brothers)

The revolution in women's clothes in the 1920s is apparent in this news photograph taken in 1927. The original caption reads: "Miss Suzette Dewey, daughter of Assistant Secretary of the Treasury and Mrs. Charles Dewey, snapped beside her roadster." (Library of Congress)

Among the earliest ready-made garments were this black silk skirt and cotton shirtwaist, about 1904. (Division of Costume, Smithsonian Institution)

in working conditions, pricing of garments, and such benefits as health care and pensions. The union's contribution to the industry is an important chapter in the history of ready-to-wear.

28

But women's ready-to-wear was still subordinate to men's. Store clothing was essentially for the lower-income groups; women of even moderate means used a seamstress or dressmaker until World War I required the production of uniforms in large numbers. Factories were hard put to supply the need, so facilities were enlarged.

The women's movement for equality had begun, and women were banding together to change the traditional roles assigned to them. Women in the United States could not vote until 1920. Most jobs and professions had been barred to them, and the range of work opportunities was largely confined to homemaking or schoolteaching. Wartime conditions opened the door, and some women were able to make choices of career opportunities. The entry of a limited number established a path for the many who followed. As women's roles became more varied, suitable functional clothing was required. Women, by 1920, needed freedom from restrictions of apparel and had less time for dressmaking. The need for ready-made women's clothing had arrived.

A cursory review of women's clothing up to this point shows most of all the skirt and shirt, sometimes sewn together to make a dress. Anything that was not cotton was known as silk. The introduction of rayon brought the popular-priced dress, a crucial step toward women's apparel that moved into the spotlight. Industry now had a product that could be produced in quantity, at low prices, and in styles that had popular appeal. This condition was also helped in no small way by the migration to cities. The growth of cities gave rise to common values, easy markets in which to sell goods, and relatively easy transportation of merchandise to stores. Women's clothing had entered the fashion mainstream in 1920. The photographs show the tremendous revolution in styling.

The years that followed 1920 brought about different and greater needs and greater opportunities for industry growth, the highlights of which were connected with another military conflict:

1. World War II required millions of uniforms for both men and women.
2. World War II brought about the further development of size specifications following a greater realization of different size groupings.
3. Brand identification assumed importance during World War II (see Chapter 7).

SUMMARY

The word *fashion* has a multiplicity of meanings; in its broadest sense it is synonymous with culture. Its definition includes four conditions: people, acceptance, time, and place. Therefore, fashion apparel, for our purpose, is clothing accepted by a substantial group of people at a given time and place.

When a fashion came into being can be determined only after the fact; prediction of what will become fashion is the difficult responsibility of all fashion marketers. Simply put, fashion is a resultant state—the product of acceptance. Hence, styles created by designers, featured by producers, and offered by retailers are not fashions until they are accepted by ultimate consumers. The length of acceptance is the basis for categorizing a fashion. A short-lived one is a fad, the longest can be an artifact of culture, one that is handed down from generation to generation (denim jeans). **29**

The general environmental factors that influence acceptance of a style are economics, social values, cultural aspects, technology, and political forces. Specific reasons for apparel acceptance are numerous and subjective, and include sociological and psychological values. An oversimplification of consumer purchase behavior, an encompassing motivation, is a search for a state of betterment. Included as specific reasons for acceptance are events and personalities who motivate emulation.

Interesting aspects of fashion marketing are investigating environmental factors of past eras to ascertain why certain fashions came to the fore, and then estimating the probable future degree of importance of present market offerings. Since fashion apparel is cyclical in nature, what was accepted in the past will return to prominence in an updated version. When and to what degree of importance are the questions.

Ready-to-wear had its beginning in Europe when four events occurred in the nineteenth century:

- The development of machinery to mass produce fabrics
- The invention of the sewing machine
- The creation of paper patterns
- The invention of a factory system based on the division of labor

United States manufacturers soon adopted these European developments. Ready markets for factory-made clothing included three groups—sailors, government (uniforms for Civil War soldiers), and plantation owners, who had to provide clothing for slaves. Fifty-five years later, about 1920, modern ready-to-wear was established for the production of women's clothing, when availability of skilled immigrant labor, the development of rayon, and more liberalized attitudes about women's role in society created a favorable environment. The importance of the American fashion industry is based on mass production for mass acceptance.

QUESTIONS FOR DISCUSSION

1. Explain how each of the following is an influence on fashion:

   Social values
   Cultural values
   Technology
   Economics
   Political climate

2. Explain the need for fashion in products other than apparel.
3. Discuss at least five motivations that influence people in their apparel purchases.

4. Identify three fashions that were the result of specific events.
5. Do subcultural values play a part in fashion acceptance? Illustrate with two fashions.
6. List the events that led to the establishment of modern ready-to-wear.
7. Discuss why the development of modern ready-to-wear started with men's apparel.
8. Manufacturing and retailing of ready-to-wear in America started in Massachusetts. Why?
9. Discuss the development and significance of a factory system in the production of ready-to-wear.
10. What is the relationship of the industrial revolution to ready-to-wear?

2 FASHION APPAREL MARKETING PRACTICES

Marketing is a total business interaction which includes the planning, pricing, promotion, and distribution of consumer-wanted products and/or services for a corporate profit but with regard for social obligations. Marketing is a complete study in itself; here we will discuss only the highlights in the context of fashion apparel. The definition implies the need to plan what to make and at what prices; how to communicate with potential customers and when, where, and how to sell a product or service. It also presupposes a knowledge of consumer orientation: knowing what people want, when they want it, at what price they will buy it, and in what quantities they can absorb it.

Classically, there are nine marketing activities:

Merchandising Activities
1. Product planning and development
2. Standardization and grading
3. Buying and assembling
4. Selling

Physical Distribution
5. Storage
6. Transportation

Supporting Activities
   7. Marketing risk-bearing
   8. Marketing financing
   9. Obtaining and analyzing marketing information

These activities apply to all types of businesses. The list also indicates the distinction between **marketing** and **merchandising,** although these terms are often used interchangeably. The total range of the listed activities is known as marketing; the first four, the merchandising aspects, are used to determine market need and/or stimulate market demand.

A manufacturer of dresses, for example, must determine consumer preferences in styles, fabrics, colors, silhouettes, and details to create merchandise for ultimate consumer satisfaction. In addition, for the proper functioning of the business the manufacturer must consider the size and location of the market and the nature of the competition; plan how to make consumers aware of the product; make it available at places and times that are convenient to prospective customers; and offer it at prices that are acceptable to potential customers and still yield a satisfactory profit.

The reason for being in business is to make a profit. Profits are maximized when business activities are coordinated and include a system whereby information is gathered, analyzed, and used as a basis for decision-making. Marketing practices are directed toward this end. Marketing is fundamentally a process in which a business functions and people are organized in their efforts to produce products or services that fit market need. Figure 2–1 suggests how all the activities of marketing begin and end with the customers.

FASHION MARKETING

American business operates in a competitive, consumer-oriented society that can be characterized as a **buyer's market** (where supply exceeds demand) in which the ability to produce goods does not assure profit. Even after finding success through customer acceptance, a firm can find its business drifting away to competitors. Consumer demands change, the environment is always in a state of flux, and given product features can become less acceptable due to

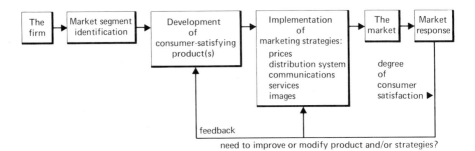

Figure 2–1 How marketing activities are applied.

technology, competition, and a host of other external developments. Every organization must therefore be alert and constantly reassess the market environment (people and industry) to determine current effectiveness of the product line and/or service. This is true for all firms, regardless of the nature of the business.

In this chapter we will examine two important factors: (1) what makes the marketing of fashion apparel different from other marketing operations and (2) why fashion marketing is a career specialty. First we will discuss the values and conditions that make for uniqueness in fashion marketing.

Intrinsic value

Fashion as a product changes and accommodates the time. What is fashionable today may be "old hat" tomorrow. Further, fabric, workmanship, and other costs may have little relation to the retail price at which a fashion item can be sold if the item is offered at the wrong time. As a case in point, a pair of men's slacks made of the finest English worsted wool that features pegged pant cuffs and waist pleats may be worth $100 in terms of intrinsic value of material and workmanship. But who would buy that style of slacks in today's market? The loss of value is a result of the refusal of customers to buy a garment that is not in fashion. Most stores, in fact, would not buy it at any price for fear of customer rejection of a garment that is passé and also for fear it might reflect lack of store fashion sophistication. Conversely, a dress consisting of three yards of material worth $50 could be retailed successfully at $1000. In this case the value would come from style currency and the designer's importance. Other products—garbage cans, for example—can be out of fashion and still sell at prices fairly close to original retail value. Why? The intrinsic value is recognized by the consumer. But who wants to wear clothing that is "old"?

The obsolescence factor

Product obsolescence exists when any product is depleted or no longer usable: it can no longer serve its intended purpose. In apparel this is also true, but with the difference that the product is usually still serviceable. The obsolescence is in the mind of the consumer, a psychological state that induces the owner of apparel to conclude that the product value has diminished or evaporated. The usual course of action is to dispose of such garments, most often by contributing them to a charity. They will, of course, be worn again: someone will be the recipient of clothing that is perfectly wearable.

In fashion marketing, apparel that does not sell well becomes obsolete. Producing and retailing have one goal—selling at a profit—and a slow selling rate is costly in terms of both tied-up capital and the loss of having produced or purchased the wrong goods. Once there is a judgment that merchandise is not "right," sellers mark it down and dispose of it.

A healthy fashion inventory is one that reflects newness, what is currently wanted. If we accept the premise that a strong element in fashion is change, then inventories should reflect what is new and avoid the old. In merchandising terms we therefore refer to **stock turn,** essentially the number of times during a given period the stock is sold out and replaced. Stock turn is determined by dividing sales by average inventory. Certain manufacturers, of course, produce only one collection a year; others offer six or seven. A marketer who offers one or two lines a year had better be right. In fashion, being out of trend is disastrous.

How many times have you gone into a store and found the stock about the same as when you visited it three months previously? If you saw the same merchandise, you were disappointed and probably came to the conclusion that the store did not know its business, risking a possible loss of customer patronage.

Change of stock is a necessary condition for all organizations in the fashion business. Older is cheaper. What is old is not fashionable. What is old is not exciting for customers who like to shop and buy—or simply admire. What is new has the best opportunity of being sold at the price intended by the producer.

High markdowns

Lack of intrinsic values leads to the necessity of re-evaluating merchandise on the basis of current salability. Since all goods are produced or purchased for resale, what does not sell at the anticipated rate must be considered not wanted. What does not sell well enough ties up capital and inhibits profit. The way to attain profit is to sell, rebuy, and sell, repeating this process over and over.

When the selling is slow a style becomes unwanted merchandise, and the course of action is clear: mark it down. A **markdown** is the difference between the original and the new lowered price. The degree of markdown is variable with the product, the price, the time of offering, and other conditions. In a business based on calculated estimates of what customers will select, there must be a fair share of markdowns—higher than those of most industries, particularly ones that deal in products of slow fashion change. It is axiomatic that any product that has a high degree of fashion is vulnerable to obsolescence. High markdowns are part and parcel of the fashion apparel business, and what is not in customer demand is a victim.

Seasonality

Products of all industries are updated from time to time. Manufacturers are aware that products go through a life cycle from growth to saturation. But few industries other than fashion apparel must offer up to six new lines a year. A retail season, which is the basis for offering lines at wholesale, lasts from two to three months, so changes are fast, merchandise ages rapidly in comparison to most products, and it is difficult for producers to maintain a constant standard of excellence.

The practice of fashion accommodating seasons creates an inherent problem. Therefore, not every manufacturer produces goods for every season; some concentrate on a single big one, as in the bathing suit sector. Normally, manufacturers make collections for two or perhaps three seasons of the year. Retailers

High markdowns bring customers in for bargains. (Photo Abigail Heyman/Archive Pictures, Inc.)

observe the greatest number of seasons, although some stores basically restrict them to spring, summer, fall, and winter. Higher-priced stores add a transition period between summer and fall and a winter cruise season. Every season stresses newness in an attempt to make the old obsolete and cause the potential customer to discard the old in favor of the current versions. That is the name of the game!

But up to six hits a year are hard to produce. The retailer is in a relatively stable position, as is the fabric producer, but the manufacturer is often under pressure. The weakest link in the chain on which goods flow to the ultimate consumer is the manufacturer.

The nature of the product

Clothing is a product of conspicuous purchase, and we know the reasons for wearing clothing, but who is sufficiently perceptive to determine the specific fashions for the coming season? (The ability to operate in an atmosphere of imprecision and make profits is the reason merchandisers and marketers earn high incomes.)

The ability to understand consumer preference is one of the most highly desirable attributes for a purveyor of fashion in all business sectors. Techniques vary with sector and price level, but no one ever knows all the answers. Who could have foretold the advent of hot pants, denim, see-through blouses. pant suits, platform shoes, sweatshirts, maxi-skirts, bobby sox with high-heeled boots, and slogans on T-shirts? One cannot say "never" about fashion. Fashion is as variable as people.

Fashion acceptance involves emotional value, and on that basis alone rational predictions are often defied by the electorate—the consumers. Every level of fashion selling also involves dramatic value, which goes hand in glove with the emotional reason for consumer preference. There is no product that needs more psychological analysis than fashion or is more difficult to predict. The inability to keep pace with consumer preference is a sure road to failure.

It is with reason that the fashion business has been called "The Wild West of Industry." It is a business of extremes: high markdowns, fast turnover, dramatic presentation, greatest profit on investment but the lowest rate of return on sales for manufacturers. It is a business in which the product is often conceived and purchased emotionally.

36

THE DIFFUSION OF FASHION APPAREL

Design

Apparel rarely becomes fashion because of the expressed wishes of customers for specific styles, but fashion must start with precursors who are sensitive to the environment and who create styles. Some styles are accepted and others are not, and those that are not are discarded at some point in the marketing process. Styles are abandoned by the manufacturer because of lack of store buyer interest, and a retailer similarly disposes of merchandise for the same reason—lack of ultimate consumer interest.

There are two classes of creators who have the sensitivity to what may become fashion, the designers in both the textile and the manufacturing areas. The textile fashion experts must be aware of trends, the direction in which fashion is headed, because fabrics must accommodate specific styles. When the trend tends toward soft dressy styles, for instance, a fabric like chiffon will assume importance.

The other group of creators, the designers of apparel, must be sensitive to both the broad and the specific influences to which consumers are being exposed. Some are more daring than others, but as a group they are the originators who bring about the fashion offerings. Sometimes newness is offered as an introduction for the future, the top of the line—more for consensus than selling depth. This is more usual with moderate-priced merchandise. At higher-priced levels the European and American designers offer seasonal newness with a complete array of prophetic styles. (The methods and practices of domestic and foreign manufacturers are discussed in Chapters 7 and 8.)

In the fashion apparel industry are experts with the responsibility of predicting the fashion trends of fabrics, styles, and colors—the combination that is found in both the textile and the manufacturing sectors.

Figure 2–2 shows the dynamics of the fashion industry as well as the influences on each group impinging on the development of merchandise that becomes fashion.

Not every manufacturer or textile company employs creative people or presents collections that are unique. In fact, the vast majority in both fields are copyists. In the main, the popular- and moderate-priced fields are devoted to copying or knocking off someone else's success. (**Knocking off** is an industry market term for copying another's style and usually offering it at a lower price.) The fashion industry has always been willing to steal, mutate, or improvise on those styles that look promising or have been proved to be in customer favor. Since there is no law against piracy of styles, it is a usual method of styling. The only patentable fashion item is a fabric design, and even in this area there is copying;

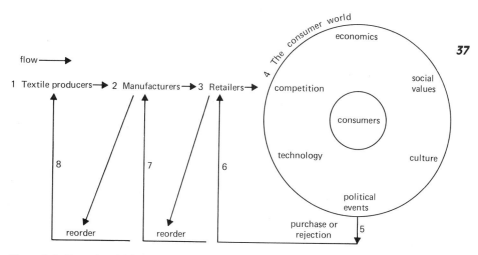

Figure 2–2 Dynamics of the fashion industry. *Timing factors:* Textile producers: 12–18 months to prepare lines. Manufacturers: 2–5 months to prepare lines, depending on merchandise type and price level. Retailers: purchase opening inventory for new season 2–4 months in advance, depending on retail location and price level (purchases from foreign producers require extended delivery terms). Reorder lead time is shorter and variable, depending on market, product, availability, delivery destination.

most originators do not seek damages or an injunction, although a few have done so.

Consumer acceptance patterns

Fashion is evolutionary, as we have seen. Acceptance of the new requires a rejection of the old and a period of time before it is embraced by a substantial number. Figures 2–3 and 2–4 show the process of fashion acceptance and life span based on the usual pattern of new clothing starting out at better-priced

Figure 2–3 Fashion acceptance: consumers, prices, stores.

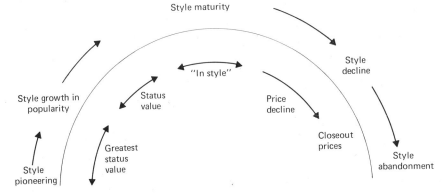

Figure 2–4 Product life span of fashion.

levels. The vast majority of consumers are fashion imitators; the initiators are only about 2.5 percent of the market, a very small group. Most people do not have the sensitivity or the courage—and some do not have the money—to accept newness.

The percentages in the diagram of fashion acceptance are approximations of when groups accept a given style, under average conditions. The initiators are normally people with sufficient income or knowledge to indulge their fancy; the style-conscious are those who have the wherewithal and the desire to be up-to-date; generally, the later acceptors are those who must or prefer to buy when the price and/or the fashion is right; and, finally, there are those who have little feeling for fashion but buy on the basis of intrinsic value or for replacement need.

As a corollary, when a fashion is first offered, its position in the diffusion process is in the introductory stage; it then rises, reaches the peak of greatest popularity, declines, and finally reaches the abandonment level.

There are three theories of how fashion can flow: vertically downward, vertically upward, and horizontally. The most common one is that a style or fashion is embraced by upper-level-income people and then is later accepted in copied form by the early acceptors and later by the general acceptors, pretty much as diagrammed. The second is the horizontal movement theory, which is more up-to-date and more in line with the way fashion acceptance is generally imagined. The theory assumes that since most ready-to-wear is at moderate price levels and marketers are most concerned about the broadest population group, what is created—regardless of the price or origin—is immediately available at most prices. In today's world of instant communication, what is the length of time between the introduction of a French **couture** (high-fashion) style and its appearance in moderate- and even popular-priced copies? This theory holds that no single social group has an advantage over another in the ability to purchase new fashions: technology has democratized fashion completely. The third theory is that fashion can start at the bottom of the price spectrum and work its way up. Youth in the 1960s fostered new fashions that were gradually adopted at higher prices. What was the clothing of dissent became the garb of the majority.

TYPES OF FASHION

In theory, it should be simple for marketers to make or buy and sell what is wanted. In practice, the trouble stems from the inability to assess what is wanted, when it is wanted, and for how long.

Change is what makes for excitement in the marketing of fashion. When fashion acceptance is established, the road to what to make or buy for consumers is relatively easy. The problem for all marketers is how long the fashion will remain in favor, a consideration of utmost importance. Here is a comparative scale of fashion's tenure:

- A **fad** is a short-lived fashion, one that is here today and gone tomorrow.
- A cyclical fashion can last anywhere from a year to several years (with seasonal detail and color changes).
- A classic fashion is a basic style that continues in some degree of acceptance for years, sometimes the most important fashion of a period.
- Some fashions become part of our heritage, the culture itself: the longest fashion term.

A fashion buyer's problem is the difficulty of assessing the term of importance. It is all too easy to buy an item that is on the upswing and in great demand, deal in big numbers, and then suffer the consequences of being overstocked. Fashion merchandising is an opportunistic business that involves change, and the trick is to discern the speed of change. Customers want newness, but how new? When does the new become old, when do you mark goods down and abandon them? These are merchandising problems that are inherent in fashion merchandising, which involves a unique product.

We have seen that fashion acceptance follows a set pattern. Figures 2–5, 2–6, 2–7, and 2–8 show a few variations of fashion acceptance patterns, beginning with the classic one. Figure 2–6 traces the path of the debacle of the Nehru suit, a fad that came in fast and went out fast during the late 1960s. Figure 2–7 shows a steady growth of acceptance and a fast decline. The men's turtleneck sweater of several years ago is a good example. It took about six months to reach the zenith and one month to descend almost to the nadir.

Seasonal goods have a characteristic acceptance pattern. In the case of bathing suits, customer demand is strong from April until mid-June and then declines, even before the period of end use. Customers know when the bathing suit selling season is in its ending days. Manufacturers and retailers attempt to reverse the downward demand. Promotional goods with lower prices are offered by both and the selling pattern is accelerated, so the graph of activity can be shown as in Figure 2–8. These dates vary somewhat with locale. In some areas or stores, the price-break date is the day after July 4 and the season extends another week.

The timing of fashion has a strong relationship to the timing of merchandise

Figure 2–5 The classic evolution of a fashion.

Figure 2–6 A fad.

Figure 2–7 A fashion with a fast cut-off.

Figure 2–8 Acceptance pattern of seasonal goods (bathing suits).

availability. We noted that fashions often start at highest prices and then become available in greater quantities successively at lowered prices in different types of stores. Each new entrant into the marketing of the fashion—manufacturer or retailer—is saying, "I have the fashion." In the ordinary course of events, this availability is not newsworthy; there is no introduction of creativity. The offer is actually a statement of "Me too; I am now in the act." Consequently, the marketer must offer some justification for entry and has two choices: (1) to make the fashion or style with some feature that is newer than the original, or (2) to make it available more cheaply. In the main, to be late is to be cheaper.

In summary, our definition of fashion indicates the most important merchandising principle of all: fashions are made by customers; their acceptance is the only condition for what fashion is. How many people accept a given fashion and for what period of time gives the word a qualitative meaning.

A high fashion is accepted by a relatively small group of people, such as the very wealthy who embrace a style at a very high price. Or a style can be created by either wearing or mutating a manufactured garment, changing the details, colors, or silhouette. Cutting down denim pants to ragged shorts, tie-dying, and superimposing decals on jackets are among the "abuses" of fashion that became the fashion.

A fad is fast fashion—in and out.

Fashion relates to a time and a place. The place is not quite so important now as previously, when different parts of the United States had sharply defined attitudes about newness and when there was greater reluctance to abandon accepted local values. Television has tended to make for commonality of ideas. However, regional values due to climatic and cultural considerations make for different degrees of acceptance of given fashions and the time it takes for that acceptance. Among the evident considerations are that in warm-weather areas heavy winter coats are not sold, some dark colors are not important, and garments with full-length sleeves are of minor sales value. Some areas are considered fertile for the introduction of new fashion ideas while others are known as slower adopters.

Fashion acceptance is evolutionary and cyclical in nature. As an excellent example, women's hemlines move up and down, interestingly in tandem with the economy, as already noted. In every recession, hemlines went down and in every boom period they rose. Witness skirt lengths in the period 1923 to 1929 (flapper era). The lengths went down as a reflection of the depression and did not return until the 1960s. Interestingly, in the early 1980s, with the nation grappling with the effects of a stubborn recession, some designers are featuring styles with raised hemlines, apparently an effort to give hope for an upward bound economic direction. In essence, the raising and lowering trends are related to the attitude that the covering of the body parts is reflective of a somber mood, the exposure of more body of a buoyant spirit. One can observe any fashion of the past and see its importance in a later period. Of course, fashion never comes back in its original form. Manufacturers would be foolish to bring back styles customers could resuscitate from an attic collection.

The evolution of fashion is much slower than generally conceded: it took some five or six years for consumers to reject midcalf- in favor of knee-length hemlines, a movement pace of an inch a year. Another interesting note is the relationship of skirt lengths to automobile height, where some make a case for another tandem pattern. In the 1970s, for example, skirt lengths became lower and automobiles became higher, the same trend—a lengthening process.

A classic fashion is a long-term fashion, examples of which include loafer shoes, blazer jackets, and shirtwaist dresses. They are always produced by manufacturers and stocked by retailers in quantities that vary with acceptance level. At certain times classics become most important consumer needs.

Fashion is not a price; it is acceptance itself. Whatever is accepted is the fashion, whether it is high fashion or a general fashion, high-priced or low-priced. Fashion is also a reflection of life style that changes with the times. The merchandising axiom of greatest importance for the marketer is that the cardinal sin is to be out of trend—a condition of obsolescence or miscalculation that causes heavy markdowns.

MARKETING PRACTICES

Although the focus of all sectors of the fashion industry is on the electors—the ultimate consumer—each must operate from a different frame of reference because each has a different timing requirement and a different connection with the group for which fashion apparel is intended. The retailer obviously has the closest associations, the manufacturer is one step removed, and the textile producer farthest away in both time and position.

In a large organization the marketing duties are assigned to specific jobs, and the larger the organization the more specific and narrow the area of re-

42 sponsibility of the assigned positions. Figure 2–9 shows a marketing structure that could be used for a moderate-size firm. Following here is a summary of responsibilities for each position on the chart. Remember that structures vary with organizations, and functions are assigned to departments which individual firms feel are most appropriate for their purposes.

It is the responsibility of top-level management to formulate organizational policies and objectives and the manner in which they are achieved.

The marketing director, usually a vice-president, is given the responsibility for marketing functions that respond to the mandates of corporate objectives. The marketing director has under his or her supervision a staff of department directors who are responsible for specified marketing activities.

The director of research is in charge of personnel who gather, analyze, and interpret information for support of such business decisions as marketing opportunity, alternative solutions for specific problems, and the implementation of marketing strategies.

The director of advertising and sales promotion is concerned with communications from the organization to customers, channels of distribution (immediate customers, manufacturers, or stores), and ultimate consumers. The communications involve the creation of advertising messages, artwork, layout, publicity releases, fashion shows, and other forms of messages to create sales, good will, and a desired market image.

The director of product planning is charged with the development of a line of merchandise that will find customer acceptance. To help the effort, the director has as staff personnel who include designers, stylists, artists, and other creative people sensitive to the current environment and/or trends.

The director of sales personnel or sales manager directs and controls the sales staff and has seven basic responsibilities: to recruit, select, train, allocate, remunerate, motivate, and evaluate salespeople. A staff function that helps the

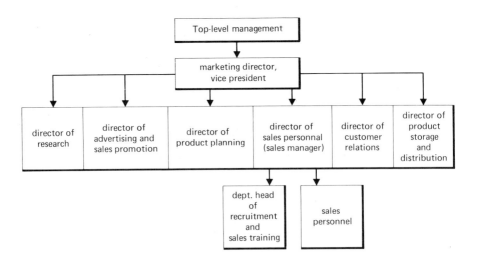

Figure 2–9 Marketing structure: moderate-size firm.

sales manager is handled in a department that recruits potential sales personnel and maintains a formal training program for selected candidates.

The director of customer relations heads a department that has two func- **43** tions: (1) to advise customers how the firm conducts its business; (2) to ensure that the business is conducted in accordance with management's policy of how its product or service is delivered to customers.

The director of product storage and distribution directs personnel who handle all merchandise. This department receives finished goods produced for proper warehousing, selects merchandise against orders, and then arranges for transport and ships goods to customers.

Observe that all departments are interlocking in their activities, and that marketing is a total business interaction. This is true regardless of the size of the firm. The marketing-structure chart reflects a large-size producer of goods, a textile company or manufacturer (large size in the fashion industry is equivalent to moderate size in most industries). Smaller firms may not have a formal marketing structure because personnel is limited and people tend to function as generalists rather than specialists. Different types of organization charts, including those used by retail organizations, will be found in later chapters.

BUSINESS ORGANIZATION

The terms *producer*, *firm*, *company*, *manufacturer*, and *retailer* refer to an organization doing business. As a basis for carrying on the activities of any kind of business, there must be an organization. There are three types of business structure: sole proprietorship, partnership, and corporation.

Sole proprietorship

Sole proprietorship is the most frequent form of business organization in the United States, although this kind of business firm is usually a rather small one. Since ownership is vested in one person, all profits accrue to the owner. Other advantages are the ability to execute one's own judgment in all business matters, the limitation of income tax (payment is made as an individual), and the right to terminate a business at will. Disadvantages include the facts that the length of the life of a business is dependent on that of the owner, any liabilities of the business are assigned to the owner, and the amount of capital available for expansion or other business opportunity is restricted.

Partnership

When two or more people own a business, it is a partnership, a structure that has an almost endless variation of form. The participants agree to the nature of the relationship by mutual consent, establishing the conditions of partnership, the contribution of each partner to the business, the division of profit, and the authority and liability of each member. The contract, not required by law, is known as the articles of co-partnership. In this type of ownership, there are two basic kinds of partners, general and limited. In a limited partnership, an owner is only liable to the extent of his investment. A limited partner can be a silent, secret, dormant, or nominal partner. A silent partner takes no active part in the business. A secret partner is not known to the public. **44** A dormant partner is a combination of silent and secret partner. A nominal partner is a person who lends his name to an organization but is not a partner and is neither liable for debts nor shares in the profits. The disadvantages of partnership are that there can be unlimited liability (in a general partnership); the nature of the relationship can cause disagreements, especially when duties and authority overlap; the termination of the association upon the death of a partner; the difficulty of dissolving the relationship in terms of establishing value and sale price; and the difficulty in raising capital, although capital accumulation is greater than in a single proprietorship since the assets of partners can be used for loan collateral purposes. Partnerships are most frequently used by firms of limited size.

Corporation

The third business organization is the corporation, an artificial being that may legally own property, transact business, enter into contracts, sue and be sued, and engage in other business activities. Individual states grant charters creating corporations. Each state sets its own requirements for these charters.

The owners of a corporation are its stockholders, who hold its stock certificates that define the extent of their ownership. Some major corporations, like General Motors and Exxon, have millions of stockholders. Stockholders receive corporate profits in the form of dividends declared by the directors at periodic meetings. Usually, however, not all profits are distributed, some part being retained for working capital and growth purposes. Dividends are not mandatory; in fact, some corporations do not pay them, preferring to use the cash for growth purposes. Thus the value of the stock can be increased and the stockholders rewarded with an asset salable at a higher price. The stockholders' interests are safeguarded by a board of directors elected by them. The board sets policies and controls the company, and also appoints the president and other officers.

Before any dividend is declared, taxes must be paid. A corporation must pay income tax, which is one present disadvantage of a corporation: stockholders pay federal tax twice—once at the corporate level and then again as private citizens. The advantages of a corporation, however, are considerable: stockholders are not liable for corporate debts; the life of a company is not terminated by the loss or death of personnel; the value of individual ownership is established and salable; and corporations often have the ability to raise capital by issuance of more stock.

The sole proprietorship is by far the most prevalent type of American business organization; there are six times as many sole proprietorships as there are corporations and more than ten times as many as partnerships. But the greatest volume of business and total investment rests with the corporations, many of which are vast entities. The organizational structure of firms in the fashion-apparel industry runs the gamut from sole proprietorship through various kinds of partnership to corporation. This brief sketch of the kinds of business organization will be useful background for our later discussions.

The fashion industry marketing practices are unique because they deal with a product that often defies prediction. As one of the largest industries of the country, the volume and profit potentials are great—for the successful. Each sector of the industry has an abiding interest in and sharp focus on the consumer—the elector of fashion. Obsolescence, change, copying, time, and the capriciousness of consumer taste are elements of an opportunistic business that offers high rewards for good marketing and failure for miscalculations.

One thing is certain, it is never dull, a fascinating vocation for those who qualify.

CAREER CONSIDERATIONS

In the three sectors of the fashion industry—textiles, manufacturing, and retailing—there are hundreds of different career entry jobs, a range of opportunity that can confuse interested applicants.

How does one start? An excellent beginning is the selection of a particular part of the industry: the textile area, manufacturing, or the retailing (or supporting) sector. Options should be predicated on the knowledge of:

- How the market functions
- The candidate's abilities and personal traits gauged against the industry's needs
- The opportunity within the chosen sector to achieve the candidate's goals

How does one obtain this information? First, carefully note the background, practices, and opportunities discussed in the following chapters. Follow up with a visit to the library to review books, periodicals, articles, trade publications, and other sources for complete details. Then:

1. Visit the market. Observe the people and the tempo of activities. This may require an investment if you live far from the marketing scene, but the reality is that the headquarters of the textile sector, for example, is in New York City. Textiles are sold in regional markets, but the main action, marketing activities particularly, takes place in the fashion capital.

2. Arrange to meet executive personnel. Visit two or three firms to obtain a general point of view. Arrangements can be made by mail or telephone, or simply by an unheralded visit. The latter is often unproductive and is not recommended for those who must travel from distant places.

3. Arrange to meet as many professionals as you can and obtain firsthand information.

4. Visit industry trade associations; each industry sector has them. The best-known will be found in the appropriate chapters. These organizations have personnel who will be helpful and can also supply brochures that list names of firms, personnel, location, and specialties.

5. Write a dossier on yourself that includes the reasons for your selection of

the industry. Even if you are a year or two away from job entry, it will be valuable for the purpose of self-evaluation and as part of a resume for actual job-seeking.

46

The successful selection of the area and then of a position with the right company in the right industry is a major accomplishment that takes application and effort. The successful accomplishment of these "rights" leads to good training, valuable knowledge, a stepping stone for a bigger job or a different one in the same industry, and a running start in building a career. These steps will take time and ingenuity, but they are worthwhile and realistic. The timing depends upon the individual, when there is sufficient knowledge backed up with adequate research.

The industry is always interested in self-starters—people who are motivated, those who are curious. More often than not, executives are pleased to take the time to meet and talk with those who fall into the self-starting category.

The first important step is to decide which area of the fashion industry seems most appealing to you. Appendix A contains summaries of the most popular fashion-career options. Refer to them after reading the discussion of the industry that most appeals to you. The relationship of each sector's dynamics and demands will come into sharper focus and help your research efforts. Appendix B has examples of a standard resume form and a recommended application letter that can be tailored to your own use.

SUMMARY

Every business organization is a marketing structure that operates to make a profit. Marketing activities are classified into three groups: merchandising, physical distribution, and supporting activities. How the activities are carried out depends on the nature of the product and market competition. Because the product and level of competition of the fashion industry differ from those of other industries, this market's tempo, strategies, and tactics are different.

The vast majority of manufacturing firms are small in a highly competitive market that produces a unique product. Fashion merchandise has relatively limited intrinsic value, is completely dependent on consumer acceptance, and is subject to change. These conditions make slow-selling styles candidates for high markdown and require manufacturers to produce goods when they are most likely to be accepted.

What is consumer-wanted is a manufacturer's constant concern. Consumer orientation—knowing what is wanted, when, at what price, and in what quantities—is a key factor. A manufacturer knows that fashion apparel's life span can range from a period of weeks to years, a fashion is not necessarily accepted at a particular price, and the cardinal sin is to be out of trend.

Although apparel firms are small, most are corporations; in total, apparel making is one of the largest industries in the United States.

The marketing of fashion merchandise for retail selling is an opportunistic business that must accommodate change. When this product is in line with consumer acceptance, the rewards are high; when merchandise timing is miscalculated, the result is failure.

The one certainty is that fashion marketing is a business that is always exciting and fascinating for those who qualify.

QUESTIONS FOR DISCUSSION

1. Explain the difference between marketing and merchandising.
2. Discuss the necessity of a marketer's understanding of consumer orientation.
3. What are the reasons for the uniqueness of fashion apparel marketing?
4. Define the term *consumer obsolescence.* What is its significance to fashion marketing?
5. Take a pro or con position on the statement "Fashion bursts on the scene."
6. Explain the possible financial loss a marketer can incur from investment in a fad.
7. Of the three sectors of the fashion industry, which is the weakest link in the distribution to the end user? Why?
8. If you were starting out in business for yourself, what type of business organization would you establish? State the advantages.
9. Define *fashion apparel.*
10. Define the term *knocking off.* Explain why it is a widespread fashion-apparel industry practice.

The primary component of most apparel is fabric. Cloth—whether silk, wool, cotton, linen, or a synthetic—is an evidence of man's progress, even though the essential processing of natural fibers is basically the same today as before recorded history; the changes are modifications, improvements, and methods of production through the use of machinery.

Textiles were the chief industry of Britain until the industrial revolution, when technological breakthroughs gave rise to heavy industry. Indeed, for hundreds of years, the textile industry influenced the course of history, foreign relations, and domestic policies of England, then the leading power in the world.

The textile sector, which now includes the chemical companies, affects almost every phase of our lives and has a longer history of commercialization of scientific discoveries than any other industry. This sector produces the materials of clothing and a tremendous variety of plastics and other synthetics used in modern living.

A full study of the textile industry requires more space than is available here.

PART II

SOURCES OF THE MATERIALS OF FASHION

Any interested reader can find in a technical library many shelves of books that range from textile history to technical discoveries and their applications. Our discussion is directed toward the appreciation, understanding, and importance of textiles as they affect ready-to-wear. In this part we concentrate on the important industry specializations, how and why they function, and where an interested applicant can seek an entry job.

The objectives of Part II, therefore, are these:

1. To examine some of the important events of the industry's development, its economic importance, and its relationship to the fashion industry
2. To furnish information for those considering a career in the industry so that they can identify entry-level and career job opportunities
3. To motivate the reader to research areas of interest

This part also includes a discussion of two nonfabric materials of fashion: leather and fur.

Photo Bruce Davidson/Magnum

3

THE TEXTILE INDUSTRY

The art of textile making very possibly accompanied the first use of fire for cooking and caves for shelter. The earliest civilizations made use of available raw materials: the skin, sinews, and intestines of animals, flax, wool, and tree bark. Excavations in Egypt and Latin America have revealed the existence of beautiful manufactured fabrics thousands of years before the time of Christ. Flax fabric of very great age has been unearthed in England.

HISTORICAL DEVELOPMENTS

Spindles and looms very much like those in use today date back as far as the Bronze Age, and the designs worked into fabrics made on them are remarkable for the artistic use of needle and thread. Eastern textile artisans not only became proficient very early in **spinning** (drawing and twisting fibers or filaments to form a thread) and **weaving** (making cloth on a loom by interlacing warp and filling yarns); they also developed the skills of dyeing and ornamentation. Methods of weaving wool, flax, cotton, and silk developed in the East. Among nomadic peoples wool was long the most important fiber because they possessed flocks and herds. Linen and silk, which became important later, were considered luxury fabrics.

Silk was woven and decorated exquisitely in China before 2500 B.C. Cotton **51** fabric is thought to have originated in India, and carpets and shawls to have first been produced in Persia. As much as three millennia before Christ, Egyptians produced linen of a quality that has not yet been equaled. The pre-Columbian civilizations of Central and South America fashioned silklike textiles with great art in unusual high shades, and the brilliantly colored blankets made by the Navaho Indians of the North American Southwest have long been famous. Polynesian artisans of the south Pacific perfected an unusual cloth called *tapa*, made by beating the soft inner bark of certain trees.

As civilization moved westward across the continents the processes for making fabric were introduced successively to Greece, Italy, Spain, and the rest of Europe. The invasion of England by William the Conqueror in 1066 was followed by the migration of Flemings and Normans who had textile skills. They helped develop the English textile industry, which over centuries became the world's most important. (Some five hundred years later, Queen Elizabeth I employed Flemish artisans to help nurture the industry, by then centered in Lancashire in northwest England.) Although practically every country of the world was involved, England had the greatest influence on textile development leading to the start of what we now call ready-to-wear.

MODERN PRODUCTION

Mass production as we understand it presupposes a factory system. Although a primitive form existed in medieval times, when a combination of workers united into guilds for the production of goods for commercial purposes, not until the eighteenth century did the necessary ingredients combine into the formation of the factory we know today. In the modern sense, a factory is a commercial centralization of three elements: skilled workers, capital, and machinery.

The third vital element, machinery, is a product of the industrial revolution, that era of invention when machines replaced hand labor. Many of the inventions were a response to need, and this need motivated inventors' efforts to improve textile production methods. Several people made noteworthy contributions.

Early highlights

We already know the name of Richard Arkwright, the so-called father of the factory system. His improvement of the spinning frame and the erection of the first cotton mill (1768) are among his achievements. His later mill, located in Cromford, was powered by the river Derwent. For the first time, the entire operation of cotton spinning took place in one location. Sadly, concomitant with the operation of this mill was the use of child labor. The broken ends at the rollers could best be tied by children, who had great finger dexterity. This led to an abuse that was later decried and still later prohibited by law.

Arkwright's spinning machine, 1767. (Photo Ralph Stein)

Arkwright's success gave tremendous impetus to the cotton industry, and Lancaster took on all the trappings of a factory town, a new phenomenon that featured factory buildings, smokestacks, and crowded streets. The ambience went rapidly from that of a rural town to an urban environment. This was the beginning of widespread urban blights: increased population, overcrowded centers, poverty, hazardous working conditions, sweatshops, child labor, and the many other abuses caused by the imbalance of the employer/employee relationship.

In 1733 John Kay invented the fly shuttle, which greatly increased the quality of cloth, lightened labor, and doubled output. John Hargreaves made a major improvement in spinning in 1764 with the invention of the spinning jenny, named for his daughter. Samuel Crompton in 1775 perfected the process with his mule spinner, a cross between the spinning jenny and the spinning frame, which made possible the production of fine yarn. In 1785 Edmund Cartwright patented a loom that stopped automatically on breaking a thread and thus was the first practical power loom for making fabrics.

These technological advances required one further invention to make them suitable for mass production: the application of reliable power to run machines. This was achieved by improvements made on the steam engine by James Watt, a Scottish engineer. Water power had a drawback: it depended on the water level, and lack of rain could restrict its use. Watt obtained his first patent in 1769. In 1784 he produced a steam engine that could be applied to machinery of all types, and one of his models was developed for the use of textile machinery. By the early 1800s textile machinery was making fabrics in full-scale production essentially as they are produced today.

Another noteworthy figure in the story is Joseph Marie Jacquard, a Frenchman who by 1804 had perfected a power-loom attachment whereby any desired design might be woven into a textile fabric. In the Jacquard loom the design **53** is laid out on squared paper, then punched on cards that are laced into a continuous chain rotated on an overhead mechanism. The cards come into contact with needles controlling individual wires that lift a heddle of the loom when the needle passes through a hole in the card.

The American contribution was slow in beginning but major. In the colonial period the range of fabrics manufactured, technology, and factory methods were based on British experience and practice. English textile manufacturers understandably wanted the American market to remain a purchaser of finished goods, not a competitor in production. To protect its exports, England took every possible step to make certain that neither machinery nor technical information crossed the Atlantic. Ingenious Yankee entrepreneurs tried unsuccessfully to smuggle machines through France piece by piece and attempted to obtain precise drawings of English textile machinery. The Americans were

A modern Jacquard loom. *(American Fabrics & Fashion Magazine)*

finally able to secure some designs and models of English machinery by 1770, but not the one they really wanted—the Arkwright mechanism.

54   The American textile industry remained insignificant even after the end of the American Revolution and stayed so until December 1790, when English-born Samuel Slater activated a mill near Pawtucket, Rhode Island, the first to make yarn with machinery powered by water. While an apprentice in an English mill partly owned by Arkwright, Slater had read about the rewards offered in the United States to encourage cotton manufacturing. He emigrated to New York and then contacted Moses Brown of Providence, Rhode Island, a mill owner. Brown, who was unable to construct a machine, met with Slater, who asserted that he could build from scratch one that would work as well as any in England. Slater entered a partnership arrangement with William Almy and Brown under which he was to receive half the profits and half interest in the machines. The backers would supply the necessary capital and own the other half. Their first plant, located on a bridge over the falls of the Blackstone River, was destroyed by a flood. Work to complete the machine continued and it finally became part of a complete plant in Pawtucket in 1793. Alexander Hamilton reported, "The manufactory of Providence has the merit of being the first in introducing to the United States the celebrated cotton mill." Slater's success with the use of the Arkwright machine brought him fame and fortune and put cotton manufacturing on a firm basis in the United States.

Early in the year that Slater's factory in Pawtucket went into operation, 1793, an invention of Eli Whitney (who had graduated from Yale the year before) revolutionized the cotton-textile industry. Cotton, at one time hardly more than a garden plant in North America, was of little commercial importance in the early 1790s, primarily because the fiber of short- and medium-staple cotton had to be separated from the seed or boll by hand. One person could clean about a pound of cotton a day. Eli Whitney's invention, basically a toothed cylinder revolving against a grate that enclosed the cotton seed, enabled one person to clean up to 5000 pounds a day. This invention put cotton into the forefront of the American textile industry, and "King Cotton" was not dethroned until 1968.

The War of 1812 created great demands for both cotton and wool, and textiles became a major industry in the United States. There was a tremendous business surge in a very short period: in 1805 total cotton consumption in the United States was about 1000 bales, in 1816 about 90,000 bales. In 1816 all the cotton textiles made in the United States were valued at $50 million, by 1836, $250 million. At the beginning of 1816 there were 94 mills in Rhode Island, 57 in Massachusetts, and 14 in Connecticut. The first mill in North America to perform all the operations of converting raw cotton to cloth was the Waltham Company, formed in 1813. This factory, built by Francis Cabot Lowell, Patrick Tracy Jackson, and others, was an outgrowth of the knowledge Lowell gained during a visit to England in 1810.

The middle years

The industrial revolution reached the United States in the mid-nineteenth century. The factory system for the manufacturing of textiles was established,

Eli Whitney's cotton gin, 1793. (Photo Ralph Stein)

chiefly in New England, and ready-to-wear clothing was in the incubation stage. By 1850 the number of cotton and wool factories was approximately 1000. The population of the United States was also growing rapidly. At the time of the Declaration of Independence, Americans numbered 2.5 million; by 1850 the figure was 23,191,876. Fabrics were naturally in great demand in a country of such expanding population.

Then came tragedy—the Civil War. The need for uniforms challenged textile manufacturers to produce cloth for both military and civilian use. The industry was equal to the task; the combination of workers, capital, and machinery had been established. The industry grew still further and reached a new level of importance. Increased production brought further technical know-how and the ability to improve quality levels.

Toward the end of the nineteenth century, some textile concerns began to realize advantages in relocating in the South, the source of cotton. Southern states also recognized the need for industrialization for regional growth and offered manufacturers such incentives as tax advantages, reduced utility rates, and support of transportation needs. Another advantage for the manufacturer was the availability of low-cost labor. And so the exodus began and continued, and the South remains the major textile-producing area of the United States.

The twentieth century

Even catastrophic international and national events can have beneficial side effects. Such an event was World War I, which again demanded textile products in unprecedented quantities. Mills strained facilities to accommodate military needs in addition to civilian demands. The American textile industry was nearly **56** the largest in the world. In 1911 the first commercialization of a chemically dependent fiber was introduced—rayon, a new member of the textile fiber family, revolutionized the industry and, even more, the manner in which we live.

CURRENT PRACTICES

Four important developments in the textile industry will be noted here. First, during the 1950s and the 1960s industry leaders embraced the theory that big-firm efficiency could be developed by integration, whereby one firm performs all the functions of textile marketing. This led to what is known as a **vertical operation** (or *integrated operation*), the control of all production and marketing procedures within one organization. The business had become more complex with the addition of a wider variety of fabrics, more industries to serve, and the coming of age of the ready-to-wear industry in 1920. The complete concentration on production by management was no longer consistent with the market environment. Specialization by larger firms was difficult; the path to success, satisfactory profit results, and organizational growth could only be achieved through fiber and/or fabric diversity and a structured marketing system. Large companies accordingly bought or merged with other companies, and huge complexes emerged, firms that controlled the manufacturing processes and marketing steps, with sales staffs that controlled the advertising and distribution of their products. In the vanguard of this movement were two textile market firms that have an annual sales volume of over $1 billion, J. P. Stevens and Burlington Industries.

Mergers have slowed since the 1970s as a result of Federal Trade Commission guidelines. Textile firm mergers that result in combined roles or assets that exceed $300 million are prohibited. Also, coalitions that increase the market share to over 50 percent or acquisitions of suppliers or customers that result in a concentration of 10 percent in any market are also prohibited.

The second noteworthy factor was the rise in importance of the **converter.** Converters are firms that take **greige goods** (fabric as it comes off the loom), woven or knitted fabrics, and put them in a form in which they can be sold "ready for the needle" to apparel makers. Greige goods can be dyed, patterned, and finished to a manufacturer's specifications. The converter is a stylist sensitive to the needs of the manufacturing industry. Although cotton was traditionally the chief fabric converted, the advent of man-made fibers widened the range and made the converter even more important. Organizations that convert are specialists that either buy or produce greige goods; currently the largest is M. Lowenstein. When a producer both makes greige goods and converts, it is of course an integrated organization.

These are some of the many apparel-industry segments served by the converters:

Women's wear	Men's wear	Children's wear
Blouses	Slacks	Dresses
Loungewear	Shirts	Shirts and blouses
Slacks	Pajamas	Pajamas
Scarves	Underwear	Underwear
Pajamas	Robes	Rainwear
Dresses	Bathing trunks	Play clothes
Negligees	Raincoats	Slacks
Underwear	Jackets	Jackets
Sportswear	Scarves and ties	Bathing suits
Rainwear	Suits	
Housecoats		
Skirts		
Bathing suits		
Coats and suits		
Foundation garments		

Woolens are rarely converted because pattern goods are most often made from yarn that is already dyed; hence the styling is done on the looms. Technically, with the use of some synthetics in fabric, it is possible to **cross-dye** (one or several synthetic yarns in the fabric will take only specially prepared dye, so an overlay of color can be achieved), but this is a minor part of converting.

A third area of interest is the role of the **sales agent.** From the beginning, in colonial days, the English sold fabrics in America through people who worked on a commission basis. When the industry was first founded in this country, the owners' primary interest was in the technical and production aspects; selling and marketing was of small concern. What was produced could be sold. But as the business became more complicated with growing competition and diversity of product and consumer demand, marketing gradually became an integral part of most firms' operations and sales staffs were developed. Sales agents are still important even though many producers and converters sell their own output.

The fourth development—**factoring**—has an interesting background. Textiles sold to manufacturers of apparel who change the nature of the product in the manufacturing processes must be financed. Apparel manufacturers have to buy goods in advance, assume the responsibility for labor and overhead cost, and then extend credit to their customers. The textile market responded to manufacturers' financial needs and provided long-term credit. Some went into the banking business—factoring, the buying of accounts receivable. (Factoring, of course, was not developed by the fashion industry. In one form or another, the exchange of cash for an asset has been carried on for centuries.)

If an apparel manufacturer has money due him from retailers for delivery of merchandise, he can go to a commercial bank or factor and sell or take a loan against these accounts receivable. The bank charges interest and the factor who buys the accounts receivable charges a fee, the rate cost dependent upon the current cost of money and how long the debt must be carried. A manufacturer has the choice of carrying his own accounts receivable or selling them to a factor.

58 If the choice is to sell, an agreement is signed with a factor. The charge for the service is a stated rate. The arrangement calls for the manufacturer to submit all customer orders daily for the factor's credit approval. After the factor checks the credit rating and approves the amount of the transaction, the manufacturer is notified and shipment can be made to the retailer with the assumption of the credit risk by the factor. (However, if a store claims damaged goods delivered, it becomes the manufacturer's problem.) When the goods are shipped, the factor pays the manufacturer and the store is advised that the bill is to be paid to the factor.

It is not uncommon for the manufacturer to procure a loan at an agreed rate of interest from the factor in advance of a season against future business. The advantages of using a factor are the continuity of credit facilities, the elimination of a credit department (credit manager, space, and personnel), and the assumption of responsibility for contingent bad debts and collection by the factor. One well-known factor is United Merchants and Manufacturers, part of which is Cohn Hall Marx, the textile organization. The disadvantage of selling accounts receivable is the higher cost of money, which reduces profit.

TEXTILE MARKETING PROCEDURES

The textile marketing process can probably be explained best by an organization chart. Figure 3–1 was prepared with the aid of the marketing director of one of the country's largest textile firms, which manufactures and converts its own goods. Corporate officers and some staff departments have been omitted in order to focus on the levels most directly involved in the movement of the merchandise.

The multifaceted character of the marketing practices of a large firm is evident. Most companies have a variety of products that require assignment of responsibilities for the development of each product line (department manager), sales to the proper distribution channels in the appropriate markets (sales manager), overseeing each product division (divisional merchandise manager), disposal of merchandise considered over-age to jobbers (divisional merchandise managers), and personal selling of goods (salespeople). Firms recognize that out-of-town markets, particularly, require top salespeople in areas of limited sales potential. In order to obtain the greatest market share of these volume-restricted areas, some textile firms employ as sales agents top professionals who carry the lines of several manufacturers. These professionals are top earners because they have entree to important users as well as the advantage of being in business for themselves.

Note that the marketing director, who is usually an executive vice-president, has responsibility for the functioning of all divisions.

Figure 3–2 shows a typical converting process and seven positions of responsibility.

1. The department manager is assigned the task of the entire styling process.
2. The stylist shapes the product collection into salable form: as the salespeople will present it to the customers.

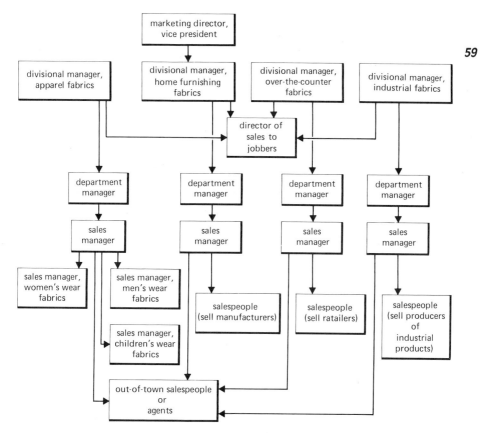

Figure 3–1 Textile marketing structure: large firm.

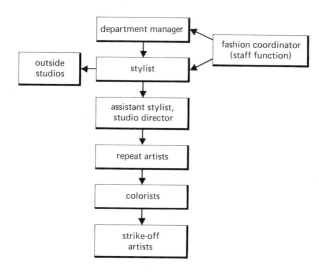

Figure 3–2 Product development in converting.

3. The fashion coordinator or director is a staff person who researches and advises on general fashion trends, fashion apparel trends, specific patterns of importance, and colors of fashion importance.
4. The assistant stylist is the studio director and makes assignments to lower echelons.
5. The repeat artists draw the designs of the various patterns and often make improvisations for customers who request them.
6. The colorists work on the designs in various color combinations and make different colorings to complete a color range. They too make special renderings for customer special orders.
7. The strike-off artist has a special skill and fills an important position in a converting organization. When the designs are set, the strike-off artist visits the plant to put them into production. This person must know machine capability and dye acceptability and must also know exactly what the finished products will look like. If there is any question about the quality or feasibility of the product, the strike-off artist can use his or her judgment and make changes on the spot.

As the supplier of fabric, the most basic need of the fashion industry, the textile sector plans and produces earlier than any other area of the fashion apparel industry. Marketing and production also have a long span because the industry must accommodate to future fashion need with a product that requires numerous and complicated production processes.

Textile selling

Since New York City is the world fashion capital of mass-produced apparel, textile firms maintain their marketing offices in midtown Manhattan, where apparel manufacturers are located. This concentration leads to a unique selling-assignment pattern.

Most salespeople are employees of the firms they represent. The problem is how to assign responsibility for accounts to be serviced. With apparel manufacturers clustered in a single small area, it would be folly to make assignments on a geographic basis. Each salesperson is therefore assigned specific manufacturer accounts. In some instances, salespeople are given buildings to canvass, a process known as "cold" selling, in which every manufacturer in a building is solicited without appointment. Larger firms may also break a particular industry segment into separate markets; for instance, the dress market may be divided into makers of garments costing up to $19.75; moderate-priced vendors, from perhaps $21.75 to $49.75; and vendors of garments at $55 and up (these are wholesale prices).

Although sales agents represent some smaller firms in New York City, they are of greatest significance for textile selling to apparel manufacturers located outside New York City.

Textile selling begins with a representative's visit to a manufacturer's office, at which time he or she displays samples and color ranges. When a maker expresses interest in particular styles, a sample quantity, up to ten yards, is ordered to determine how the fabric lends itself to a finished garment. After receipt of the sample and the making of finished garments, the manufacturer is ready to negotiate a purchase in manufacturing quantity.

This selling process is unique to this sector of the industry because the price **61** is usually negotiable. Price is often dependent upon two factors: the time the order is placed and the depth of the commitment. A textile manufacturer is particularly eager to go into production against early orders, a much sounder economic step than producing without commitments. Too, a larger order insures the most economic use of machinery, the guarantee of machine time— again an economic advantage. These circumstances lead to a battle of wits, the final stage of which is settlement on price.

As a general rule, better-priced makers place orders earliest and popular-priced manufacturers latest. Large popular-priced manufacturers, however, knowing that quantity orders can mean a price advantage of use in a highly competitive market, may also make heavy commitments very early in the season, sometimes even before the textile producer has gone to his machines. A large fabric commitment provides the opportunity to obtain a price advantage.

Once the season is under way, the manufacturer may wish to reorder from the textile maker. Depending on production needs later in the season, the manufacturer may need small quantities or fabrics no longer available from the textile producer. In this case, the apparel manufacturer seeks a **jobber,** a middleman who does not produce, but buys from producers and resells the product. Jobbers service manufacturers, allowing them to extend the season by supplying fabrics no longer produced, and they also liquidate the textile makers' stocks, which keeps capital working for new production.

Fashion colors

One of the intriguing aspects of the fashion business is the selection of colors by the marketers as candidates for popularity in a given season.

The selection is made by an informally structured interrelationship among fashion directors of such companies as Celanese, Direct Yarn, Avtex Corporation, Du Pont, and Hoechst Fibres. They are joined by trade groups, the best known of which are the Wool Bureau, Cotton, Inc., and the Tanners' Council of America; by fashion magazines like *Mademoiselle, Vogue, Seventeen,* and *Glamour;* and by such color and fashion associations as Promostyle of Paris, Color Association of N.Y., Nigel French of London, and IM of New York.

Members of this group consult one another and consider what would be suitable as changes from existing popularity, remembering that fashion apparel needs seasonal newness in shades appropriate to projected styles. This interaction might be considered like that of a group of artists who compare their thoughts and share techniques that evolve into a school of painting. Specific shades are prepared in the form of swatch books that textile firms offer to their customers, the manufacturers. In due course selections are made for the colors of purchased fabric. The consensus then becomes the touted color selections of the season.

The input of the leather industry is important to fashion color since it supplies the accessory market and therefore must develop shades that complement the major fashion items of each season. The following is part of a fashion-projection report from the Color Bureau of the Tanners' Council of America **62** for fall and winter 1978:

Women's Leather Colors

The Color Bureau recommends the following leather colors for Fall and Winter, 1978:
Royal Treasure: Ruby, Lapis, Tiger's Eye, Emerald, Dark Amethyst, Onyx
Balances:
    Light: Winter White, Chino, Ivory, Palomino
    Dark: Winter Khaki, Loden, Tobacco, Charcoal
Autumn Leaves: Adobe, Caramel, Camel, Fruitwood, Rocky Mountain, Brick 3, Golden Honey, Chestnut, Spur, Mecca, Coronado, Black Walnut
Victoriana: Evergreen, Antique Taupe, Rose Clay, Gypsy Blue
Lalique: Misty Toffee, Crystal Ivy, Frosted Claret, Bronze Luster, Black Pearl
Fort Knox: Gold, Silver, Platinum, Copper, Bronze, Black Metal

Color and fashion associations research and advise textile companies and related fashion sectors of the industry; the textile companies develop their own research and relate to other textile companies; and textile industry consensus is more or less established. There are, of course, different interpretations of shades and degrees of importance of particular colors. Apparel manufacturers have the same sources of information (including the leather market) and have a point of view when reviewing the lines of textile producers. The orders placed by apparel manufacturers, the points of view of fashion magazines, and color preferences of store buyers add up to the colors of the season as predicted by the industry.

The final step, the big one, is acceptance or rejection by the customer. With acceptance, a color becomes a fashion.

Economic impact

The textile industry is huge. In 1982 it operated more than 7000 plants, serviced about 25,000 apparel manufacturers, and was one of the nation's leading business sectors. Its current annual volume is reported to exceed $60 billion. Another sense of the size and economic impact of the textile industry on United States life can be gained from Table 4–1 (next chapter), which shows textile fiber consumption.

The leading textile-producing area is the South, although there are plants in every state of the nation but five.

The textile industry employed 555,900 workers in 1979, excluding hundreds of executives. The eight states with the largest textile-industry employment in 1980 were these:

North Carolina	279,000
South Carolina	148,000
Georgia	117,000
Virginia	43,000
Alabama	42,000
Massachusetts	36,000
Tennessee	33,000
New Jersey	31,000

Production workers represent 88 percent of all employees, as against 72 percent in all other manufacturing industries.

Employment by type of industry is as follows:

cotton	662,000
wool	175,000
man-made fiber	113,000

Billions of dollars are invested in plants and equipment, and each year approximately $600 million is spent on expansion and improvements.

The industry distribution of its products of different kinds is broken down as follows, in terms of percentage of dollar volume:

apparel	50%
household	30%
industrial	20%

UNIONS

The International Ladies' Garment Workers' Union represents apparel workers. Textile workers are similarly represented, but not with the same degree of solidarity. The history of textile unions is marked by internal strife that started with fragmented organizations in 1935. Out of the conflict of the goals of the two factions emerged the United Textile Workers and The Textile Workers Union. In 1976, The Textile Workers Union merged with the Amalgamated Clothing Workers Union, an organization founded in 1914, to represent men's wear apparel workers. The coalition is known as Amalgamated Clothing and Textile Workers Union and has a total membership of 510,000, 150,000 of whom are textile workers. In 1979 the 25,000 members of the United Shoe-workers of America were merged into the ACTWU and designated the union's Shoe Division.

SUMMARY

The textile industry has a long and interesting history that includes art, craftsmanship, inventions, chemical developments, and active participation in the founding of modern industrial practices. Fulfilling a basic human need, it is the earliest human art form and a fundamental industry of all nations.

Textile producers must have a grasp of international fashion trends because fabric designs, colors, and yarns must be selected one to one-and-a-half years in advance of their showing to customers. Production takes place in widely scattered areas of the United States, with greatest concentration in the South. To gain fashion trend information, textile designers and color experts seek input from apparel manufacturers, and, not infrequently, request information from fashion directors of retail organizations.

The marketing process by which textile products are distributed to manufacturers and ultimate consumers requires a well-organized personnel team. Large firms maintain a multilayered organization to fix responsibility on specialists concerned with style development, production, and selling.

64

One point should be emphasized. Bigness is not the overwhelming characteristic of textile companies. Although there are many giant-sized firms, there are more small organizations—the relationship is about 55 percent to 45 percent. However, the combined sales of larger firms far exceed the total revenues of the small-sized producers and distributors. Larger firms are those doing a business of over $100 million, small firms those with an annual volume under $50 million. The industry gives employment to hundreds to thousands of people and requires deep annual investment to maintain production competitiveness. It is a significant part of the nation's industrial society.

QUESTIONS FOR DISCUSSION

1. Discuss the textile industry's part in the development of modern big business.
2. What events led to the founding of the American textile industry?
3. Relate the reasons for the integration of larger textile firms of the United States.
4. What is factoring? Why did this institution come into being?
5. Discuss the economic role of a converter.
6. What practices are unique to the selling of fabrics?
7. Explain the activities that lead to the fashion colors for a new season.
8. Why are production facilities of the textile industry located largely in the South?
9. Explain the textile industry's importance to the economy of the country.
10. Prepare a list of five textile trade associations, five textile organizations listed on the New York Stock Exchange, and two textile firms that do an annual volume of more than $1 billion.

4

THE CHEMICAL COMPANIES AND MAN-MADE FIBERS

Chemistry is one of the earliest sciences, but the rapidity of recent discoveries and the broadening of knowledge have given us a variety of products beyond the wildest dreams of early experimenters.

The long history of the textile industry in commercialization of technological breakthroughs can be illustrated by a modern series of research applications—fibers developed in laboratories.

RAYON

As early as 1665 the great English physicist Robert Hooke suggested the possibility of making artificial silk, duplicating the delicate cocoon filament spun by the silkworm, the source of raw silk. During the next two hundred years there was growing interest in the development of artificial filaments, some intended for fabric applications and some for other uses. In 1841 Louis Schwabe, a silk manufacturer in Manchester, England, demonstrated a machine he had invented that produced filaments spun from glass; these were not practical for use in apparel fabric, however. Joseph Wilson Swan, an English chemist and physicist, made an incandescent light using a carbon filament in 1860, twenty

years before Edison's electric bulb. Swan, who was knighted in 1904, also experimented with a variety of man-made fibers. In a parallel development—
66 as a result of which most paper since about 1860 has been made of wood pulp rather than cotton cuttings and similar "rag" material—interest focused on the possibilities of cellulose, the chief component of the cell walls of plants.

The first artificial textile fabric was produced in 1884 by a French scientist, Hilaire de Chardonnet, who patented what he called *une matière textile artificielle resemblant à la soie* (an artificial textile resembling silk), which he began to manufacture commercially in 1889. Chardonnet's process used cellulose, originally from cotton linters, later from wood pulp. The substance was washed, bleached, and pressed into sheets, then dissolved in chemicals and forced under pressure through tiny holes in a metal cap called a spinneret. These filaments united to form a single continuous filament that solidified when it passed through an appropriate solution or through warm air. Chardonnet treated the cellulose with nitric and sulfuric acids. His accomplishment was a great one, but there were significant drawbacks: the filaments were flammable, and the resultant fabric was both too lustrous and difficult to launder.

These disadvantages were overcome when the English chemist Charles Frederick Cross and his collaborator Edward John Bevan developed the **viscose process** in 1892. Cellulose was treated with carbon disulfide, then dissolved in caustic soda, forced through a spinneret, and hardened in sulfuric acid. Viscose rayon is still the most important commercial type, used in apparel fabrics, furniture fabrics, and carpets. By the turn of the century the Viscose Development Company had been established in England; it was taken over by Courtaulds Ltd in 1904, and large-scale manufacture of viscose rayon began in Courtaulds' silk-weaving mills in 1909.

A third important development in rayon manufacture came with the **acetate process,** in which an acetate derivative of cellulose is made by steeping the cellulose in acetic acid, then treating it with acetic anhydride. The end product is rayon that is more resistant than viscose to stains and creasing, is plasticized by heat, and requires special dyes, which permits two-tone effects with a single dye when acetate is used with other fibers. There were patents for acetate early in the twentieth century. Henri and Camille Dreyfus (who made the first commercial application and coined the name *Celanese*) produced acetylcellulose dope for British military aircraft in World War I. Saponified rayon acetate was originated in Britain in 1918, and after World War I British Celanese Ltd. brought its manufacture to a new high level of technology with improved methods of weaving and knitting that included the use of shuttleless and circular looms.

The first practicable man-made fiber continued to be known as artificial silk until 1924, when the term *rayon* was substituted by the U.S. Department of Commerce and various industry associations.

Rayon was one of the primary elements in the establishment of what we know as ready-to-wear. In the beginning, in 1920, rayon was still in the early stages of commercial use; dresses made of it were shiny and had a tendency to show dirt. Many women were reluctant to buy garments made of a fabric

Polyester fiber in ropelike tow form moves toward a drawing machine that stretches the fibers to give them strength. Another strand is added from each huge can. This is one of many steps necessary to produce fibers ready to be shipped to textile mills. (DuPont/*The New Encyclopedia of Textiles,* Doric Publishing Co., © 1980)

At a textile mill, a technician develops a pattern on a computer system. When the pattern is ready, the computer will control the knitting machine in the background, which will make the fabric. (American Textile Manufacturers Institute)

68

that was inexpensive and obviously imitative. At that time insiders called the ready-to-wear business the "rag business"—one that produced cheap clothing of inferior quality.

In the early 1930s, rayon delustering techniques were developed as well as processes to reduce its tendency to show dirt. At the same time, tensile strength was increased, and yarn use was extended from clothing to such items as automobile tires. In the 1940s additional advances included color-fastness, still greater tensile strength, and yarn uniformity. In the two decades that followed, rayon became the predominant tire yarn for original-equipment vehicle tires. Use of rayon as an apparel fiber declined during the 1950s because of the competitive pressure from newly developed man-made fibers, particularly nylon and polyester. In the 1960s new processes helped rayon recapture many of the apparel and home-furnishings markets. Rayon is presently used as a blending fiber with polyester, especially in permanent-press fabrics. Polyester has replaced rayon as the fiber of original-equipment tire-cord yarns.

Two rayon processes are currently employed:

1. Cuprammonium—filaments of regenerated cellulose are coagulated from a solution of cellulose in ammoniacal oxide
2. Viscose—filaments of regenerated cellulose are coagulated from a solution of cellulose xanthate

Leading registered trademarks include Polynosic, Zantrel (American Enka); Avril (Avtex Fibers); Bemberg, Cupioni (Beaunit); Coloray, Fibro (Courtaulds).

Rayon has a wide variety of clothing uses:

Women's and children's wear

Dresses	Rainwear
Suits	Lingerie
Blouses	Accessories
Sportswear	Millinery
Coats	Coat and suit linings

Men's and boys' wear

Sports shirts	Jackets
Summer and year-round suits	Raincoats
	Work clothing
Rugged underwear	Ties
Slacks	

Rayon was man's first achievement in synthesizing cloth for the making of apparel. Complete dependence on nature for the supply of fabric was no longer a fact of life. The availability of chemical products serves a wide range of human needs, has great economic value, and touches all our lives. From the sheets on which we sleep to the furniture and decorations we use at home and office to the tires that give us mobility, new materials have changed our ways of living.

NYLON

In 1926 E. I. du Pont de Nemours & Company's laboratories embarked on a series of research projects devoted to the creation of fibers made *entirely* of chemical compounds. The result, after ten years of work, was polymide fiber—synthetic thermoplastic material—with many useful characteristics and an exciting potential. The most practical of these, first identified as Fiber 66 and **69** then introduced in 1938 under the trade name **Nylon,** is made from hexamethylene amine and adipic acid. Nylon has great versatility and many desirable qualities: unusual strength, elasticity, smoothness, resistance to abrasion and chemicals, low moisture absorbency, easy dye acceptance, the capacity to be permanently set by heat, and moth-repellency.

Its earliest uses were as monofilaments for toothbrush bristles (1938) and as multifilament yarn for hosiery and sewing thread. In 1940 nylon became available in stores throughout the United States. The medical field began to use it for sutures; sportsmen fished with nylon line thread; women wore nylon hosiery; and the fiber name became part of our vocabulary. When the United States entered World War II, the government directed that nylon production be used for military needs: parachutes, flak vests, combat uniforms, vehicle tires, and many other requirements of the armed forces. At the end of the war, civilians were able once more to take advantage of the prewar chemical breakthrough. Du Pont then decided to license other companies to produce the fiber under Du Pont patents, and nylon products proliferated quickly.

Nylon was soon adopted for use in woven fabrics, industrial applications, and carpeting. In due course improvements in the yarn led to major changes in its processing, revisions to suit particular use needs. During the 1960s Du Pont introduced Antron, a yarn with unique visual properties, particularly sheen; Nomex, a heat-resistant version that can stand temperatures up to 1000 F.; Cantrece, a yarn with built-in coil or crimp; and Qiana, a luxury fiber that feels like silk.

Other manufacturers were also busy. Monsanto's ribbon form of nylon fiber goes into Astro Turf, the surface of many football fields. American Enka markets Crepeset, characterized by a crinkly surface. Allied produces Source, a nylon matrix with polyester for the luxury carpet market.

Many-purpose nylon fiber has yielded some of its apparel applications to newer man-made fibers but it is still extremely important and a major member of the family of synthetics. It has never lost its dominance in the hosiery business, and even where it is no longer a primary component in outerwear garments, it is often used in such garments as a strengthening fiber.

Nylon uses are approximately the same as those of rayon, with greater importance in tires and in hosiery and lingerie.

Some of the major producers are these:

Allied Corporation	UniRoyal Fibres and Textile Divison of UniRoyal, Inc.
American Enka Corporation	Dow Badische Company
Beaunit Corporation	E. I. du Pont de Nemours & Company, Inc.
Courtaulds North America	Enjay Fibres and Laminates Company
Monsanto Company, Textile Division	Fibre Industries, Inc.
Phillips Fibre Corporation	Firestone Synthetic Fibers and Textile Company
Rohm Haas Company	

Nylon marks the beginning of a new era—the synthetic world. The industrial uses of nylon are numerous, particularly for products that require material with fiber strength. Nylon is a versatile fiber with a multiplicity of uses.

ACRYLICS

70 **Acrylics** are fibers made from a special group of vinyl compounds, chiefly acrylonitrile. Recognizing that no fiber can meet all requirements, even after the introduction of nylon chemists continued to seek new developments to suit specific needs. Up to this point, laboratory output had synthesized silk and produced a man-made fiber with a variety of excellent characteristics. But not one had synthesized the natural fiber wool.

In the early 1950s, Du Pont introduced the first acrylic of major importance under the trademark Orlon. This fiber had new dimensions: warmth and a luxurious feeling, not unlike that of cashmere. It also draws moisture from the body and prevents clamminess, has lightness and fluffiness, resists harmful elements like mildew and moths, and accepts dyes readily.

In due course additional acrylics were developed by other producers: Acrilan by Monsanto, Creslan by American Cyanamid, Zefram by Dow Badische Company. Whereas acrylics do not have the tensile strength or durability of nylon, they do resist sunlight and chemical degradation and have a unique **hand,** a pleasant reaction to fabric of the sense of touch.

Out of the acrylic research, modacrylic, trademarked Dynel, was produced by Union Carbide Corporation. This fiber's properties make it suitable for products that simulate furs and for fleece linings, industrial fabrics, nonwoven fabrics, curtains, scatter rugs, stuffed toys, wigs, and decorations. Dynel's characteristics are resiliency, shape retention, easy dyeability, flame resistance, and quick drying.

Acrylic fibers have a wide variety of uses in apparel, home and industrial fabrics. They are used in many products:

blankets	sweaters	water softener filters
coverlets	men's hose	stiffening fabrics (interfacing)
draperies	resist yarns	molded fabrics
upholstery	filter cloths	infants' wear
pile fabrics	dust-fume bags	men's suiting
snowsuits	shirtings	floor coverings
scarves	work clothing	knit dresses
swimsuits	insulation fabrics	hand knitting yarns
paint rollers	doll wigs	

Acrylic blends are becoming increasingly important; hangtags on garments featured on retail racks indicate their wide use by manufacturers, some of whom are these:

Acrylic	*Modacrylic*
American Cyanamid Company, Fibers Division	Tennessee Eastman Company, Textiles Division
Dow Badische Company	Union Carbide Corporation
E. I. du Pont de Nemours & Company, Inc.	Monsanto Company, Textiles Division
Monsanto Company, Textiles Division	

Acrylics may be considered another step forward in the enlargement of the family of man-made fibers. They supplied what was lacking in the synthetic story—a luxurious hand and the imitation of another natural fiber, cashmere wool. The first products had retailer support but were far from satisfactory

At a textile mill, a Jacquard loom weaves a fabric with an intricate pattern. (American Textile Manufacturers Institute)

from the consumer's point of view, something that was rectified when additional processes, like bulking, were added.

The man-made-fiber story continues with another major advance, polyester.

POLYESTER

Du Pont's British counterparts concentrated on their own versions of laboratory-made fibers, and polymer chemistry became known to the world. Polyester, a man-made fiber that has excellent applications in textile manufacture, is produced by the polymerization of the product that results from the reaction of an alcohol and an organic acid. The fiber developed by the Calico Printers Association in England was known there as Terylene. Du Pont obtained exclusive right to produce this polyester fiber in the United States in 1946 and immediately set about determining practical commercial uses.

At a press conference in 1951 Du Pont displayed the new fiber in the form of a garment that had been worn, washed by machine without pressing, and appeared fresh. Polyester was launched toward popularity and the way was cleared for the marketing of a new man-made fiber.

Du Pont took Celanese in as a marketing partner. Celanese started to produce polyester under the trade names Mylar and Celanar. The most important use of the Celanese fibers is in metallic yarn laminations, but they are also used for computer and recording tapes, electrical and electronic installation, and packaging. Producing licenses were eventually granted by the owners of the original patent rights to organizations in France, Italy, Germany, Japan, Australia, South Africa, Portugal, Czechoslovakia, and the U.S.S.R.

Polyester is known for its remarkable wrinkle recovery and continued freshness of appearance. This fiber has earned a highly important place in the fabric family and is usable in the wide range indicated for rayon and nylon, both by itself and blended with other fibers. On the list of trademarks and trade names of man-made fibers in the United States it will be seen that the number of companies involved in producing polyester has expanded and that it is available under many different brand names (see Table 4–3, page 80).

CURRENT DEVELOPMENTS

Although polyester is the most recently developed man-made fiber, extensive research efforts have been successful in producing innovations to meet specific industry and consumer needs. For example, nylon required for sweaters is different from nylon needed for carpeting. Fibers have now been modified to embody the characteristics most suitable for such specific products as hosiery, undergarments, outerwear, and carpets.

Some of the ways fibers can be modified are as follows:

1. Chemical additions
2. Chemical modifications
3. Physical modifications like surface change
4. Permanent crimping: pressing into small folds, frilling, corrugation
5. Cross-section modification: changing fiber shape to create new luster and feel

Man-made fibers have been successful because they have a series of advantages that accommodate modern living style: they have esthetic value, are easy to care for, have controlled shrinkage, are pleat- and crease-retentive, and require little or no ironing. Economically, they have been a stabilizer in the price level of ready-to-wear because they resisted price increases until the oil shortage affected the cost of production.

The overwhelming advantages of man-made fibers have resulted in their overcoming natural fibers—in 1968 "King Cotton" was toppled from first place. Man-made fibers have assumed the dominant role in use for apparel, ranging from nearly 100 percent of hosiery and pantyhose to more than 80 percent of women's dresses, 70 percent of sweaters, and so on down the list. Indeed, the new king of fabric fibers is an important figure, all-pervasive, powerful, and firmly entrenched in importance with the constituency it serves. Just how important man-made fibers have become can be seen from Table 4–1, which shows comparative United States mill consumption of fibers from 1975 to 1981.

Future research efforts are likely to develop fibers that will

1. Respond to temperature changes, becoming warm in the winter and cool in the summer
2. Be capable of conducting electricity or heat

TABLE 4–1   U.S. Mill Consumption of Fibers, 1975–1981
(totals, percentage distribution, per capita)

	Total (million pounds)	Share of fibers	Per capita[a] (pounds)
Man-made fibers[b]			
1975	7,416.5	69.9%	34.7
1976	8,052.5	69.5	37.5
1977	8,887.5	72.9	41.1
1978	9,227.7	74.4	42.4
1979	9,446.0	74.7	41.6
1980	8,760.1	73.2	37.5
1981	8,722.5	75.3	38.0
Cotton			
1975	3,068.7	28.9%	14.9
1976	3,389.0	29.2	16.9
1977	3,169.8	26.0	15.8
1978	3,040.4	24.5	15.8
1979	3,066.4	24.2	14.8
1980	3,064.4	25.6	14.7
1981	2,703.0	23.4	14.3
Wool			
1975	132.0	1.2%	0.7
1976	145.9	1.3	0.9
1977	133.9	1.1	0.9
1978	141.6	1.1	1.0
1979	134.4	1.1	0.9
1980	137.8	1.2	0.9
1981	152.7	1.3	1.0
Total, all fibers[c]			
1975	10,618.2	100.0%	50.3
1976	11,590.2	100.0	55.3
1977	12,192.8	100.0	57.8
1978	12,411.7	100.0	59.2
1979	12,648.3	100.0	57.3
1980	11,962.3	100.0	53.1
1981	11,580.2	100.0	53.3

[a]Domestic consumption (mill consumption adjusted for import/export balance)
[b]Includes textile glass fiber
[c]Total includes silk

SOURCE: Textile Economics Bureau, *Textile Organon*, March 1982

3. Change from transparent to opaque and back again

4. Be self-cleaning

5. Be capable of reflecting different colors

CHEMICAL COMPANIES AND READY-TO-WEAR

The textile industry reached a peak just before World War II. With a growing population, the democratization of fashion, improved income, other affirmative demographic factors, and technological advances, a change was taking place. But the war put a damper on the growth of civilian products, and the wartime experience had far-reaching implications. Due to the shortage of apparel, manufacturers were in a **seller's market** (where demand exceeds supply) and in a position to set the terms of retail store purchases. Accordingly stores had to agree to publicize the vendors' names to receive maximum quantities from manufacturers. The result was the introduction of brand names in the women's apparel industry. The use of brand names—branding—in male clothing had long been an industry practice because of style stability—slow change—and men's reluctance to shop and to accept new fashion ideas. Later, men's attitudes about clothing changed—a subject to which we will return.

This branding during World War II was picked up by the chemical companies after the war. Since they are large and powerful (two of the most important are Du Pont and Celanese), they had the wherewithal to make inroads into the apparel industry; they had money for cooperative advertising, marketing expertise, and research that is technically based but applicable to such marketing activities as color and style forecasting, fashion acceptance, and other important aspects of fashion professionalism.

The chemical organizations and large textile companies were now fully in the apparel business, a business that offers high returns. In addition, the chemical companies realized the variety of end uses of the fibers they could produce and knew that brand importance could help influence consumer purchase of products from paint to sweaters. Cooperative advertising became the lure to attract spinners, weavers, knitters, manufacturers, and consumers. The battle of the giants was on.

Retail stores were filled with a new array of garments constructed of man-made fibers with hangtags featuring the chemical company name, the brand name of the fiber, and the name of the apparel manufacturer. The consumer was bewildered—and to a great extent continues to be. A polymer chemist or a textile expert, of course, knows the meaning of *triacetate*, but how many consumers do? And how many know the meaning of *trilobular fiber*? The list that follows, from the hangtag of a current multifiber outerwear garment, is interesting both in showing the number of fibers used and in the featuring of generic names. Once again, though, how much do you think these terms mean to the average consumer?

Shell
100% Nylon

Quilted to Polyester
Pile Lining
Face 50% Acrylic
     50% Polyester
Back
100% Polyester
Sleeve Lining
100% Acetate
Stitched to Polyester
Pile Trim
80% Modacrylic
20% Acrylic
100% Polypropylene Back

The advertisement on page 76 further illustrates the combination of brand names regularly present in the promotion of today's apparel goods. This ad features the Du Pont polyester fiber Dacron, presented by brand name; the fabric producer, Klopman; the fabric producer's parent corporation, Burlington; and the manufacturer, Wilroy.

A new dimension was added with the entry of the chemical companies into the fabric industry. Big companies, especially those heavily dependent on research, approached the business with a degree of professional analysis never before practiced by the textile industry. Because of the necessity to plan early, the need for the investment of great sums in machinery and personnel, and the requirement to establish a rationale for business decisions, specialists are used in every area of marketing, from product development through the place-

A technician tests textile finishes in a plant laboratory. The many finishing processes include dyeing, bleaching, durable press, sanforizing. (American Textile Manufacturers Institute)

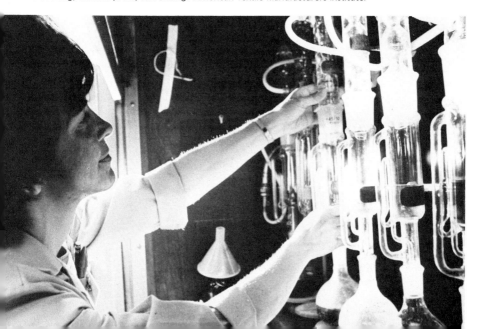

76

Klopman believes all polyester fabrics should look and feel like natural fiber fabrics.

Take our Crepe Berenda:
It looks, feels and drapes like silk crepe.

We begin by weaving it from a unique 100% polyester yarn. **Today's Dacron**.

Then Klopman's superior technology gives it its silk crepe characteristics.

The result is an elegant, non-glitter fabric in a practical form.

Crepe Berenda.
Wilroy chose it for this nostalgic ensemble that can travel wrinkle-free. On you or in your luggage.

When the fabric is Klopman, the feeling is natural.

LEAN ON KLOPMAN FABRICS
a division of Burlington ⊞ Industries

Klopman fabrics advertisement. (Klopman Mills)

ment of products in proper channels of distribution—to customers and their customers' customers.

Research is continuous. European markets are searched for fashion styles and colors. Contacts with important retailers are a source of important information: selling trends, competition, consumer attitudes, and, above all, future trends.

The entry of chemical companies into the fashion industry widened merchandise availability and consumer conveniences and added a new force in the promotion of apparel. The vocabulary of end users has been expanded, but there does not yet exist an educational program through which consumers can become knowledgeable enough to make wise purchase decisions. Technology has outstripped our ability to cope with it judiciously.

No description of the growth and impact of the development of man-made fibers and of the chemical companies on the apparel-fabric industry could serve as well as Tables 4–2 and 4–3. The first is a chronology of the commercialization of man-made fibers in the United States from 1911 on. The second, which will also be useful for ready reference, is a listing of current trademarks and trade names of man-made fibers in the United States.

CHEMICAL COMPANY CAREER OPPORTUNITIES

Since they are industrial giants, the chemical companies have to set up a chain of command and decentralize their various business activities into areas of responsibility. The list that follows, from the organizational directory of one

**TABLE 4–2 Chronology of Commercialization
of Man-Made Fibers in the United States**

Date of commercial introduction	Generic classification	Trade name	Company
1911	rayon		Avtex Fibers, Inc. (American Viscose Division, FMC Corp.)
1916	rayon		IRC Fibers (subsidiary of American Cyanamid Co.)
1925	acetate		Celanese Corp.
	rayon	Bemberg	Beaunit Corp.
1927	rayon		Beaunit Corp.
1928	rayon		American Enka Corp.
1929	acetate	Acele	Du Pont Co.
1930	acetate		Avtex Fibers, Inc. (American Viscose Division, FMC Corp.)
	acetate		Eastman Kodak Co.
1935	glass	Fiberglas	Owens-Corning Fiberglas Co.
1939	nylon 6,6		Du Pont Co.
	saran		Dow Chemical Co.
1940	saran monofilament		Amtech (National Plastics Products Co.)
	vinyon		Avtex Fibers, Inc. (American Viscose Division, FMC Corp.)
1948	metallic	Metlon	Metlon Corp.
1949	modacrylic	Dynel	Union Carbide Corp.
1950	acrylic	Orlon	Du Pont Co.
1951	polyester	Dacron	Du Pont Co.
1952	acrylic	Acrilan	Monsanto Co.
	rayon		Courtaulds Alabama, Inc.
1954	fluorocarbon	Teflon	Du Pont Co.
	nylon 6		Allied Chemical Corp.
	nylon 6,6		Monsanto Co.
1955	nylon bcf		Allied Chemical Corp.
	nylon 6		American Enka Corp.
	triacetate	Arnel	Celanese Corp.
1956	modacrylic	Verel	Eastman Kodak Co.
1957	acrylic		Dow Badische (Dow Chemical Co.)
1958	nylon bcf		Du Pont Co.
	olefin monofilament		Thiokol Chemical Corp.
	polyester	Kodel	Eastman Kodak Co.
	spandex	Lycra	Du Pont Co.
1959	acrylic	Creslan	American Cyanamid Co.
	metallic	Brunslon	Brunswick Corp.
	nylon bcf	Cumuloft	Monsanto Co.
1960	nylon	Antron	Du Pont Co.
	olefin		Hercules, Inc.
	polyester	Fortrel	Fiber Industries (Celanese Corp.)
	rayon	Avril	Avtex Fibers, Inc. (American Viscose Division, FMC Corp.)
	rayon	Zantrel	American Enka Corp.

Sources of the Materials of Fashion

**TABLE 4–2 (continued) Chronology of Commercialization
of Man-Made Fibers in the United States**

Date of commercial introduction	Generic classification	Trade name	Company
1961	acrylic	Zefkrome	Dow Badische (Dow Chemical Co.)
1962	polyester		American Enka Corp.
1963	aramid	Nomex	Du Pont Co.
1964	nylon	Cantrece	Du Pont Co.
	nylon 6		Courtaulds North America, Inc.
	nylon 6,6	Celanese	Fiber Industries (Celanese Corp.)
	nylon 6,6	Wellon	Wellman, Inc.
	polyester		IRC Fibers (subsidiary of American Cyanamid Co.)
	spandex	Numa	Ameliotex, Inc.
1965	olefin	Polycrest	Uniroyal, Inc.
	polyester staple	Blue "C"	Monsanto Co.
	rayon	Nupron	IRC Fibers (subsidiary of American Cyanamid Co.)
1966	nylon	Cordura	Du Pont Co.
	nylon 6,6		Beaunit Corp.
	polyester	Avlin	Avtex Fibers, Inc. (American Viscose Division, FMC Corp.)
	polyester	Fillwell	Wellman, Inc.
	polyester	Wellene	Wellman, Inc.
1967	polyester	Trevira	Hoechst Fibers Industries
1968	acrylic	Acrilan	Monsanto Co.
	metallic	Feltmetal	Brunswick Corp.
	nylon	Qiana	Du Pont Co.
	nylon/polyester		Allied Chemical Corp.
	biconstituent olefin	Polyloom	Chevron Chemical Co.
1969	anidex	Anim/8	Rohm and Haas Co.
	nylon 6		Dow Badische Co.
	olefin	Patlon	Amoco Fabrics, Patchogue
	polyester		Dow Badische Co.
1970	glass	Hycor	PPG Industries, Inc.
	glass	Trianti	PPG Industries, Inc.
	nylon 6	Shareen	Courtaulds North America, Inc.
	olefin		ACS Industries, Inc.
	olefin bcf		Concorde Fibers, Inc.
	polyester	Spectran	Monsanto Co.
	rayon	Aviloc	Avtex Fibers, Inc. (American Viscose Division, FMC Corp.)

**TABLE 4–2 (continued)   Chronology of Commercialization
of Man-Made Fibers in the United States**

Date of commercial introduction	Generic classification	Trade name	Company
1971	modacrylic	SEF	Monsanto Co.
	nylon 6 (solution dyed)		Camac Corp.
	olefin	Fibralon	Fibron, Inc.
	olefin	Fibrilawn	Fibron, Inc.
	olefin	Fibrilon	Fibron, Inc.
	polytetrafluoroethylene	Gore-tex	W. L. Gore & Associates, Inc.
1972	nylon 6	Type 90	Courtaulds North America, Inc.
	nylon polyurethane biconstituent	Monvelle	Monsanto Co.
	polyester filament		Monsanto Co.
1973	aramid	Kevlar	Du Pont Co.
	nylon 6	Starbrite	Star Fibers, Inc.
	nylon 6	WonderThread	Shakespeare Co.
1976	acrylic	Fina	Monsanto Co.
	nylon	Ultron	Monsanto Co.
	nylon 6,6	Vecana	Chevron Chemical Co.
	rayon	Avril II	Avtex Fibers, Inc. (American Viscose Division, FMC Corp.)
1977	olefin		Elizabeth Webbing
1978	rayon		North American Rayon Corp. (Beaunit)
1979	olefin		Twine Products Corp. (Intl. Harvester)
	olefin		WaynTex (Thiokol Fibers)
1980	olefin		Meyers Fibers, Inc.
	olefin		Fiber Industries, Inc.
1981	polyester		Omega Yarns (Texfi)
	olefin		Camac Corp.
1982	polyester		Toloram, Inc. (Meyers)
	olefin		Toloram, Inc. (Meyers)

Note: Since 1976, the primary changes in the manufacturing of man-made fibers in the United States have been in ownership and in the production of variants of current fibers, often for very specialized purposes. Many of these variants are not given trade names. When they are, they are likely to be names derived from existing names; for example, Avtex is producing modifications of its rayon fiber Avril as Avril II, Avril III, and Avril Prima, each of which has specific properties. In the past few years no major new trade names have been introduced.

SOURCE: Textile Economics Bureau

TABLE 4–3 Major Trade Names and Manufacturers of Man-Made Fibers in the United States (by generic classification)

Acetate
Acetate by Avtex—Avtex Fibers
Ariloft—Eastman Chemical
Avron—Avtex Fibers
Celanese—Celanese
Chromspun—Eastman Chemical
Estron—Eastman Chemical
Lanese—Celanese
Loftura—Eastman Chemical

Acrylic
Acrilan—Monsanto
Bi-Loft.—Monsanto
Creslan—American Cyanamid
Fi-lana—Monsanto
Fina—Monsanto
Orlon—Du Pont
Pa-Qel—Monsanto
Remember—Monsanto
So-Lara—Monsanto
Zefran—Badische

Aramid
Kevlar—Du Pont
Nomex—Du Pont

Modacrylic
SEF—Monsanto
Verel—Eastman Chemical

Nylon
A.C.E.—Allied Fibers
Anso—Allied Fibers
Antron—Du Pont
Blue "C"—Monsanto
Cadon—Monsanto
Cantrece—Du Pont
Caprolan—Allied Fibers
Captiva—Allied Fibers
Celanese—Celanese
Cordura—Du Pont
Courtaulds Nylon—Courtaulds
Crepeset—American Enka
Cumuloft—Monsanto
Eloquent Luster—Allied Fibers
Eloquent Touch—Allied Fibers
Enkalure—American Enka
Enkasheer—American Enka
Golden Touch—American Enka
Lurelon—American Enka
Matte Touch—American Enka
Multisheer—American Enka
Natural Touch—American Enka
Natura Luster—Allied Fibers
Shareen—Courtaulds
Shimmereen—American Enka
Softalon—American Enka
T.E.N.—American Enka

Ultron—Monsanto
Zefran—Badische
Zeftron—Badische

Olefin
Herculon—Hercules
Marquesa—Amoco Fabrics
Marvess—Phillips Fibers
Patlon—Amoco Fabrics
Polyloom—Chevron Fibers
Vectra—Chevron Fibers

Polyester
A.C.E.—Allied Fibers
Avlin—Avtex Fibers
Blue "C"—Monsanto
Caprolan—Allied Fibers
Crepesoft—American Enka
Dacron—Du Pont
Encron—American Enka
Fortrel—Celanese
Golden Glow—American Enka
Golden Touch—American Enka
Hollofil—Du Pont
Kodel—Eastman Chemical
KodOfill—Eastman Chemical
KodOlite—Eastman Chemical
KodOsoff—Eastman Chemical
Matte Touch—American Enka
Natural Touch—American Enka
Plyloc—American Enka
Polyextra—American Enka
Shanton—American Enka
Silky Touch—American Enka
Spectran—Monsanto
Strialine—American Enka
Trevira—American Hoechst
Twisloc—Monsanto

Rayon
Absorbit—American Enka
Avril—Avtex Fibers
Avsorb—Avtex Fibers
Beau-Grip—North American Rayon
Coloray—Courtaulds
Durvil—Avtex Fibers
Enkaire—American Enka
Enkrome—American Enka
Fibro—Courtaulds
Rayon by Avtex—Avtex Fibers
Zantrel—American Enka

Spandex
Lycra—Du Pont

Triacetate
Arnel—Celanese

Vinyon
Vinyon by Avtex—Avtex Fibers

Note: The generic names for the three cellulosic fibers are: acetate, rayon, triacetate. The Federal Trade Commission has assigned generic names to 18 noncellulosic fibers. Of these the following 12 are currently being produced in the United States: acrylic, aramid, glass, metallic, modacrylic, nylon, olefin, polyester, rubber, saran, spandex, vinyon. The other six are: anidex, azlon, lastrile, novoloid, nytril, vinal.

SOURCE: Man-Made Fiber Producers Association, *Man-Made Fibers: A New Guide*, 1982

of the nation's largest fiber producers, Celanese, gives an idea of the many areas of activity and responsibility in a giant fiber-producing organization. It will help put into perspective the complexities of servicing the various industries and the numerous products that are marketed. It suggests a range of executive positions that could be considered for career goals, since each line is a department within the organization and employs numerous people, some at entry level.

Celanese Fibers Marketing Company
Organization Chart Index

President's Staff
Textile Marketing Staff
Woven/Fiberfill Markets
Woven Markets
Home Furnishings Merchandising
Fiberfill Markets
Knit Markets
Warp Knit Markets
Circular Knit Markets
Throwster/Spinner Markets
Merchandising
Textile Markets Plans & Programs
Apparel Merchandising
West Coast Marketing
Regional Marketing
Advertising/Public Relations/Marketing Services
Advertising
Public Relations
Marketing Services
Administration & Technical
Textile Products Development Staff
Textile Products Development Weaving & Fiberfill Department
Textile Products Development Warp & Circular Knit
Textile Products Development Dyeing, Finishing, & Evaluation Department
Special Products Development
Special Products Development Industrial Products, Tire & Rubber Reinforcement
    Development
Special Products Development Floor Coverings Development & Technical Service
Special Products Development Smoking Products & Mirafi Development & Technical
    Service
Product Performance
Sales Order & Pricing
Product Distribution
New Business Ventures
Industrial & Smoking Products Marketing
Industrial—Tire Cord—Mirafi
Mirafi
Industrial

Tire Cord
Cigarette Tow/ Floor Coverings
Floor Coverings
Cigarette Tow
International Marketing
Personnel

SUMMARY

During the past 150 years one fiber development has followed another and has had impact on what we wear, how we furnish our homes, and even what type of napery we use when we dine—just to mention a few applications of fibers born in a test tube. Indeed, the evolution of man-made fibers that started in the mid-19th century is a remarkable progression of scientific developments.

Man-made fibers are successful because they have characteristics that accommodate modern life style: esthetic value, ease of care, minimum shrinkage, pleat- and crease-retention, permanent press. Economically, they have been a price stabilizer because their supply is predictable, not subject to price increases caused by unfavorable elements (rain, drought, disease). It is true, however, man-made fiber costs increased considerably due to oil price escalation during the 1970s. Petroleum is a basic element in the process of making man-made fibers.

In 1968 "King Cotton" was toppled from its throne, and man-made fibers became sovereign. Their dominance in apparel usage is shown by the following percentages: almost 100 percent in hosiery and panty hose, over 80 percent in women's dresses, 70 percent in sweaters.

Chemical companies, obviously, make deep investments in research and marketing of man-made fibers because they serve not only ready-to-wear, but a wide spectrum of other industrial uses. As part of their marketing practices, they display their brand names prominently, as well as their product features. The competition among chemical firms is strong, but the rewards are high.

Man-made fibers are an integral part of our lives. They are certainly a significant factor in an age of technology.

QUESTIONS FOR DISCUSSION

1. Discuss the role of chemical companies in helping to create a "synthetic" world.
2. Visit a fashion department of a store and study the hangtags on fashion merchandise. What are your thoughts about a consumer's ability to buy with sufficient knowledge of fabric serviceability or fashion advantage?
3. Select and discuss at least four newspaper or magazine advertisements that have cooperative textile market (including fiber-producer) support for a manufacturer or retailer.
4. Carpets were traditionally mostly of wool before the advent of man-made fibers. What percentage of carpets are presently manufactured of this natural fiber? What are the reasons for the loss of its importance?

5. What percentage of your wardrobe consists of man-made fabrics? What percentage is blends?
6. Discuss the converter's importance to fashion development.

7. Explain the importance of name brands to giant textile or chemical fiber producers.
8. Assume the unlikely possibility that man-made fibers become as costly as wool. What would be the effect on present consumer preference for apparel of man-made fabrics?
9. As a consumer, identify the man-made fiber brand names that you know. What brand do you seek when making an apparel purchase, if any? Why?
10. Discuss the reasons for Du Pont's decision not to maintain nylon as an exclusive product but to allow other companies to make it under a licensing agreement.

5

LEATHER AND FUR

The use of animal skin and fur as human body covering predates the art of making textiles, ancient though that craft is. The ability to process leather has been traced to all early civilizations and is a technique that has been handed down from generation to generation. Once our ancestors learned to make cloth, it became the primary material for apparel, but leather and fur have remained important items of fashion apparel throughout history—leather for shoes, gloves, and handbags, and fur for coats. Leather garments, in fact, are an important contemporary fashion element. As the modern leather and fur industries are highly specialized, we will discuss finished products as well as the raw materials.

LEATHER

Historical artifacts show hunters wearing skins of animals as early as what is assumed to be 20,000 B.C. The art of ancient Egypt pictures kings and gods followed by servants carrying leather sandals, evidently a symbol of rank to be worn on solemn occasions. In the Hebrew culture, sandals were part of the

Models show leather jackets by Gianni Versace, March 1982. (*WWD*/The Fairchild Syndicate)

marriage contract, exchanged at the end of the ceremony as a pledge of marital fidelity.

In early cultures, products made of leather were considered to have magical powers and were used as protection against snakes and evil; pagan priests slept on leather robes in the belief that they gave the power to interpret dreams. In some Amerind societies, men of authority and warriors who distinguished themselves in battle were accorded the honor of wearing buckskin shirts.

The **tanning** of leather, the process of treating hides and skins to make them usable, dates back to the Bronze Age, around 2500 B.C., and according to Genesis 3:21 the first clothing worn by Adam and Eve after expulsion from the Garden of Eden was animal skins. In most cultures the art of tanning was a carefully guarded secret. Leather guilds in Europe and North Africa issued charters to restrict the dissemination of information about the craft to outsiders. Such guilds still exist in North Africa, and the leather craftsmen still use the traditional processing methods, operating from the locations of their forebears and passing their knowledge from father to son.

In North America, the first tanning was practiced by the Indians, using methods somewhat different from those employed in the Old World. When the New World was settled, the immigrants brought their own tanning processes but also improvised on some of those used by the Indians. In 1623, the first colonial tannery was set up in Plymouth, Massachusetts.

Over the centuries, leather-tanning methods have been improved through expanded scientific knowledge and the development of new instruments and machines. In modern production, machines make it possible to broaden the assortment of leather products with new finishes, new grains, new patterns, and new properties.

Types of leather

Leather is a highly specialized material, the hide or skin of an animal, usually mammal or reptile, that has been preserved by **dressing**—tawing, or tanning. *Hides* refer to leather from such large animals as horses, cows, and buffalo. *Skin* is leather from small animals, like calves or kids. Hides are usually cut into smaller sections for easier handling. Leather is priced by the square foot and is available in various thicknesses, indicated by weight of from one to twelve ounces or more. A cattle hide yields 40 square feet, a sheepskin about 6.5 square feet.

Leather is used in many end products:

belts	pillows
briefcases	sculpture
furniture	upholstery
apparel (including shoes, hats, and accessories)	wallets, key cases, and similar small products
handbags	bookbindings
linings	

There are numerous varieties and treatments of leather:

Kinds of Leathers and Their Uses

alligator   Alligator, crocodile, and related types.

belting   Usually supplied in a roll in round or flat narrow continuous stripping.

buckskin   Deer and elk skins, having the outer grain removed.

bull hide   Hide from a male bovine, capable of reproduction.

cabretta   A hair-type sheepskin; specifically, those from Brazil.

calfskin   Skin from a young bovine, male or female.

capeskin   From a sheep raised in South Africa.

carpincho   A water rodent native to South America; like pigskin.

cattlehide   General term for hides from a bovine of any breed or sex, but usually mature; includes bull hide, steerhide, cowhide, and sometimes **kipskins.**

chamois   The product of oil tanning the underneath layer (called a **flesher**) that has been split from a sheepskin.

cordovan   From a section of a horsehide called the shell.

cowhide   Hide from a mature female bovine that has produced a calf.

deerskin   Deer and elk skins, having the grain intact.

diploma   Usually vegetable-tanned sheepskin used in making diplomas.

doeskin   From sheep or lambskins, usually with the grain removed.

English bridle   A high quality cattlehide oak-tanned in a bridle-tanning process; excellent for tooling, sandals, and a wide variety of applications.

flesher   The underneath (flesh side) layer of a sheepskin that has been split off. Used to make **chamois.**

glove   Sheep, pig, deer, and kidskin that has been tanned to produce a soft, stretchy leather for dress gloves. Also, cattlehide splits, sheepskin, and others that are tanned for garden and work gloves.

glove horse   A supple horsehide used for garments given exposure to weather.

goatskin   Skin from a mature goat.

hair calf   Skin of a calf with the hair intact. When hair is clipped short it is called *hair calf clipped.*

hair sheep   Sheep from several species whose "wool" is hairlike.

harness Vegetable-tanned, cattlehide leather finished for harness, saddlery, and sculpture.

heifer A female bovine, under three years of age, that has not produced a calf.

horsehide Hide from a horse or colt.

kangaroo From the Australian kangaroo or wallaby.

kidskin Skin from a kid, or young goat.

kipskin Skin from a bovine, male or female, intermediate in size between a calf and mature animal.

lambskin Skin from a lamb, or young sheep.

latigo Cowhide sides tanned with alum, gambier (a yellowish catechu), and oil. Used for saddle strings, lacing, carved forms, sculpture.

lining A shoe leather used for lining the inside portions. Made from all kinds of hides and skins, either grain- or suede-finished.

live oak Vegetable-tanned cowhide producing a clear and even grain. Good for tooling, sculpture, and many other uses.

lizard Any of a great number of the lizard family.

mocha Middle East hair sheep, usually with the grain removed.

novelty Any of a variety of leathers, frequently vegetable tanned, used for billfolds and small leather goods.

ostrich From the two-legged animal native to North Africa.

patent Leather, heavily finished to give a highly lustrous, baked-enamel appearance, often used for shoe uppers. Generally from cattlehide.

peccary From a wild boar native to Central and South America; like pigskin.

pelt An untanned hide, or skin, with the hair on.

pigskin Skin from pigs and hogs.

raw stock General term for hides, or skins, that a tanner has received in a preserved state preparatory to tanning; a tanner's inventory of raw material.

saddle skirting Very heavy cowhide sides vegetable tanned for saddles. Good also for sculpture.

sharkskin From certain of the shark species.

shearlings Wooled sheep and lambskins, tanned with the wool intact with a nap of ¼ to ¾ inch.

sheepskin Skin from a mature sheep.

skiver The thin grain layer split from a sheepskin.

slunk Skin of unborn or prematurely born calf tanned with hair left intact.

snake Any of a number of the snake species.

steerhide Hide from a mature male bovine, incapable of reproduction, having been raised for beef.

suede Leather-finishing process whereby the flesh side or top of a split is buffed to produce a nap. Exceedingly difficult to tell kind of skin, or hide, used.

upholstery Large cattlehide, split thin, and tanned for use as furniture and automobile seat coverings.

walrus Skin from a walrus; also, sometimes sealskin.

water buffalo Flat-horned buffalo, primarily from the tropics.

The processing of skins and hides

Leather processing starts with animals that are bred or trapped, most obtained from ranchers or farmers. As cattle are the major source of leather, an important source is the meat processor. Converters purchase hides and skins

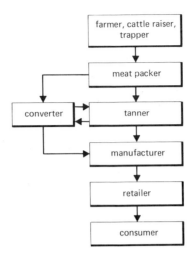

Figure 5–1 Leather industry flow chart.

from the meat packer, have them processed at contract tanneries, and sell them to apparel or other manufacturers. The manufacturers develop lines of merchandise that are sold to retailers, followed by the ultimate transaction— sale to the consumers.

Figure 5–1 diagrams the flow of skins from sources of supply to consumers.

Economic impact

Leather-industry statistics are often approximations because of the difficulty of obtaining precise base figures. According to the U.S. Bureau of Commerce 1979 Industrial Outlook, manufactured leather products were estimated to total $7.5 billion in 1978, a figure that can be translated into $15 billion at retail, with the largest proportion shoe sales. During 1978, the total retail value of shoes was almost $12 billion, of which slightly less than half were produced in foreign countries.

In 1978 the meat industry slaughtered 39,534,000 cattle, 4 million fewer than in 1976. The decrease was due to the reduction of the size of cattle herds by farmers responding to the increase in feed prices and the low return on beef in 1976. The result was that the 1979 price of beef as well as of its by-product, leather goods, increased considerably. Cattle hides represent 80 percent of all processed hides, with an additional 10 percent coming from sheep hides, the greatest part of which we import from New Zealand.

Since foreign manufacturers import hides and skins from the United States and then produce products for our domestic markets, there is strong sentiment in the United States leather industry for government protection. As a case in point, foreign producers of shoes control approximately 50 percent of the market. In 1966, the total shoe imports were 96 million pair; ten years later, the figure was 404 million. We will examine the industry dislocation caused by imports in Chapter 8.

The leather business is one of high specialization. Some 500 tanneries in the United States employ about 25,000 workers. Some tanneries are owned by meat packers; for instance, Esmark owns A. C. Lawrence Leather Company. Most of **89** the tanneries are located in the Northeast and north central states because that is where the major users, the shoe and glove manufacturers, are located. However, most manufacturers of finished products maintain sales offices in New York City. Of the several unions to which leather workers belong the Amalgamated Meat Cutters and Butchers Workmen of North America has the largest membership.

FUR

Furs are treated differently from leather: the skins or pelts of fur-bearing animals are dressed in a way that allows the hair covering to remain while leather processing removes the hair or wool. Fur processing results in a luxurious material to be used for a garment or as a trimming.

Originally, skins, pelts, or hides were probably used in their natural shapes, with the animal feet tied over the shoulder or around the waist of the wearer. In due course, garments that resembled capes were fashioned, with a head-sized hole in the middle. Over the centuries, apparel became more sophisticated, and fur was fashioned into garments much like those worn today and often used in trimming as a sign of social distinction. Roman generals wore fur garments as early as the third century B.C. In the fourteenth century, Edward III of England made ermine with black spots of lamb a royal fur. Early clerical rules limited the wearing of luxury furs to the upper level of the church hierarchy. The garment of greatest status was a long coat with a combination collar-cowl, lined with gray squirrel or ermine; a short, front-buttoned ceremonial cape is still reserved for certain levels of the clergy. The wide-shouldered, puff-sleeved fur robe is associated with Henry VIII, although many nobles also wore this type of garment. Through the ages the privileged wore luxurious furs, and the common people warmed themselves with garments of sheepskin.

The history of the American fur industry goes back to the exploration of the country, when early pioneers were often fur trappers and traders. Trading posts were set up to deal with the fur catches of the Indians. Out of these settlements grew many important cities, including Chicago, Detroit, St. Louis, and Minneapolis. Furs were big business in the New World as early as the sixteenth century. The colonies offered the Old World trading companies the opportunity to obtain a valuable raw product in quantity that had easy marketability in the form of skins and finished garments.

In the beginning, fur was used in the Western world essentially as a garment lining; only in the Arctic was fur used on the outside. (People living in colder climates realized that fur as an outer facing had superior heat-holding qualities.) However, improved methods of processing made fur more attractive and therefore usable as a garment material rather than a lining. Not until the twentieth century did "hair-out" become a custom of the Western world.

King George III of England in the ermine robes of royalty; portrait by the studio of Allan Ramsay, about 1767. (National Portrait Gallery, London)

The marketing of fur

The nature of fur, the required steps of processing—including the manner of obtaining animals—and the customs of the industry are a unique part of the apparel business.

Fur farmers and ranchers belong to associations like the Emba Mink Breeders Association and the Great Lakes Mink Association that provide means, time, and place to buy and sell skins at auction. The price of skins is set on the basis of quality, with the added factor of supply and demand. Prices can fluctuate sharply. Trappers, on the other hand, accumulate their catches and sell them to collectors, who in turn sell them to dealers and at auctions. The price fluctuation of fur skins can be illustrated by the current price of raccoon skins, which were once in the popular-price range. Raccoon today can be more costly than mink.

Most American fur manufacturers are undercapitalized, and the fact that auction sales are held long before a garment is made, sold, and paid for creates pressures on the producer. The average manufacturer has a yearly sales volume ten times his capitalization and therefore must strain to pay labor, buy a costly material, and finance his accounts receivable. Accordingly he seeks support from specialized banks that employ personnel fully conversant with the marketing of fur garments. Suppliers of fur manufacturers often take interest-bearing notes to cover the necessary purchases.

Another custom of the fur business is to sell on **consignment** (a contracted obligation to take back unsold goods), although this practice has lessened during the past few years as a result of improved business conditions. Obviously, this method of selling is based on weakness and is not in the long term good for the industry. The practice still continues in some degree, and many a retail sale is in reality a transfer of title from manufacturer to ultimate consumer.

For many years, the styling of most producers was staid and repetitive, with the exception of a few innovative furriers. Within the past few years, however,

One step in making a fur coat: A skilled worker tacks wet skins to a board, fur side down, in the exact shapes needed in the finished coat. When they are dry, the skins will hold their shapes. (Manning, Selvage & Lee, Inc.)

The actress Marlene Dietrich in an ermine robe. (Bettmann Archive)

that has changed, with famous designers offering their names on a franchise basis, among them Yves Saint Laurent, Givenchy, Oscar de la Renta, and Bill Blass. This trend is assuming real importance, and some designers of furs have now become famous. One well-known name is unusual because it refers to an entire family—Fendi of Italy—that includes five sisters and their husbands.

Fur garments, an international product, are featured at fashion shows in many countries. In the United States, fur shows are held in New York City during a three-week period in June. In West Germany, at the West German Fur Fair, the shows are the first week in April. In Paris and Milan they are held about the same time, but not on the same dates.

Two significant new markets for furs are Japan and Hong Kong, which have become important areas for United States exports of both skins and finished garments. For the five-year period 1972–1976, United States business in mink showed these increases:

	Skins	
	Units	Dollars
Japan	42%	517%
Hong Kong	24%	359%

The figures for both areas increased approximately 45 percent in each of the ensuing years.

Many specialty-store retailers in the fur business are also manufacturers who **93** will make an item to order, a custom-tailoring practice. Potential customers located near big cities, New York City in particular, know that manufacturers maintain showrooms for retail trade. Of course, manufacturers of coats, suits, and dresses open their doors for the same purpose in some instances, but the total business is hardly significant. In the fur market, retail trade is a sizable portion of the volume of many producers.

New York City has the largest aggregate of fur manufacturing establishments in the United States, a group that contributes to the importance of the fashion capital of the world. The New York City market is clustered in a small area, located in midtown, from 26th Street to 32nd Street.

Figure 5–2 is a flow chart of the fur industry.

Animals used for furs

The range of animals used for the purpose of making **plates**—skins joined together so that they have a form tantamount to woven fabric ready to be cut— is vast. The list is almost long enough to make a pocket-sized dictionary and includes such exotic items as white weasel, panda, reindeer, and zebra as well as some unexpected ones—bison, cat, coyote, dog, dormouse, musk-ox, platypus, tonky, and wombat. The list is long, but the extent of use is another matter.

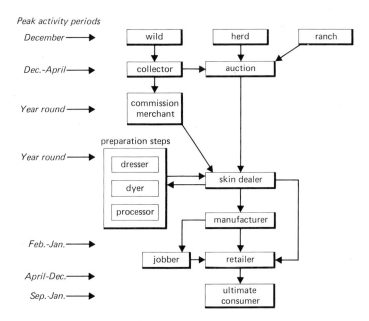

Figure 5–2 Fur flow chart: from catch to consumer. Auctions are arranged by permanent trade associations, e.g., the Emba Mink Breeders Association. Some skin dealers sell direct to retailers. Commission merchants often sell direct to manufacturers.

The commercial fur industry concentration is approximately

mink	62%
fox	15%
raccoon	15%
sable	5%
miscellaneous	3%

Mink is both bred and trapped; the figures are about 150,000 wild (trapped) as against 3 million raised on farms. Fox is trapped and bred. Raccoon is all trapped. Sable is imported.

The U.S. Bureau of Wildlife and Fisheries cooperates with state agencies that enforce laws that give partial protection to certain animals to control killing, give full protection to certain animals classified as endangered species, and give no protection to animals that are too numerous or predatory and for which extermination or thinning out is encouraged. A complete listing is available from the Bureau in Washington. This protection is considered inadequate by those who decry the killing of mammals, reptiles, and birds for apparel, apparel accessories, and sport. In fact, there are those who consider the killing of animals for these purposes as immoral. Obviously, they are not customers for apparel made of animal skin or fur.

An interesting aspect is the development of man-made fibers that simulate furs from mouton to mink. In the 1950s, fake fur women's coats were confined to mouton at popular prices, retailing from $79.95 to $100. But over the years

Metzger fake-fur garments: a herringbone-patterned mink-look jacket, left, and a chevron-patterned "foxy" jacket. Retail prices are slightly under $300 each. (Sportowne/The Metzger Group, Inc.)

TABLE 5–1   U.S. Retail Fur Sales, 1942–1981

Year	Sales	Year	Sales
1942	$331,907,150	1962	$ 304,140,000
1943	520,555,480	1963	301,600,000
1944	440,925,235	1964	296,450,000
1945	428,991,820	1965	346,253,000
1946	492,549,135	1966	319,937,772
1947	426,633,315	1967	355,450,865
1948	365,504,985	1968	332,346,559
1949	268,676,890	1969	294,459,051
1950	244,074,730	1970	279,147,180
1951	277,042,630	1971	293,383,686
1952	258,241,955	1972	361,626,000
1953	199,125,000	1973	440,841,000
1954	350,785,000	1974	441,000,000
1955	272,460,000	1975	525,000,000
1956	290,560,000	1976	554,000,000
1957	299,340,000	1977	612,500,000
1958	282,840,000	1978	750,000,000
1959	301,280,000	1979	858,400,000
1960	298,880,000	1980	944,300,000
1961	297,330,000	1981	1,027,000,000

Note: During the years that the Retail Fur Excise Tax was in effect, 1942–1964, fur volume was computed on the basis of tax collections. Since taxes were not filed or paid until the quarter following sales, there are discrepancies; however, these are the best figures available. From 1965 through 1981, with the tax no longer in effect, the sales figures are based on samplings taken by the Retail Fur Council of the National Retail Merchants Association, projected by the NRMA into approximate overall amounts. The 1972 through 1981 figures were provided by The American Fur Industry. These figures closely approximate retail fur sales volume since 1942.

technological advances have broadened fake-fur manufactured styles to encompass versions of precious types, including chinchilla, that are difficult to tell from the real thing and now retail for hundreds of dollars. As an example of the importance of fake fur, one of the oldest women's coat manufacturers, owned and managed by the third generation of the Metzger family, confines its styles solely to fake furs.

Economic impact

Table 5–1 shows estimated retail fur sales in the United States from 1942 through 1981. Note that in the latest year sales exceeded $1 billion. The table note explains the basis for the statistics.

The fur industry employs 30,000 workers. Its workers' union is the same as the one for the leather industry, the Amalgamated Meat Cutters and Butchers Workmen of North America. There are 7400 fur retail establishments nationwide, with 600 fur manufacturers in New York City alone. Employment opportunities are afforded 250,000 people, directly and indirectly.

The fur business was not touched by the new designers who appeared on the scene during the 1950s and the 1960s and who gave life to the rest of the apparel business. During this period mink remained the traditional fur. But at the beginning of the 1970s fur gained a new image. New textures, revolutionary styling that included new combinations of skins, new processing, and new combinations of colors resulted in new fashion applications. "Fun" furs, occasionally of garment types, designer name importance, and more aggressive industry practices spell a bright future for the business.

96   The fur business is conducted on an international basis and offers positions in selling, designing, and administration in the major markets. The trade publication that reflects the international aspect is the Winckelman *International Fur Bulletin*, published in London. Its advertisements are in many languages, including Russian.

SUMMARY

Although the use of leather and fur is almost as old as mankind, their place as the most basic clothing materials dwindled when the art of making cloth was developed. The list of the types of animal skins used in making apparel and other products is longer than most realize.

The production flow of leather products involves many specialists, with the most dominant role played by the meat packers. The international marketing trend of the early 1980s has put domestic manufacturers of leather products under pressure because foreign producers have made deep penetration into the United States market. At this time, domestic manufacturers have not been able to combat foreign competition with any degree of success. The largest users of leather are the shoe and glove industry.

Fur is an international product which has a long history of association with nobility and a relationship to events related to the founding of our nation. During the past fifteen years the industry has taken an aggressive attitude toward styling and marketing. With the help of creative designers, styles have become more exciting and more appropriate for a widened group of ultimate consumers. Exciting fur fashion shows receive international media coverage and help to stimulate the demand for fur products.

Although the economic contribution of the leather and fur sectors is well below the major areas, they have considerable importance because their products accessorize and glamorize fashion.

QUESTIONS FOR DISCUSSION

1. What is the economic significance of the leather industry?
2. Discuss the interest of youth in leathercraft, a phenomenon that was an outgrowth of the 1960s.
3. Discuss the uniqueness of the practices of the fur industry.
4. What are the international aspects of fur marketing? Do they differ from other parts of the fashion industry?
5. To what extent has the selling of furs been influenced by manufacturers' recognition that fashion encompasses the condition of change?

6

CAREER OPPORTUNITIES IN THE FASHION MATERIALS MARKET

The United States textile industry (including leather and furs) provides one of our basic needs, the primary requirements of clothing, as well as products for industrial and household uses. It also provides employment: more than a million people work in the manufacturing, marketing, and research and development aspects of the industry. Some 7000 textile plants located in forty-two states produce about 17 billion square yards of fabric yearly, not counting leather and furs.

The industry offers career opportunities in a sector that has a long history and a distinguished place in our economy. It is an area that offers stability because, whatever scientific advances are made, the industry will respond with an application and thereby add to the range of available products. This ability to absorb new products is a matter of record.

Its scope and variety are so immense that there is perhaps no other industry in the world that can use the same diversity of talents. To list several, consider the following fabric-industry occupational needs:

- Artists
- Scientists
- Sales personnel
- Skilled workers

- Designers
- Chemists
- Researchers
- Accountants
- Engineers
- Marketing managers
- Technicians
- Administrators

So far we have discussed the production, channels of distribution, and uses of cloth as the primary product of the fashion-materials industry. In a single year, more than 10,000 different patterns, designs, weights, and textures of cloth are produced to supply the manufacturers of apparel. This output is about 50 percent of the production of the industry; another 20 percent is used for general industrial applications. The remaining 30 percent is for household purposes, in such products as sheets, towels, carpets, draperies, and upholstery fabrics. This leads again to a diversity of specialized industry career opportunities.

Many aspirants obtain training in vocational high schools for required mechanical skills. Others attend college and specialize in the art, science, management, and operation levels of the industry. These people have established a particular entry and/or career position. But the field must also have trained personnel with skills applicable to a business of a size that requires a structured marketing system. So, with a liberal arts background as well, a student can opt for a place in this primary market. For example, sales personnel, copywriters, and administrators do not have to come from the ranks of those who selected the area as part of their formal school training. A student trained in home economics, fashion merchandising, or retailing could be considered for positions that involve the development of the line (**stylists** put the designers' output in salable form), fashion coordination, or working with manufacturers, to mention only a few possibilities.

The location of plants is widespread and employment opportunities are numerous in certain geographic locations where there is a concentration of production and administration. Plants are not located in New York City or Chicago or Los Angeles.

New York City is the marketing capital of the world of mass-produced apparel, so opportunities for artists, designers, marketers, and converters are most numerous in and most often confined to that city. Sales personnel are required for regional markets or for selling to out-of-town manufacturers.

OBTAINING A POSITION

There are basic steps to take before applying for a position. First survey the market—visit a public library and obtain a comprehensive list of textile or textile-related firms. There are many trade and trade association books, including *Davison's Textile Blue Book*, Davison Publishing Company, P. O. Box 477, Ridgewood, NJ 07451, and *Textile and Apparel Industry Directory*, Fairchild Books and Visuals, 7 East 12th Street, New York, NY 10003. Also, you will find many leads in the latest roster of the 180 or so members of the Textile Distributors Association, Inc., 1040 Avenue of the Americas, New York, NY 10018.

From such sources you can determine the specialization of firms and prepare a list of your own preferences. (More precise information about larger companies that are listed on the stock exchanges can be obtained from a local stockbroker or through company or industry reports.) **99**

You should then prepare a well-documented resume that gives your background and your entry-job and career goals (see Appendix B). Send out a hundred resumes, or as many as you feel are necessary, each accompanied by a short individualized cover letter explaining that you are applying for employment. The solicitation of many firms should bring some affirmative responses, one of which could lead to employment.

Some of the larger textile firms maintain formal training programs, but all firms have a means to educate entry personnel. Some firms use an on-the-job method, others the rotation system, putting an applicant in a series of areas to obtain an overview. The textile and chemical industries, which are technically based, recognize that despite formal school training much is to be learned, especially about the products and business methods of particular firms.

SUMMARY

Jobs in the textile industry offer a wide scope of opportunities, ranging from those that require artistic talent to create design to those requiring the ability to sell. There is a place for applicants trained in almost every discipline.

For those who plan a career in the industry, it is well to consider locations of employment and whether relocation would be a satisfactory condition of employment.

The information about where to apply is easily obtained. The industry offers lists of every firm in the United States (and in the world). How to apply is discussed in Appendix B.

QUESTIONS FOR DISCUSSION

1. List six man-made fiber producers.
2. List five giant-size textile companies.
3. Prepare a sample resume to obtain an entry-level job in the textile or chemical industry.
4. Write a letter of transmittal to accompany the resume.
5. Why do textile organizations have so many departments of responsibility?
6. Discuss the sectors of the industry that are of interest to the marketing activities of a chemical company.
7. What advantages can you visualize from employment in the textile industry?
8. Discuss the textile industry from the point of view of job opportunities, number of employees, types of available jobs, and career viability.
9. What are the essential differences between the textile and chemical sectors of the fashion industry?
10. List five entry-level positions in a chemical company, not including those associated with chemical research.

The United States apparel industry, the largest in the world, is a major component of the apparel textile/fiber complex, which is the nation's largest industrial employer. Here we will concentrate on its economic importance and practices and the methods by which the finished product reaches the retailer. Chapter 7 examines the domestic market, Chapter 8 looks at the global market, and Chapter 9 focuses on career opportunities in the industry.

PART III

THE MANUFACTURERS OF FASHION APPAREL

The objectives of Part III are to explore

1. The relevance of the industry to the economy
2. Relationships between the industry, its suppliers, its retailer customers, and consumers
3. The manufacturing sector as a possible career

7

THE DOMESTIC MARKET

The latest survey published by the United States Department of Commerce shows that in 1979 the total apparel industry employed 1.3 million workers in 22,554 establishments throughout the United States. There were twenty-three states in which employment was 10,000 or more and thirteen states in which it exceeded 30,000. In recent years, the apparel industry, like the textile industry, has been attracted to the South by a lower regional wage structure and proximity to textile supplies. Southern states currently employ 45 percent of the apparel work force.

Only a few years ago, though the migration to the South had made considerable inroads on the number of northern apparel plants, the top five states in numbers of employees were New York, Pennsylvania, California, New Jersey, and Massachusetts. In 1979, however, North Carolina and Georgia had moved up to the top five (and Texas was not far below this group). The 1979 rankings were:

	Employees	Establishments
New York	193,321	6285
Pennsylvania	133,046	1714
California	120,255	3759
North Carolina	80,655	638
Georgia	76,030	569

Apparel plants have been declining nationwide. According to industry statistics, between 1969 and 1973 the number dropped by 4560. However, plants with 250 or more employees increased 64 percent, from 711 to 1165. The greatest decline was in plants that had fewer than twenty employees. Thus in the same period the average number of employees per plant increased from 43 to 61. From 1969 to 1972 men's furnishing plants decreased only 7 percent, while those producing children's outerwear declined 41 percent and women's and children's underwear producers dropped 35 percent. The size of plants has increased and the smaller ones have been adversely affected by recent competitive forces.

These figures and others that follow are not all current and often are approximate. The Department of Commerce Census figures and those of other government departments are accumulated and analyzed every five years. In order to update them, it is necessary to add recent related industrial figures and apply them to obtain the best approximations. However, the available figures give relevant dimensions.

For example, the U.S. Department of Commerce figures on numbers of plants and employees cover plants producing apparel and related products. This different base naturally produces somewhat different results from figures for apparel plants only. Nevertheless, the trends are interesting. In this broader category, over the longer period from 1969 to 1979 the number of plants dropped by 2073, or 8.4 percent. Plants with 250 or more employees also decreased, from 1110 to 1068, or 4 percent. Plants with fewer than twenty employees declined slightly more, from 11,692 to 11,113, or 5 percent. The average number of employees per plant increased from 57 to 59.

Table 7–1 compares the wage conditions of the plant workers in women's and men's apparel with the wages paid in selected other manufacturing industries for the period 1961 to 1981.

The apparel industry is the sixth largest employer in the entire manufacturing sector but first in employment of women. Of the total work force, 81 percent is women. In another context, of all women employed by the manufacturing area, one-fifth are employed by apparel makers.

Although our economy has been beset by an unprecedented rate of inflation during the past fifteen years, the price of apparel commodities (except footwear) increased less than any other major segment of manufactured commodities. The latest figures available show that for the ten-year period 1968–1977 consumer prices increased 74 percent while apparel prices increased only 42 percent. However, prices in the early 1980s kept pace with the national rate of inflation.

In 1974, wholesale prices of apparel products increased 9 percent which was the largest increase in at least thirty years and a reflection of higher textile costs. The price peak was reached in January 1975; thereafter a downward price movement due to significant decreases in fabric prices continued until July 1975. In the remaining months of 1975, wholesale prices of apparel increased and continued to increase through 1976 and the following years. Prices for men's and boys' clothing rose at double the rate for those of women's and girls' apparel.

TABLE 7–1 Average Hourly Earnings, Women's and Men's Apparel and Selected Other Industries, 1961–1981

	1961	1971	1976	1977	1978	1979	1980	1981
Women's apparel								
Coats, suits, skirts	$2.23	$2.99	$3.61	$3.89	$4.09	$4.34	$4.82	$5.21
Dresses	1.82	2.76	3.52	3.66	3.92	4.27	4.60	5.03
Blouses	1.53	2.39	3.21	3.42	3.64	3.90	4.24	4.58
Knitted outerwear[a]	1.64	2.52	3.52	3.70	3.85	4.17	4.56	4.95
Children's outerwear	1.48	2.31	3.12	3.24	3.49	3.82	4.12	4.47
Other outerwear	1.55	2.28	3.27	3.46	3.78	4.04	4.39	4.76
Corsets, brassieres	1.60	2.40	3.36	3.58	3.75	4.14	4.33	4.59
Underwear, nightwear	1.41	2.21	3.00	3.18	3.48	3.74	4.05	4.40
Knitted underwear[a]	1.47	2.30	3.17	3.41	3.71	4.03	4.52	4.82
Men's apparel								
Suits, coats	1.90	2.97	3.99	4.33	4.80	5.06	5.39	5.70
Shirts, nightwear	1.33	2.14	3.01	3.13	3.45	3.75	4.05	4.43
Separate trousers	1.37	2.14	3.13	3.30	3.67	3.93	4.30	4.72
Work clothing	1.27	2.08	3.00	3.18	3.51	3.78	4.10	4.47
All manufacturing	2.29	3.52	5.09	5.52	6.01	6.56	7.06	7.79
Non-durable goods	2.09	3.21	4.58	4.98	5.40	5.85	6.30	6.98
Durable goods	2.45	3.74	5.46	5.89	6.40	7.00	7.54	8.33
Automobiles	2.79	4.71	6.98	7.68	8.27	9.05	9.56	10.81
Primary metal industries	2.84	4.12	6.61	7.07	7.94	8.75	9.45	10.55
Printing, publishing	2.73	4.10	5.59	6.01	6.39	6.81	7.34	8.02
Rubber and plastic products	2.33	3.31	4.58	5.08	5.33	5.85	6.27	6.98
Cotton fabrics	1.57	2.54	3.63	3.96	4.28	4.68	5.10	5.49
Silk and synthetic fabrics	1.64	2.58	3.67	4.00	4.35	4.72	5.15	5.60
Wool fabrics	1.73	2.66	3.64	3.94	4.33	4.60	5.09	5.55
Coal mining	3.05	4.76	7.60	8.12	7.89	9.96	10.52	11.35
Building contractors	2.98	5.22	6.92	7.41	7.81	8.38	9.01	9.51

[a]Men's and women's

SOURCE: U.S. Bureau of Labor Statistics

An interesting relationship is the ratio between women's and men's expenditures for clothing. It would have seemed that with the advent of the Peacock Revolution male expenditures would narrow the gap. But U.S. Department of Commerce figures over the years show that the ratio of 65 percent for women's and children's clothing to 35 percent for men's and boys' remains almost constant.

THE MARKETS

New York City

Apparel is the largest industry in New York City and New York state. Although manufacturing takes place in most states, the dominant designing, manufacturing, and selling in the industry takes place in New York City and makes it the capital of the fashion world. This position is a result of socioeconomic events of the late nineteenth and early twentieth centuries.

Lewis Hine's famous photograph of an Italian immigrant carrying a bundle of clothing on the Lower East Side of New York City, 1910. (International Museum of Photography at George Eastman House)

During the period 1880–1910 there was a mass migration of people from Eastern Europe. After arduous trips by ship, they landed on Ellis Island in New York harbor where they were processed and finally arrived in the New World. With no knowledge of English and little or no money, they lacked mobility and remained in the area of first settlement—New York City. Many had tailoring skills that could be used by an industry that was in the incubation stage. Despite harsh conditions these people—who were accustomed to poverty—were willing subjects to the demands of factory owners. The developing industry now had one of the important elements for factory-produced clothing: labor.

Another necessary element is the material for clothing. New England was the region of fabric manufacturing and is relatively close to New York City, although the source of raw material was in the South and other regions. But New York City was close to a midway point. Hence, two important elements were in favor of New York City as the industry's logical location.

The last dimension was the cosmopolitan spirit of the city. It was home for the leaders of society, a mecca for theater and other arts, and it attracted talented people who felt the need to function in an atmosphere of creativity. So the additional elements of design ingenuity and the garments of the fashionable for copying purposes were added to the needs of the industry; the combination of these various elements created ready-to-wear. By 1920, the incubation period was over and ready-to-wear was a growing industry.

Manhattan is the focal point of the apparel industry. This area is so small that it probably produces more sales volume of manufactured goods than any other area its size in the United States. The action takes place in a "compound" that runs north from 23rd to 40th streets, bounded by Fifth and Eighth avenues (plus the men's suit market in the 50s).

The women's wear markets are segmented (or clustered) by wholesale costs. Broadway is the market for moderate-price dresses, sportswear, and house-

A ten-year-old spinner in a North Carolina mill, photographed in 1909 by Lewis Hine. (L. Pelaez Collection)

dresses. Specific buildings house large segments of a merchandise classification; for example, 1400 Broadway is a building of medium-priced missy and junior dress firms; 1410, 1407, and 1411 Broadway are, in the main, sportswear buildings; 1350 Broadway leaseholders number many firms that sell dresses by the dozen, some of which are called daytime types, garments that are somewhere between aprons and housedresses.

Seventh Avenue has a range of coat and suit houses and name fashion firms like Bill Blass and Pauline Trigère. These nationally famous firms occupy space in 498, 512, 530, and 550 Seventh Avenue. (In fact, Seventh Avenue was informally renamed Fashion Avenue in 1972.) Popular-price makers are located on the side streets off Seventh and Eighth avenues.

At one time practically all firms had their production and shipping facilities behind showrooms. But increasing rental rates, crowded conditions, difficulty in shipping goods through packing houses (designated carriers of merchandise for retailers), and the need to cut costs in a highly competitive world market added up to reasons for a considerable exodus of the manufacturing and shipping facilities to other areas, principally in the South.

The men's suit market is in two areas, 23rd to 26th streets, the older area, and uptown in the 40s and 50s, the newer one. 1290 Avenue of the Americas (Sixth Avenue) has a listing of over 125 men's wear firms, representing about 75 percent of the men's clothes produced in the United States. The Empire State Building is the giant that houses most of the sales offices of manufacturers of men's furnishings.

The reasons for the clustering are obvious. Out-of-town store buyers have limited time in New York and enjoy the convenience of visiting showrooms that are adjacent to one another. As in consumer shopping, the need is to get as near as possible to one-stop shopping. Additionally, the creation of specific markets has such manufacturer advantages as the facility to compare notes (not that Gimbels tells Macy's everything); efficient access to suppliers of fabric, trimming, and other necessary ingredients of manufacturing; and the easy **107** identification of merchandise specialization for all concerned—buyers, resident representatives, textile sales personnel, and suppliers.

Regional markets

The term *market* signifies a place where buyer and sellers meet for the purpose of transferring ownership of products. It is easy to confuse a *manufacturing area* with a market; some larger firms produce goods in Alabama or Mississippi, but that does not mean that those states are considered markets.

A considerable quantity of apparel is sold by road salespeople who visit stores and report back to New York marketing offices. In order to facilitate the greatest sales volume, they organize seasonal shows in hotels in selected major cities and attract hundred of buyers within the trading area. For practical purposes, these shows can be considered regional markets. For example, smaller stores in the Michigan area know that many major makers will be represented in Detroit periodically, a month or two before the major showings in New York City. These shows take place in every major region of the United States.

In addition, major markets, in permanent locations with full-time selling personnel, have been growing steadily, causing many New York-based producers to maintain permanent regional offices. Some of the most important regional markets are Dallas, Charlotte, Denver, Atlanta, Los Angeles, Chicago, and Miami.

These markets contain large buildings in which manufacturers are also clustered by the type of merchandise sold. The Merchandise Mart of Chicago was one of the early nationally known regional market buildings in the country. Obviously, regional markets are a matter of savings and convenience for retailers, particularly for the smaller organizations. However, they have grown in importance for larger retailers, too, especially for the seasons, such as spring and summer, when regional manufacturers in some cases assume greater importance. A Texas store, for instance, may find the California market of greater value than New York for spring and summer fashions and in fact may not even visit New York for those seasonal needs.

The enclaves of manufacturers developed through the years make for regional manufacturing importance of certain classifications of apparel. Here are a few examples of cities that are major manufacturing locations of important classifications of apparel:

- Rochester: men's suits
- Boston: misses' skirts, raincoats, storm coats, leather jackets and coats
- Los Angeles: bathing suits and sportswear
- Cleveland: knitwear
- Dallas: sportswear
- Philadelphia: women's, misses', and children's outerwear

THE WOMEN'S APPAREL INDUSTRY

108 The women's apparel industry is one of the most competitive in the United States. Since its technology is relatively simple and capital requirements are relatively low, new firms can easily go into business. It is an industry that has given many the opportunity to realize the ambition of a lifetime, owning one's own business. The early manufacturers struggled to succeed. The capital requirement was for a showroom, sewing machines, and cutting table. Someone with tailoring or selling skills harbored the dream and often teamed up with another individual. Partnership arrangements typically placed one person in the factory and the other in charge of sales.

The going was often tough and the incidence of failure high. The unique characteristics of the business taught bitter lessons to many. Even now, the failure rate continues at 17 percent per year, making for an average tenure of approximately six years. The industry is still characterized by small firms, and it is reasonable to state that the greatest number do an annual volume between $2 million and $4 million.

Specialization

Traditionally, the market was divided into distinct and narrow classifications of consumer demand: price range (popular, moderate, and better); size (missy, junior, half-size) and category (coats and suits, dresses, skirts, sweaters). Over the years the industry has become less specialized as a result of economic and fashion changes. Skirtmakers as such no longer exist; the current maker of this type of apparel also produces blouses or shirts and frequently offers sweaters to coordinate with them. It would have been unthinkable at one time to expect a pantsuit or a knit garment from a dressmaker. Fashion producers, in following the trends, had to broaden their manufacturing assortments, and although specialization continues (makers of bridal gowns, outerwear, sportswear, raincoats, and dresses), the lines of demarcation are more open.

Size and price ranges

Size specifications, the actual dimension of garments, are not standardized to the extent that the same size from different manufacturers will be the same. Each manufacturer interprets the specifications of garments produced, and the consumer comes to understand that it is often necessary to buy a larger or smaller size, depending on manufacturer.

The following are women's size ranges (not dimensions):

Petite	3 to 15
Junior	5 to 17
Misses'	6 to 20
Women's	
straight	36 to 52
half-size	12½ to 26½

Note: There are a few manufacturers making 1 and 3 in junior and 2 and 4 in misses.

In the children's range:

1 to 3
3 to 6X
7 to 14
10 to 16

The market is subdivided by the wholesalers' three price ranges.

Better   The highest prices of the category, usually featuring quality fabrics and workmanship as well as a more costly production process. Firms at these levels usually have designers, sample hands, pattern makers, and the like, which results in a high cost of doing business.

Moderate   The middle prices that appeal to the greatest number of customers. This is the price zone of concentration of most stores of the country. Most nationally branded merchandise is priced at middle-price levels.

Popular   The lowest-priced group of the price spectrum, sometimes referred to as the budget market. To a great extent, discount stores, mass merchandisers, and basement stores are its customers.

Producing the line

When a manufacturer starts to produce a line for a given season depends upon the product and the price range. A new knit collection can start as early as six to twelve months in advance of market weeks, while a popular sportswear line may be worked up as close as a month to six weeks in advance. Manufacturers must have lines ready for market weeks, when buyers visit for a new season; market weeks are held two to four months *before* the merchandise is received in the store.

We have already noted that the name of the manufacturing game is knocking off. What the better makers offer is copied by moderate-price houses, and in turn the popular-price makers watch and copy, or improvise on, the moderate-price houses. As a rule of thumb, highest-priced apparel is produced earliest and lower-priced lines later.

Here is a calendar of fashion buyer visits to New York, which is a guide for the producers:

Season	Better	Moderate	Popular
Fall	April/May	June	July
Holiday	September	Sept. 15–Oct. 15	October
Resort & cruise	Sept. 15–October	———	———
Spring	Oct. 15–November	Oct. 15–November	November*
Summer	January	January/February	March/April*
Transition	May	May/June	

*These markets start showing in these periods but continue style developments throughout the selling season. The popular market is one of fast development since it knocks off the higher-priced best sellers and therefore constantly adds to its offerings.

The production process

At better levels, the designers create a collection through their sensitivity and knowledge of the influences of the time. They have shopped the textile market, and have had reports from Paris and other fashion centers of the world. They are then ready to conceptualize and create a collection for the season.

At price ranges below the **couture** or high-fashion level, the process varies; a line can have a degree of originality through the efforts of designers or may be the styles of others that are copied, improvised, mutated, or varied to some degree. Knockoffs can be fashioned with different fabrics or details or in some way that fits the economic capability of the manufacturer.

Whatever the price level, the samples are made and then reviewed before being put into a *collection*, a term used in the better market (*line* is used to describe lower-priced merchandise). The firm's executives are interested in the potential selling level of each garment, because styles that do not sell in sufficient quantity are losers. The objective is to produce garments that will sell to both retailers and ultimate consumers. A manufacturer who produces poor sellers loses two ways: a markdown of the finished product and the loss of production capacity for the styles that did sell. A sufficient number of poor sellers in an industry known for manufacturer undercapitalization can spell failure. The axiom is "Two bad seasons back to back and you are out of business."

Many manufacturers solicit the advice of buyers they trust. In this way they obtain a consensus of the styles that are most appropriate for the new season; the goal is to whittle the line down to the styles that have the greatest sales potential. Once the line is finalized, it is ready for showing to buyers. The important decision that faces all manufacturers is what and how much goods should be put into production.

In the better markets, very little—if anything—is put into work before the placement of orders by retail buyers. To do so is too dangerous, costs are too high, and poor estimations of garments' salability can affect the firm's capital structure. Once a consensus of best-selling styles is established, however, the firm is in a position to go into production. The styles that do not receive sufficient support are discarded and never get into work. A manufacturer can start out with a hundred designed styles, discard fifty or sixty in the process of determining what looks best, show forty or fifty as a collection, establish twelve as likely winners, and end up with two or three as very strong retail sellers.

At lower price levels and in some classifications of merchandise, this process of testing buyer acceptance is not available to the manufacturer. Knitwear, for instance, requires a long production period. If initial quantities do not get on the machines in April, or at the latest in early May, there will be insufficient merchandise to deliver in June, July, and August for fall retail selling. The necessary input to arrive at production decisions, at least in quantities to establish a production rate, is a combination of sales personnel opinion, retail buyer evaluation, and executive judgment. The longer the manufacturer's production pipeline, such as a mill in Puerto Rico or an even more distant point, the greater the need to go into early production.

It goes without saying that each style is carefully weighed and a production quantity is assigned on its relative importance. Any style that has questionable salability is held up. Therefore the manufacturer goes through these steps:

- Development of a line
- Elimination of estimated poor sellers
- Buyers' confirmations of estimated best sellers (by advice and through orders)
- Actual confirmations of best sellers based on reorders, reflecting acceptance by ultimate consumers

Most moderate- and popular-price manufacturers want a small number of strong sellers and one "hot" number, which is the way to make the highest level of profit. If it were possible to have one hot style a season, practically every manufacturer would show one style. All costs are lowered with continued heavy production. For example, on the basis of 10,000 units produced and a rental cost of $1000 a month, the unit cost is .10; but if the production is 100,000, the cost is .01. Other factors have to be considered, but the crucial fact is that overhead per unit is reduced when the production rate is high. Other elements are the facts that production output is accelerated when the same garment goes through the assembly line repeatedly (operators work almost by rote) and that the materials for garments can be purchased at lower prices with quantity orders.

Once the decision is made to **chop** (go into production with) the goods, the process goes through a series of nine steps:

1. Each sample garment in a sample size must be made into patterns of a wider size range, a technique called *grading*, or *sloping*. The grading is done on cardboard and all the components or pattern pieces of a style are called *slopers*, which are kept on file for future use. A workroom usually has a collection of them hanging from nails or in a file, identified by style number. Some manufacturers also keep a file of all samples by taking Polaroid shots. These photos are identified by style, season, and any other detail that may be of later value.

2. The next step uses a wide sheet of paper rolled out to the length of the cutting table. The sloped patterns are laid out on the marketing paper with each part of the pattern so placed that the least amount of fabric will be wasted. Of course, the cardboard pattern placement is by individual size.

3. The graded cardboard pattern is then traced onto the marking paper and removed. The result is a *marker*, a master layout—the tracing of the components of each size. In modern plants the marker is put through a photocopying machine to obtain additional copies for additional cuttings.

4. The fabric itself is then spread. At one end of the cutting table a bolt of material is stretched to the end of the table. Once the end is reached, the fabric is reversed and brought back to the beginning so that each extension and return results in two layers of fabric. This process is repeated until all the cloth required for the number of garments to be produced has been spread. In a volume operation, the layers of fabric are many, or, as it is said in the market, "as high as the knife will go."

"I'm a refugee from China. I sew pockets on pants. Everyday I have work, and living here is easy. . . ." From *Working I Do It for the Money* by Bill Owens. (Photo Bill Owens)

5. Once the spreading is complete, the marker is carefully placed on top, and the stacked fabric is ready to be cut. Operators using electric knives or cutting wheels carefully follow the lines on the marker to cut through the fabric.

6. The operator now has layers of fabric cut by size into components of a style. Each component within a size is then tied together and coded by style and size. These are called *bundles* and are ready to be assembled by the operators.

7. The assembling can be done in the shop either of the manufacturer or of a contractor who sews (and sometimes cuts) garments for a manufacturer.

8. The garment components next go to the plant, where the final assembly is organized on an assembly-line basis. Each worker performs a particular function, after which the uncompleted garment is passed to the next worker, who does additional work on it. The process is repeated until the garment reaches the last person in the assembly line, who puts the final needle on the garment, often the label.

9. From the assembly line, the garments go to the finishers, who press, examine, and arrange them according to the way they will be hung, boxed, or packaged for shipment.

Variations of these procedures are those used in the tailoring process. Some garments require special workmanship and must be made one at a time. A bridal dress is probably as good an example as any. In this case, one person makes the entire garment from beginning to end. In other instances, a very expensive dress may be made first in muslin on a figure and then scaled to the individual size. These are both variations of the practices of traditional tailoring and dressmaking shops.

Contractors

A **contractor** is someone who is hired to do the sewing, and occasionally the cutting, of the garment. Many producers frown on cutting by contractors; **113** the adage is "You make money on the cutting table." Expert cutting ensures both the greatest use of fabric with the least waste of material and sizes of garments to specifications.

The contractor is almost as old as ready-to-wear. There are advantages to hiring a contractor. When one wants to establish a manufacturing firm, more often than not capital is limited, and the establishment of a plant demands a heavy investment. By arranging for contract work, the new entrepreneur has only to rent a showroom, sell goods, and buy fabric. This is something of an oversimplification, but if one has the ability to recognize what will sell well and then sells it, most of the battle can be won. After all, the major problem of fashion marketing is to keep pace with customer preference.

By hiring a contractor a manufacturer eliminates many burdens: running a plant, hiring workers and keeping them working steadily, and administering personnel. It is a difficult task to keep workers busy fifty weeks a year in a business that is subject to change and seasonality as well as many other ups and downs.

In the assembly-line system, also called **section work,** the workers are paid on a unit basis, called **piecework.** In union shops, a price is set for each process and every worker's output is tallied as the basis for pay. When the initial collection is completed, the labor prices for each style are set by negotiation between union representatives and the manufacturer. In a nonunion shop it is a matter of negotiation between owner and employee.

Pricing

It is said that the fashion business yields the largest sales on investment but the lowest profit on net sales. What appears as the tip of the iceberg is not always the reality of the fashion-producing business. The simple statement that if a garment's fabric costs about $5 and the labor about $4, a wholesale price of $40 should yield an enormous profit is far from the truth. The difference between the manufacturer's selling price and the cost of goods sold is the **gross margin.** The **net profit,** the final figure, is the gross margin less all other expenses of doing business, including salaries, selling commission, rent, telephone, and advertising. Therefore, although many manufacturers' profit-and-loss statements show a gross margin of 40 percent, the bottom line, the net profit, is often between 2 percent and 4 percent of net sales.

Manufacturers' costs vary with the firm and are dependent upon a myriad of variables. In some instances, the wholesale price is based on the direct cost of material, trimming, and labor figured as 40 percent of the net wholesale price after trade discount. Others double the direct costs.

The form shown in Figure 7–1 is from a dress manufacturer who used the base $10.97 for labor and material. He added 200 percent—twice the direct cost—for the mark-up factor (overhead and profit). He also added $3.89 per

SIZE SCALE: _10 To 16_   **CALCULATION TICKET**   STYLE NO. _711_

ITEM: _COTTON SHIRTWAIST DRESS_

_5/16_ 19 _83_

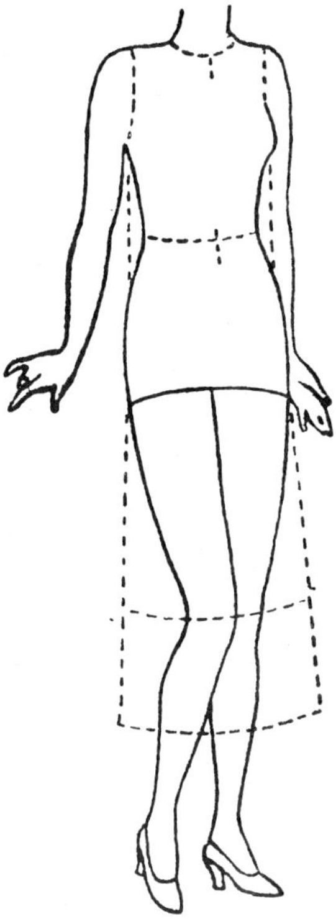

WIDTH	YDS.							
_54"_	_2.24_	Material +5% = 2.35 YDS @			2	75	6	46
_36"_	_.25_	Material +5% = .2625 yd @				75		20
		Binding						
		Buttons						
		Zippers						15
		HOOPS						02
		THREAD						15
		Labels						10
		Boards, Hangers, Bags						10
		Carton						
		Total Materials					7	18
		Cutting						65
		Sewing					3	14
		Floor						
		Total Labor					3	79
		Total Cost					10	97
		SELLING EXPENSE 11½%					3	89
		Mark Up Factor					21	94
		Cost Per ~~Dozen~~/Unit					36	75 *

REMARKS *_ADJUSTED To PRICE POINT_

Figure 7–1 Calculation ticket used by a dress manufacturer. (The metric system of measurements, not generally used in the U.S. fashion industry, is expected to be gradually adopted.)

garment for selling expense. The wholesale cost was thus established at $36.80. The industry practice is to use wholesale prices that end in 75 cents, so the price was adjusted to $36.75. This wholesale price is the quoted showroom price. The actual delivered price to the retailer is the wholesale price less the

Figure 7–2 Organization chart: women's apparel firm: sales volume $1.5–2 million a year.

trade discount. The discount is 8 percent in women's apparel; thus $36.75 less 8 percent equals $33.81, the net wholesale price. (The 11½ percent selling expense is derived from the net wholesale price.) As for the retail price, one store ran an advertisement that featured this dress at $78.

Organization

The charts here show two types of garment-manufacturer organizations. Figure 7–2 is the organization used by a firm that does $1.5 to $2 million in business a year. There are three tracks: sales is headed by one partner; production is managed by the other partner; the finance division is run by a paid employee. This is a typical ready-to-wear business chart of organization. In this setup, the firm owns no production facilities but uses contractors.

Figure 7–3 shows the structure of a large firm with an annual volume of $20 to $25 million, a size that is not typical. This firm has three factories and uses one contractor. Note that contractors are used by firms when they are unable to produce sufficient goods due to great demand, or when their facilities are unable to handle certain categories of merchandise, or when they own no production facilities. A sweater manufacturer may have machinery only for *fine-gauge* garments, like knit shirts, for example, and must employ contractors with *coarse-gauge* equipment for heavier-weight garments like bulky sweaters. Fashion therefore may dictate the need to use outside services. When all garments are made within an organization, it is known as an **inside shop;** when work is given out, it is called an **outside shop.**

A manufacturer must be certain that contractors are reliable and capable of quality work. The manufacturer often finances the contractor and holds it "captive" to make sure that required work is available when needed, particularly at the height of the season. It is incumbent on the maker to keep his contractor busy; otherwise the position of strength is lost.

One could ask how a "manufacturer" can be a firm that does not actually manufacture goods. Normally a middleman is considered a jobber. In this industry, however, whoever is the producer of goods—that is, conceives the line and sells it, whether goods are put together by the firm or not—is called a manufacturer. Other synonyms are vendor, maker, seller, and resource.

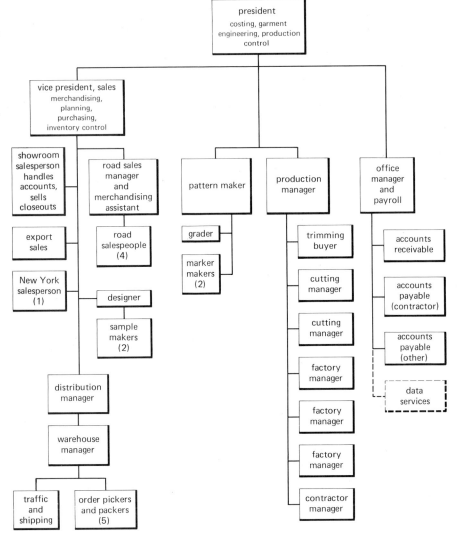

Figure 7–3 Organization chart: women's apparel firm: sales volume $20–25 million a year.

Selling

A fundamental requirement for all producers is the ability to sell to selected retailers in various locales in sufficient depth to obtain desired consumer acceptance. The optimal manufacturer strategy is to reach the retail buyer early and get a share of the budget before it is fully allocated. An additional goal is to obtain orders in such quantity as to ensure prominent retail display or advertisement.

All firms have sales personnel; most have traveling salespeople who are assigned specific territories and, in most cases, work on a commission basis. These people are considered sales agents and not employees. Large firms contract with sales agents for exclusive representation; when the potential selling is limited, the sales agent may carry one or more noncompeting lines.

The average salesperson travels approximately thirty-nine weeks a year and often comes to New York during market-period weeks of fall buying, the second and third weeks of June, to meet his customers in the showroom for added selling. Many of them are members of NAWCAS (National Association of Women's and Children's Apparel Salesmen).

Salespeople visit stores well in advance of market weeks and attempt to obtain early orders to give directions to their firms, and, of course, to earn a commission. Orders received early provide a manufacturer with valuable knowledge: (1) the importance of the line to retailers (compare this year's order with last year's); (2) the styles that will require greatest production concentration; (3) need to make line additions and deletions; and (4) the basis for making a realistic sales forecast. The sales manager in New York collates orders daily for the purpose of production control.

Showroom sales personnel wait on buyers who visit the showroom. Some office salespeople also call on New York representatives at buying offices, chain-store headquarters, and local stores. These visits are usually in the mornings but can be in the afternoons by appointment. When these salespeople return from their rounds, they spend the rest of the day in the showroom, conferring with visiting trade (retail store buyers and resident buying office personnel).

Some popular-price makers concentrate their selling efforts in New York, without road personnel. Their major business is with the chains, which have their own central merchandising organizations with personnel who buy for all member stores located throughout the country.

The practices of the selling staff differ with the type of goods sold, the customer, and the price range of the merchandise. The moderate-price market most usually sells goods through traveling salespeople.

Advertising and promotion

The women's apparel industry spends less than 1 percent of net sales on advertising, a very low figure. There are several reasons for this low advertising percentage. First, advertising must be planned months in advance of publication dates, and a product that is not a fashion until it is accepted is difficult to select as a winner for national advertising. Most firms are therefore unwilling or unable to afford the luxury of featuring merchandise of questionable fashion value. Why should a manufacturer select a garment or two and risk thousands of dollars on them in a fickle market? Larger firms that are interested in brand identification are bigger advertisers and run most of the national advertising. National advertising does not give large immediate returns. It has little effect unless the ads are repeated.

Some producers have cooperative programs in which a manufacturer shares a retailer's advertising cost based on a given percentage of delivered goods for advertising purposes. Any advertising money given to one store must be proportionately available to all others, to be in compliance with the 1936 Robinson–Patman Act, a federal law concerned with unfair price discrimination and inequitable quantity discounts.

Alert manufacturers use a variety of techniques other than advertising to help sell goods. Some of the more popular are these:

- *Trunk showings*, in-store fashion shows of new lines; stores can take special orders for displayed merchandise
- *Displays* and display fixtures to highlight merchandise
- *Displays* and other promotional aids to tie in with national advertising
- *Statement enclosures*, sent with monthly statements or special mailings
- *Manufacturer pm (push money)*, a sum given to retail sales personnel for each item sold
- *Educational booklets* for salespeople and customers
- *Use of manufacturer personnel and electronic data processing* to aid in reordering of goods

In some unusual cases, manufacturers have used television in conjunction with a supplier (a larger textile firm) to advertise the textile fiber (the fabric), the manufacturer, and the store.

Distribution

A manufacturer must sell to a sufficient number of appropriate retailers, those best qualified to sell the product. Some products can be sold to anyone who can pay for them, but the distribution of fashion goods is another story.

Retail stores are highly competitive with different types serving the needs of customers. Retail stores are in race for consumer patronage, and through their communications (a total range of messages that includes advertising, fashion shows, interior display, window display, and the like) try to instill reasons why consumers should prefer to shop in their establishments. The mix of retail efforts will be discussed in depth later; here the retail price of merchandise is our important concern. In some cases, prices must be sufficiently high to attract the highest-income-level consumers. Conversely, other stores with relatively low prices use price as a major attraction for customers with less money to spend. A store is advantaged when it can show that the price of a product reflects high value, particularly when competitors have the item at a higher price.

Fashion goods are vulnerable to price reductions by some retailers who need to obtain a competitive edge over stores that have more prestigious ratings. This vulnerability is accentuated by a product that is produced in a highly competitive market, where there are more producers than needed. In this situation the buyer often has the greatest power in the buyer-seller relationship.

The manufacturer who wants to maintain retail price levels has only one strength—the selling rate of his or her goods. If a retailer marks a manufacturer's goods down, the manufacturer only has one recourse—not to ship any more goods to the culprit store. But if the merchandise is not sufficiently important, the manufacturer loses two ways: the probable loss of patronage of stores that marked the goods down and stores that want no part of a manufacturer whose goods are being **footballed,** the industry term for selling goods at discount prices.

The producer must therefore select a distribution system that can provide a **119** sufficient number of outlets to obtain the estimated business volume, to represent merchandise in the selected areas of the country, and to prevent unfair competition among customers.

A manufacturer cannot sell to a store that maintains normal retail price levels and to a discounter in the same locale. In fact, it is not uncommon for some stores to avoid buying from manufacturers who sell closeout merchandise to discount stores in any area. Stores are often suspicious of a manufacturer's distribution system, and the first question a buyer will ask a new resource is "Who do you sell to in my area?" or "Do you sell to discount operations?" Therefore, a manufacturer must make up his mind, and select one of three systems:

- *Franchise:* a form of exclusivity in a trading area
- *Select:* limiting the number of stores in a given area, usually on the basis of population, number of stores, and so on.
- *Open:* selling to anyone who can pay, a method restricted to popular-price makers

Brand names

The entry of chemical companies into the industry and World War II shortages gave many manufacturers the opportunity to gain brand-name importance, an advantage new to the women's fashion industry. The practice of cooperative advertising still continues although not quite at the previous rate. Conditions have changed in the 1980s. Chemical companies are well identified and are in a position to be more selective, and the cost of doing business has risen dramatically and cut down on their ability to be generous.

Brand-name status is highly desired by a producer because it influences consumer purchasing. The ultimate state of a brand-name position is consumer rigidity, the refusal to accept any product other than the specific brand. It is hard for a manufacturer to reach the status of London Fog, for example, some of whose customers will not buy any other make of coat. However, consumers do have loyalty to a variety of brands for reasons that may include price, the key position of the manufacturer in a given store, the image the brand name carries, and garment specifications that fit properly.

It is vital to understand that a brand position in the fashion business does not depend wholly upon the amount of advertising. We have already seen that manufacturers spend less than 1 percent of net sales for that purpose. A brand position is obtained when the distributor makes the merchandise available to consumers and the merchandise is purchased on a continued basis.

Brands can be important at better, moderate, and popular prices. Designer names at highest price levels are brands; the firms of moderate-price levels usually use a contrived name, as do popular-price makers. The brands of greatest volume importance, as noted earlier, are at moderate levels.

Licensing

One of the marketing tactics used by manufacturers of products, especially on television, is to display the sponsorship of well-publicized figures. A related practice is to include the name of a famous personality, preferably a well-known designer, on a garment's label. This practice is called **licensing,** the purchase of the right to use someone else's name. (This definition can be expanded to cover a contractual arrangement whereby one sells the right of use of a product, secret, technique, or name.)

In the past twenty years, the fashion industry has adopted this technique with enthusiasm and now uses names for advertising and on garments. Cheryl Tiegs claims she uses Cover Girl makeup, Willie Mays says he uses a certain perfume, and Joe Namath—among other things—prefers a particular sheet and pillowcase maker.

Among the many fashion names that are franchised for apparel use are

Oleg Cassini	Calvin Klein
Christian Dior	Kasper
Pierre Cardin	Geoffrey Beene
Bill Blass	John Weitz
Halston	Oscar de la Renta
Yves Saint Laurent	Gloria Vanderbilt
Ralph Lauren	

This is a trend that has become so common that one can see famous-name "designed" clothes in stores featuring almost any price range. Designers are capitalizing on their fame and selling their names for every conceivable product.

CHANGES IN MARKETING STRUCTURE

Most apparel manufacturing firms are owned by two or three partners but, although these firms are partnerships in practice, they are also corporations. This form of ownership has the advantage of limited liability and also, as a private corporation, has certain disadvantages.

Going public

Before 1960 there were few corporations in the apparel market whose stock could be purchased on one of the stock exchanges (the over-the-counter market, the American Stock Exchange, or the New York Stock Exchange). Some twenty-two companies were large enough and had an ownership that wanted to **go public**—sell shares in the business to outsiders. In the 1960s a trend began and a number of firms made bids to become public corporations; by 1968 there were about 100 such firms.

Why did owners want to sell their firms and put themselves in a position that requires accountability to outsiders? One of the most compelling reasons, not always mentioned in textbooks, was the desire to gain a windfall profit. When the underwriters complete the "going public" procedure and stock is sold, the original owners receive sums for the shares they sell. Since the tax law permits a capital gains rate lower than individual income tax rates for assets sold after a specific ownership period, the owners were able to realize large profits, often in the millions of dollars. In a business where the failure rate is high and it is difficult to maintain a position of importance, going public offers financial advantage.

Another compelling reason to go public was the realization that selling a private corporation in a volatile business for fair value is difficult, particularly when one of the partners dies or leaves the firm. In small private corporations, the contribution of one partner may be the reason for the firm's success. Going public offers the chance to gain additional capital, enlarge the business, and employ specialists who bring expertise with them. In this manner a firm could better withstand the loss of a key person. Within this context, in a public corporation the number of shares gives precise value of ownership, which can be passed along to the heirs of the owner.

A number of people were interested in owning stock in the apparel manufacturing sector since it is a volatile area in which large profits can be made quickly as the result of a new trend. One interested group was the conglomerates.

The conglomerates

The apparel business gained a new respectability on Wall Street when it was recognized that firms could be built up to high volume and high profitability. The reasoning was logical; clothing is one of the primary needs. Ready-to-wear in the 1960s reached a high level of importance, accepted as an industry into the mainstream of the nation's industrial sector. Hence, in the 1960s another movement took place—the purchase of apparel firms by conglomerates. This involvement took two forms, one of them comparable to what had happened in the textile sector, horizontal expansion. Some successful firms purchased either competitors or firms that made slightly different types of merchandise. The purchasing firms ended up with ownership of other corporations that often continued to function under their original names. As an example, Jonathan Logan expanded by buying, and in some instances starting, new firms. Jonathan Logan thus became a conglomerate owning other corporations: Alice Stuart, Misty Harbor, Butte, R & K Dress Company, Harbor Master, Junior Accent, Act III, Rose Marie Reid, Villager, Modern Junior, Etienne Aigner Division (women's shoes, handbags, leather accessories), and Youth Guild. This conglomerate, sometimes referred to as the General Motors of the fashion industry, is able to generate a yearly volume in the hundreds of millions of dollars instead of under $100 million (1981 volume was $417.7 million; 1982 first-quarter sales were $96 million).

Genesco, a giant conglomerate, owns too many companies for listing on these pages, but the range of their products includes shoes, women's and children's sleepwear, sportswear, foundation garments and lingerie, Western wear, men's clothing, dresses, and others. Genesco also owns retail stores. The net sales of this conglomerate are over $1 billion annually.

Horizontal expansion follows a natural line of progress, the broadening of product lines as a means of safety in case one class of goods falls out of favor. But the second and more intriguing form of apparel-firm acquisitions is by corporations that have no relationship to apparel manufacturing. The following are all companies owned by Consolidated Foods Corporation: Hanes Corporation, Aris-Isotoner Glove, Candaelle, Inc., and Sirena, Inc.

General Mills, another food products company, owns David Crystal Division (Izod, Ltd.: men's sportswear, Alligator brand; Crystal Sunflowers, Inc.: children's wear; Haymaker Sports, Inc.: women's sportswear; Fashion Flair, Inc.: retail operations; Ernie Sabayrac, Inc.: pro shop sportswear distributor), Foot-Joy, Lord Jeff Knitting Company, and Ship 'n' Shore, as well as a retail chain, a jewelry company, and a mail-order business that sells hobby craft supplies and apparel.

The women's apparel business is a big, complex, and respectable member of the economy of the United States. (Table 7–2 gives an idea of the quantities and value of its production in 1980 and 1979.) It is a business that has unique

TABLE 7–2 Production and Value of Shipments of Women's Apparel, 1980 and 1979 (value in million dollars)

	Unit of measure	1980		1979	
		Production	Value	Production	Value
Women's blouses, total	1000 dozens	37,901	$2,602.8	38,828	$2,500.2
Women's, misses', juniors' knit outerwear, sport shirts, including sweatshirts	"	11,197	622.7	11,320	575.9
Women's, misses', juniors' blouses, waists, shirts	"	26,704	1,980.1	27,508	1,924.3
Women's, misses', juniors' dresses	1000 units	179,401	2,735.7	183,419	2,746.5
Women's, misses', juniors' suits, coats, skirts:					
Coats, excluding raincoats	1000 units	16,808	689.0	18,429	739.3
Suits	"	18,162	475.9	24,270	516.1
Skirts and jackets	"	92,535	1,226.8	86,381	1,039.0
Vests	"	1,377	15.9	2,159	17.3
Washable service apparel	1000 dozens	2,675	211.0	2,905	212.0
Swimwear	"	2,121	244.5	2,234	242.7
Slacks	1000 units	231,207	1,912.3	222,847	1,712.2
Other garments	1000 dozens	3,575	228.3	3,472	201.7
Women's, misses', juniors' sweaters	1000 dozens	4,420	346.3	4,900	379.0
Women's, misses', juniors' rainwear	1000 dozens	520	197.1	508	186.5

SOURCE: U.S. Bureau of the Census

Infants' and children's short cloaks, from the fall 1900 Sears, Roebuck catalogue. (Sears, Roebuck and Co.)

characteristics and that employs specialists who have an understanding of the ebb and flow of consumer preference. Recent events have made it increasingly difficult to become an entrepreneur, but women's apparel is still an area in which a talented person can establish a small business with limited capital.

This business offers high rewards for the deserving. It has come a long way, from the early purveyors who were first-generation Americans to some big corporations that are part of giant conglomerates. No other industry can boast of smallness, bigness, and the same degree of opportunity.

CHILDREN'S APPAREL

The modern children's wear market developed in essentially the same pattern as the women's wear sector: at about the same time, using similar production materials and in the same market locations. Like other ready-to-wear, children's clothing had traditionally been made in the home or by a dressmaker. There are differences between the adult and children's markets, nevertheless. The children's sector does less volume and therefore attracts fewer manufacturers. As a result producers make wider ranges of types of merchandise and sizes. Merchandise, to a great extent, is washable and serviceable, although fads do exist, principally T-shirts that feature such popular characters as Superman, Mickey Mouse, and Peanuts.

Merchandise is classified according to age groups and sizes:

Girls		*Boys*	
Infants	0 to 18 months	Infants	0 to 18 months
Toddlers	2 to 3X	Toddlers	2 to 4
Little Girls	3 to 6X	Little Boys	3 to 7
Girls	7 to 14	Boys	7(8) to 12
Subteens	6 to 14	Bigger Boys	14 to 20

Some merchandise is made in small, medium, and large

Manufacturer concentration can be on size range, knits, dresses, coats, and shirts; and boys' and girls'. (The boys' industry, particularly for the older group, is part of the men's industry and is discussed later in this chapter.)

It is interesting to note that industry workers belong to two unions: those who make boys' clothes from size 7 up belong to the Amalgamated Clothing and Textile Workers Union; all others are members of the International Ladies' Garment Workers' Union.

Like other fashion markets, children's wear has its brand names, some of which are shared with men's and women's apparel. They include Girltown, Florence Eiseman, Kate Greenaway, White Stag, Joseph Love, McGregor, Donmoor, Lacoste, and Wrangler.

Advertising is largely confined to the retail sector with the exception of the sales promotion efforts of such giant organizations that also produce adult clothes as Levi Strauss, Jantzen, Arrow, and Manhattan.

Children's clothing is expensive compared to adult clothing. Although it could reasonably be assumed that less fabric and labor would make smaller garments considerably less costly, this assumption is not valid. Labor cost is constant regardless of size, and fabric saving is relatively insignificant in reducing the cost of small garments.

Kiddie couture at the Sanger Harris store in the Preston Center, Dallas. (Federated Department Stores, Inc.)

The most recent children's development is "kiddie couture" clothing. Since the late 1970s Yves Saint Laurent, Louis Feraud, Jean-Charles de Castelbajac, and half a dozen other European designers have brought out lines of high-priced apparel that has sold extremely well in affluent areas. In fact, designers and firms are grossing an astounding volume. Daniel Hechter, one of the first French ready-to-wear designers to become successful, reputedly grosses about $7 million annually; 18 percent of Cacharel's revenues come from children's clothes; and sales of Pierre Cardin's young line in the United States are growing at the rate of 45 percent a year.

The prices are hard to believe:

Feraud dress	$100
Cacharel jumper	90
Muir cape	800
Zingona suit	260
Dior nightgown	35
Hechter suit (boy's)	175

It is difficult to estimate the full dollar volume of the market because of its fragmentation, but industry approximates shipments as about $12 billion annually. Table 7–3 gives relevant dimensions of the children's apparel industry in 1980 and 1979.

FASHION ACCESSORIES

One important aspect of fashion is accessories, and here we will take into account some of the highlights of this apparel-related market.

TABLE 7–3   Production and Value of Shipments of Children's Apparel, 1980 and 1979 (quantity in 1000 dozens; value in million dollars)

	1980		1979	
	Production	*Value*	*Production*	*Value*
Girls', children's, infants' sweaters	991	$ 54.5	943	$ 49.9
Girls', children's, infants' rainwear	39	7.1	33	5.2
Girls', children's, infants', toddlers' dresses and blouses, except knit outerwear sport shirts	9,623	586.7	9,634	536.5
Girls', children's, infants' coats, jackets, suits, snowsuits, vests, coat and legging sets	1,660	159.6	1,698	149.6
Girls', children's, infants' play garments, including slacks, shirts, swimsuits, shorts, playsuits, jeans, creepers, rompers	19,045	820.8	18,577	708.8
Girls', children's, infants' knit sport shirts, except sweatshirts	11,040	354.8	11,087	301.8

SOURCE: U.S. Bureau of the Census

Shoes

Shoes make up the largest accessory market. United States consumers purchase approximately 800 million pairs of shoes a year, but about 50 percent of them are imported (404 million in 1979). While shoe and slipper sales exceed $11 billion a year at retail, the industry is not doing well and is beset by a variety of ailments.

The increasing cost of raw material is one major current problem caused by sharply rising prices of cattle hide and leather, the industry's most important raw material, leading to higher end-product prices. Fairly recently, 51 percent of all domestically made shoes had uppers made of leather, but there is a current decline in favor of other materials, principally vinyl.

The inability of United States manufacturers to overcome the competition of foreign makers from Europe and the Orient has added to the woes of the industry. In an economic recession, with rising prices, domestic manufacturers are unable to make significant styling changes that would motivate consumers to buy many pairs of new shoes. One of the means to put the industry in a competitive position—innovative technology—has not been exploited because the greatest number of United States manufacturers are small- or medium-size operators unable to afford such newly available machines as computer-controlled water-jet cutters, electrohydraulic cutters, needle pacers, high-frequency flow molding, side lasters, and automatic-controlled stitchers. These innovations could reduce costs, improve the quality of the shoes, and put the industry back into a competitive position.

In 1977 the United States government signed an orderly market agreement with Taiwan, restricting the number of shoes that can be exported to the United States. The Department of Commerce's Economic Development Administration

Shoes make up the largest fashion-accessory market. (Photo Richard Kalvar/Magnum)

provides grants to stimulate the footwear economy by the development of an Advanced Fashion Information System, engineering standards, and proportional grading. The Advanced Fashion Information System also provides tailor-made courses to improve the teaching skills of those who train operators in shoe manufacturing plants, since the quality of operator training relates directly to costs in turnover, learning time, quality of product, safety, and industrial compensation. Improved styling, better quality, and reduced costs, it is hoped, can be used to stimulate business.

The United States does export some goods, but only a small fraction of production, about 1 percent of output.

The shoe industry has some giants, the largest of which is Genesco, a conglomerate which owns, among others, Cedar Crest Shoe Company, Cover Girl Shoes Company, Dimension Shoe Company, Douglas Shoe Company, Footwear Wholesale and Manufacturing Group, and Johnson & Murphy Shoe Company. In a highly competitive market, there has been a series of mergers and purchases of smaller companies by the conglomerates. Some eight companies control about 40 percent of the entire industry, an unusual fashion-industry pattern.

There are approximately 550 shoe firms that operate in nearly 1000 plants in forty states. The Northeastern region is the main production area, with concentration in Pennsylvania and Massachusetts. There is also some concentration in the Great Lakes and St. Louis regions. The most important market center, where manufacturers maintain permanent showrooms, is New York City. Showings are held twice a year. Brand names are an industry feature and, therefore, there is extensive national advertising.

In another unique industry practice, some manufacturers, like Genesco and SCOA Industries, Inc., manufacture shoes and own their own stores (**dual distribution**). Both companies own hundreds of stores nationwide.

Hosiery

The hosiery industry produces a wide variety of products, including pantyhose, knee-highs, anklets, peds, and stockings. Despite the operation of over 800 mills in the United States, located principally in North Carolina, the industry, the second largest in the accessory area, is characterized by huge firms that are part of the textile industry. These include Burlington Mills, Cannon Mills, and J. P. Stevens. (Du Pont supplies many firms with the raw materials.) The hosiery industry was of modest size until World War I because dresses covered the legs, and legwear was more functional than fashionable. When skirt lengths rose, a new industry developed.

Hosiery is made on machines similar to those used by textile mills. (Interestingly, full-fashioned sweater machinery in the United States is converted hosiery machinery.) Fiber for hosiery was first silk or cotton; in 1920 it changed to rayon, and in 1938 nylon began its dominance, although it practically disappeared from the market during World War II. The industry started to boom in the 1950s with the availability of nylon and the introduction of fashion colors and a wider range of textures and weights. Pantyhose in various forms, including the seamless styles introduced in the 1970s, added to the promotability and acceptance of the hosiery industry's offerings.

128   In due course, prices dropped to less than a dollar at retail and the makers instituted creative marketing techniques that included such new channels of distribution as supermarkets, drug stores, and vending machines. National advertising in all media is an important factor for the large firms. There are numerous national and private brands, often from the same makers. Hosiery is made on machines that can run twenty-four hours a day and require a minimum number of workers. Manufacturers with high levels of production are often their own competitors, a fact not realized by most consumers since packaging is the only product difference. One of the most unique and successful marketing operations is employed by the Hanes Corporation, which employs women who stock self-service supermarket display stands.

New York City is the marketing center for this $4-billion-a-year retail industry. Hosiery lines are reviewed by store buyers twice a year for the major seasons, spring and fall.

Gloves

New York state is the marketing and the producing center for gloves; New York City is the marketing center, and Gloversville, located upstate, is the main manufacturing area.

This accessory of fashion has symbolic and romantic meaning. At one time gloves denoted rank. In days of chivalry, knights carried their ladies' gloves into battle for good luck. Later, slapping an antagonist's face with a glove was a challenge to a duel.

In today's world, gloves are used both for protection against the elements and sometimes as a fashion accessory, although they no longer enjoy the fashion importance of long ago. Gloves come in different materials, from cotton to leather, and in different lengths and colors that are appropriate to the occasion or that complement other apparel. Knit and woven fabrics are the most important retail selling models.

Retail sales of gloves run approximately $700 million a year. This market has not been disturbed by imports, which are about 15 percent of retail sales, except for leather styles, which have relatively insignificant fashion importance.

OTHER ACCESSORIES

Cosmetics

Consumers spend over $10 billion a year at retail in products and services in their effort to reach a state of cosmetic betterment, real or hoped-for. The products include fragrances, cosmetics (lipstick, eyeshadow, face powder), toiletries (soaps, cleansing agents), deodorants, and those products that help to alter natural endowments (hair dyes, wigs, eyelashes, fingernails). Although these products and services (beauty parlors and barbershops) are not themselves apparel, they are related to one's total appearance, feelings, or both.

About half the total expenditures are for cosmetics, an industry that is controlled by such giant firms as Revlon, Estée Lauder, Elizabeth Arden, and Avon Products. They spend huge sums on national advertising, both in magazines and on television (in fact, the greatest share of net sales of all industries, about 27 percent). The industry's total advertising budget is more than $1 billion annually.

Since men today are more interested than before in cosmetics, the industry is increasingly focusing product lines and advertising on them. Practically every major company has a line of men's products; the annual retail sales volume is close to $1 billion. The use of a fashion name for a cologne is frequent; witness Chanel No. 5, a long-time favorite. What is new is the proliferation of the use of fashion-designer names for fragrances for both men and women. One can see the results of franchise arrangements on bottles featuring Dior, Givenchy, Yves Saint Laurent, Ralph Lauren, Halston, and Norell, among others.

The wig business is another related item for both men and women. Impetus was given to the industry by the youth of the 1960s, when hair became an important focus of the young. In time, hair became everyone's concern. Little did the textile industry foresee that man-made fibers would one day replace natural hair. The artificial wig industry features semiannual market weeks in New York City under the sponsorship of the American Wig Association.

Handbags

The modern handbag is a comparatively recent innovation, dating back only to the late eighteenth century. Its first form was a drawstring pouch to hold money, principally coins. Handbags were at one time made mostly of leather, but today most bags are made of other materials, including plastics, fabric, metal, straw, beads, and so on. High-priced styles are still available in calfskin, goatskin, alligator skin, and some snakeskins.

The market center is New York City, where at least two market showings a year are held. These feature bags manufactured in 500 small plants, located principally in the New York area. Retail sales are somewhat in excess of $500 million annually, of which approximately 20 percent represents merchandise made abroad.

Millinery

The hat business is comparatively small. This industry was hurt very badly during the 1950s and 1960s when hats went out of fashion focus. The current annual sales volume hovers at about $100 million and represents the production of 500 small plants, located mostly in New York City. Hats inspired only negligible consumer interest for years, but in 1979 they became somewhat more important. Manufacturers are hoping that the trend will grow and hats regain general consumer acceptance. New York City is the dominant marketing center. Clearly defined marketing weeks are lacking since styles are produced on a continuous basis. The industry is represented by a trade association, The National Millinery Institute, which engages in sales promotion activities.

Belts

Originally manufacturers of men's belts produced for both men and women. Later, as belts became a more important fashion item, costume-jewelry makers added them to their assortment of products.

As a fashion item, belts vary in importance as an accessory to the current fashion trend. It is difficult to estimate the overall retail value of the industry since production is fragmented into more than one manufacturing sector.

Costume jewelry

Jewelry products fall into one of two categories: fine jewelry made of gemstones and precious metals like gold and platinum; and costume jewelry made of base (nonprecious) metals, plastics, and other materials that fit into current fashion preferences. Costume jewelry may incorporate natural materials like shells and feathers and craftwork and has stimulated consumer buying by men and women. Costume jewelry generates more than $1 billion a year in retail sales. Manufacturing plants number approximately 750, located predominantly in the northeastern part of the United States.

New York City, the principal market center for both fine and costume jewelry, is the scene for semiannual showings. The sponsor for the showings of manufacturers, who have permanent offices in the city, is the Jewelry Industry Council.

Neckwear

One of the recent fashion trends is the use of scarves, a category that assumed importance starting in the 1950s. By the mid-1950s, scarves featuring fashion names became important. Again, this apparel classification is difficult to assess in terms of volume because the product is manufactured by makers of a variety of products, scarves being one of a product range.

Related fashion accessories

Such items as intimate apparel, foundations, and robes are significant both stylistically and financially, but we are concerned essentially with the outerwear of ready-to-wear. It should be noted, however, that intimate apparel (slips, bras, and girdles), nightwear (gowns, pajamas, robes), and loungewear have gone through many changes. The most important are that some garments that were considered "for home" now are suitable for "outside" occasions; undergarments have become less restrictive; and functional details, such as hooks, straps, and zippers, have been eliminated. Pantyhose and body stockings have become basic and important clothing accessories. With the fashion trend to more natural lines, underfashions or intimate apparel have become more functional.

FASHION ORIGINATORS

In the next chapter, the designers of Europe will be discussed. Here, it should be noted that the United States has its own couture group, one that has not been discussed in detail in connection with the development of lines or collections.

Fashion originators exist in every segment of the manufacturing industry of **131** the United States and their names are well known in many households. The best organized group is the New York Couture Business Council, Inc., of which practically every American creative designer is a member. The council sets dates for showings and acts as a trade association for couture firms, which often feature the name of the designer:

Donald Brooks	James Galanos
Halston	Geoffrey Beene
Kasper	Bill Blass
Molly Parnis	Calvin Klein
Pauline Trigère	

The growing importance of United States designers to fashion-conscious European women is a developing trend. Halston, Calvin Klein, and Ralph Lauren are becoming as well known as Yves Saint Laurent or Dior. European prices for the American designs are roughly triple the domestic wholesale cost, so the selling potential is extremely limited. But what is of high interest is that European markets are copying such designers as Calvin Klein, Bill Blass, and Stephen Burrows. That is a reversal of a longtime practice.

THE MEN'S APPAREL INDUSTRY

The men's apparel business in the United States began in the port cities of Boston, New Bedford, Philadelphia, and Baltimore and preceded the women's

Making Levi's: cutting stacked fabric. (Photo Bill Owens)

132

industry. This industry makes a significant contribution to the nation's economy through the commercial efforts of 3000 firms that support over 4100 plants in diverse areas of the country. It employs more than 500,000 workers who earn in excess of $2 billion yearly. The current annual retail rate of goods sold is almost $22 billion.

Despite recent greater male interest, the apparel purchase ratio between the sexes holds to the proportion of 65 to 35 in favor of women, with small periodic variations due to the influence of style trends. Men's apparel has been affected by national events that influenced not only styling but also the manner in which goods are currently marketed. The men's apparel business was relatively stable for many years, but it was affected strongly by a series of events that started immediately following the end of World War II.

The revolution in male attire

Styling of men's apparel from the days of the industrial revolution to the 1950s could be characterized as staid and slow to change. The average man owned a small wardrobe assortment that contained a limited number of tailored suits, one of which was reserved for important-occasion wear. The average man hated to shop and gave the chore little forethought; in fact, he tended to buy for replacement rather than newness. Suit styling was practically timeless since the sporadic changes were slight modifications of details. Outerwear fabric was almost always wool, although some cotton was worn by the intrepid minority who did not fear wearing summer "pajama suits" (cotton seersucker two-piece tailored suits). Designer names were nonexistent, and consumers who had the wherewithal for taste and quality indulgence had suits made to order. Models were selected from magazines or previously made garments. A suit or coat showed little style variation from season to season, year to year, and style predictability was precise. It was a placid, classic business that permitted longevity for well-run firms.

In the 1950s a new American phenomenon developed, the mass exodus to suburbia. Concurrently the average work week was shortened to five days. Many men had two days of leisure time when they could dress for comfort and personal satisfaction. Leisure time almost immediately led to greater interest and participation in sports: golf, fishing, hunting, tennis, and jogging. Millions of men were able to indulge in activities that for generations had been reserved for the more affluent. And the move to the suburbs caused another interest and participation: the cutting of grass and crabgrass control, a general interest in "do-it-yourself" home maintenance and repair. World War II veterans, part of the migration, had the opportunity to wear apparel that had given them great physical comfort in the past, that is suitable for lounge and casual wear—chinos and fatigues.

The scene was set for the broader acceptance of clothing that made more sense, garments that were certainly more comfortable and appropriate for weekend wear and were a relief from tailored suits and starched white shirts. In due course, a typical Saturday night suburban dinner party featured men in sport jackets, sport shirts without ties, and loafers or sport shoes.

Businessmen, in response to the casual trend, cautiously began wearing tailored sport jackets and slacks to work, principally on Fridays. Gradually this became commonplace, although there were some industries that frowned on this more relaxed attire. One of the classifications that had no industrial restraint was outerwear-overcoats. They became more casual in the early 1950s, and the suburban uniform became the raincoat. A little later, the storm coat, often with fur collar, developed into popular wear for the winter. It was during this period that traditional coat and suitmakers who did not or could not change with the trend began to lose volume.

Simultaneously with these changes, we saw the development and commercial application of laboratory efforts—man-made fabrics that encouraged the casual influence. Continued synthetic innovations gave clothing a greater variety of weights to accommodate seasonal changes, wider styling range, and price levels that had popular appeal. Above all, men were freed from the restrictions of limited fabrics and self-imposed attitudes of fashion propriety.

Attitudes about clothing changed radically in the turmoil of the 1960s. Complete conformity in clothing was rebelled against by many, and the individual was largely freed to express his own views about clothing standards. There were no universal behavior patterns, but certainly a broader tolerance for what is "right" clothing succeeded traditional expectations.

Men finally realized that apparel can bring gratification and comfort, indicate individuality, and give evidence of one's mood. Clothing as an expression of self-image became acceptable. The Peacock Revolution of the 1960s was the culmination of the influences of two eras, founded on the environmental factors of economics, social change, new cultural attitudes, technology, and political philosophy. And now that consumers of the youth era of the sixties who were "wedded" to denim are in their mid-thirties and early forties, it seems certain they will continue to favor apparel that expresses freedom of choice, comfort, and relevancy to the occasion of wear. As participants in the age of long hair and tattered jeans and T-shirts, they are not "radicalizing" their wardrobes to the tailored, structured, stiff garb of yesterday.

The conclusion must be that the outlook for casual sportswear will continue as the overriding theme for clothing of the foreseeable future, influenced in no small way by the significant percentage of males who were participants in or partisan observers of the scene of the 1960s.

Manufacturers and retailers have lost considerable power to dictate the terms of fashion. It has become the practice for all fashion marketers to listen more carefully to consumers. The realities of the 1980s are that men's fashion is not one look, that consumers must be cajoled, and that clothing need not be uncomfortable.

The events of the past twenty-five years have culminated in the following examples of current fashion acceptance:

- Unisex clothing
- The continuance of denim importance*
- The T-shirt as a major fashion

*Although there were signs of acceptance erosion, in 1979 jeans were revitalized by new styling by famous designers, chiefly Calvin Klein, Gloria Vanderbilt, and Sasson.

- Leather as a major trend
- The wide popularity of men's slacks and jacket (blazer) for business wear

Production and organization

The manner in which men's wear is produced and distributed is similar in many ways to those of the women's industry, but there are dissimilarities that result from the nature of the product and its end use. Like the women's industry, the men's industry, which also produces boys' and young men's clothing, is characterized by a number of small firms that employ fewer than 250 people. However, the larger firms generate a greater percentage of the total business than the huge firms of the women's apparel industry. Four large firms in men's wear, for example, are responsible for about 25 percent of the total value of shipments, and the top eight account for almost 35 percent.

During the 1960s, as we have seen, it became a trend for some apparel producers to sell shares to the public. The fact that some of the men's firms were of considerable size offered the opportunity to meet the requirements of the appropriate stock exchanges for listing. In fact, through mergers and acquisitions, the original corporations became conglomerates.

Cluett, Peabody & Company, Inc., owns twenty-eight divisions and subsidiaries that produce women's and men's apparel and operate retail stores. Manufacturers' ownership of retail organizations is called dual distribution. These selected well-known firms are part of Cluett, Peabody:

Manufacturing group	*Retail store group*
Lady Arrow	Lytton, Chicago
Halston for Men	Desmond's, Los Angeles
Halston Shirts for Men	Rogers Peet Company, New York
The Arrow Company	Lion Clothing, San Diego
Val Mode Lingerie	

Hart, Schaffner & Marx has sixty-one separate corporations that also manufacture and retail goods. These are some of the well-known ones:

Manufacturing group	*Retail store group*
Hart, Schaffner & Marx Clothes	Baskin, Illinois, Wisconsin
Hickey-Freeman Company, Inc.	Field Brothers, New York
Johnny Carson Apparel	Frank Brothers, San Antonio
Gleneagles, Inc.	Hastings, San Francisco and Sacramento
Society Brand, Ltd.	Silverwood's, Los Angeles and Las Vegas
Blue Jean Corporation	F. R. Tripler, New York; Wallach's, New York, Connecticut, Massachusetts, New Jersey, Rhode Island

Phillips-Van Heusen Corporation is a third manufacturing organization that operates retail stores selling men's and boys' apparel, examples of which are:

Manufacturing group	*Retail store group*
The Van Heusen Company	Kennedy's, New England, New York
Somerset Knitting Mills, Inc.	Hamburger's, Maryland, Pennsylvania, Delaware
PVH Sportswear Company	
Joseph & Feiss Company	Harris & Frank, California, Nevada, Texas

The combined current annual sales volume of these three conglomerates totals more than $1.5 billion. If one adds the men's operation of Genesco, a billion-dollar-a-year-volume producer with a share of the men's business, and **135** Warnaco, which is now in the men's field (Puritan of Altoona, Pennsylvania), the yearly conglomerate volume is astronomical. Manufacturers' ownership of retail organizations is called dual distribution.

Geographic factors and market weeks

The locations of manufacturing plants are more diverse than in the women's industry; there is no region of the United States that does not have some production. The United States Department of Commerce census of manufacturers showed this regional breakdown of production facilities in 1977 (the most recent figures):

Middle Atlantic	42%
South Atlantic	15%
East South Central	12%
Far West	8%
East North Central	7%
New England	6%
West North Central	5%
West South Central	5%

However, closer analysis shows that three states—New York, New Jersey, and Pennsylvania—account for more than 60 percent of the total dollar volume of coats and suits, which makes the Middle Atlantic the most productive men's apparel region of the United States.

New York City is the marketing capital of the industry, with showrooms clustered in three areas of the city: (1) 1290 Avenue of the Americas, which houses 125 men's wear firms that represent 75 percent of the men's clothing produced in the United States; (2) the Empire State Building, at Fifth Avenue and 34th Street, with many of the most important men's furnishing producers; (3) below 23rd Street, once the center of the men's clothing industry in the city. The 23rd Street area still has many small clothing manufacturers who maintain both manufacturing facilities and sales offices.

Unlike the women's apparel industry, the men's industry does not have clearly defined market weeks. Women's apparel market weeks are highly structured, for good reason. With a background of constant newness, the market recognized the need for specific periods of showings; otherwise the selling process could be a shambles of individual efforts. On the other hand, the lack of substantive changes in men's styling resulted in a more casual approach as to when store commitments had to be made, with the exception of tailored suits and coats. Manufacturers in these classifications have to make long-term commitments for material, sometimes a year in advance, and turn out goods that require a relatively long production period. Hence the traditional market period for fall suits and coats is in January, with January 23 to 28, when most buyers visit New York, as the peak period. Following this market period are additional weeks during January and February that are somewhat elastic and focus on sportswear and shirts.

Spring and summer goods are sold from October through December—except coats and suits, which require August order placement. The industry has recognized the importance of establishing Spring I and Spring II, the former concerned with spring and the latter with styles most suitable for warmer-weather wear. Hence, although men's wear has traditionally been marketed twice a year, the newer approach is to establish three periods: fall/winter, spring, and summer.

Brand names

We know that national brand importance in women's apparel did not come into its own until 1950. This was not the case for men's apparel. Because of limited style changes, the continuous operations of manufacturing firms, and the loyalty of men for what they purchased successfully, brand importance early became an integral part of the men's industry. The typical man tended to buy the same label suit, shoes, slacks, and jacket.

And then several developments lessened the importance of national brand merchandise. The radical changes in styling in the 1960s (somewhat like the pattern of the women's industry) became important. Some established makers could not adapt and take a new direction; and some could not compete, for example, with sportswear-firm labor set-ups in the important classification of the leisure suit. How many men would buy a leisure suit for $150 to $200 when one could be purchased for $45 to $75? It was a dilemma; the manufacturers were aware of the styling, but what could they do about it? The suit business went into the doldrums and sportswear makers with lower manufacturing costs enjoyed increased sales. The second circumstance has to do with retailers. Men's specialty stores, in their effort to maximize patronage motives, began to carry private-label merchandise. With the importance of the casual look, colored and designed shirts, smaller-size firms had the opportunity to take advantage of this trend. White shirts, a great large-manufacturer classic, began to back up in stock. Customers wanted the new styles, and the long-held loyalty to brand names was greatly diminished. The retailers, large and many small, demanded and stocked shirts with *their* names as the brand. The current shirt business is now largely privately labeled, and the name brand makers are not above selling their shirts with the label of the retailer.

Manufacturing

One of the critical aspects of manufacturing men's clothing is that fit is of prime importance, more so than in women's wear. Men's suits, for example, must be tailored with more concern for height and chest measurements. The element of height therefore includes three separate ranges of short, average, and tall, with an additional size range for portly men. Men's shirts are made to the dimensions of neck size and sleeve length as well as for style. The retail stocking of this classification alone requires a large stock. Here is an example of the problem:

A basic long-sleeve shirt requires the minimum stock range of 14½, 15, 15½, 16, 16½, and 17 neck size; 32, 33, 34, and 35 in average sleeve lengths; in the most basic colors of white, blue, and beige. This minimum assortment, if stocked in single units, one of each neck size, sleeve length, and color, adds up to seventy-two units. Of course, the sale of one piece would mean an out-of-stock condition of that unit. The manufacturer's task of manufacturing wanted styles in correct size assortments is indeed burdensome.

Some sportswear items, such as sport shirts in woven and knit fabrics, are made in small, medium, large, and extra-large sizes, which simplifies the problem to a great degree.

As in the women's industry, the manufacturer-contractor relationship exists, but the degree is more limited. From the beginning of the development of the men's wear industry, manufacturers employed people with tailoring skill; the level of skill was in fact a strength in creating brand-name importance and a higher wholesale cost. For years the manufacturers of clothing were rated by a number that designated tailoring level (number six was the finest needlework, number one the lowest), but this system is no longer used to rank manufacturer's clothing as inferior or superior.

The maker of tailored suits and coats must start his collection very early, often making piece-good commitments as far as a year in advance of showing, sometimes up to two years for fine worsted wools. Lines are shown to store buyers six months before retail need. This varies from the pattern of the women's sector, which works with a shorter delivery lead time. But men's clothing does not change so rapidly, and the trend of a season remains for the entire year; production demands and even consumer preference cannot change the pattern once it is set. The retailer must take a stand by placing an order for a good portion of the season's needs. The manufacturer, on the other hand, once he has collated his orders, plans production in sufficient quantity to cover store requirements and adds a quantity for reorders. In fact, some manufacturers offer individual cuttings to take care of retail special orders. Special orders for suits are rather common.

Another practice that is retail-related and has a bearing on store purchase depth is that some smaller retailers carry men's coats and suits over from one season to another—a practice that is anathema to retailers of women's apparel. But, again, style development pace is the key factor to the practice.

The selling process is similar to practice in the women's industry, with one basic difference. Store loyalty is greater than in the merchandising of women's apparel. With men having a background of loyalty to brand names in tailored clothing, even though this loyalty has weakened, stores tend for the most part to stay with key resources, certainly to a greater extent than the women's industry, which has a higher level of competition and a product of more limited life span.

The industry employs traveling salespeople to obtain early orders, but the coat and suit sector does not have the same concentration because it sells its goods earlier and sees retail customers at least six months before they need the merchandise.

Figure 7–4 is a chart of organization characteristic of a firm doing a yearly volume of $100 million. The responsibilities of manufacturing processes are

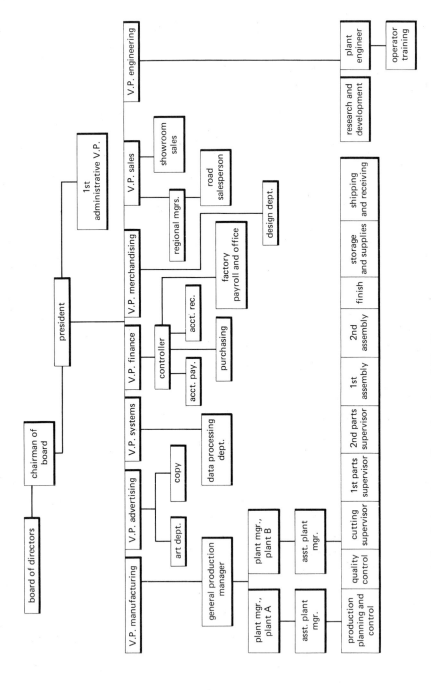

Figure 7-4 Organization chart: men's wear firm: sales volume $100 million a year.

essentially the same as those indicated on the charts of women's apparel producers. The difference is that the responsibilities are decentralized and represent a marketing structure that affords greater analysis of business information, a distribution system that reaches more customers, and an extended top layer of management.

Current industry practices

The men's business came into the fashion spotlight in the 1960s. With the idea of conformity dissipated, well-known designers of female apparel entered the men's industry. In the vanguard of the movement were Pierre Cardin, Yves Saint Laurent, Bill Blass, Oleg Cassini, and Hardy Amies. Whether they actually designed the clothing or not, garments featuring their names were produced and sold on a franchise basis. The men's apparel industry has gone along with this trend. At a recent men's wear show the following designer names were prominent in suits, coats, and sportswear that ranged in suggested retail prices from $20 to $2000: Bellini, Stanley Blacker, Pierre Cardin, Cesarani, Dimitri, Jean-Paul Germain, Alexander Julian, Norell-Tassell, Oscar de la Renta, Don Robbie, Egon Von Furstenberg, Carlo Palazzi, Bill Kaiserman, Giorgio Sant' Angelo. And just a few years ago there was not one identifiable name designer of men's apparel!

There are about 80,000 stores in the United States that have a significant interest in selling men's wear; about 30,000 specialize in men's apparel or family clothing, and more than 50,000 feature some classifications of male attire. Within the specialty store group are stores owned by conglomerates that own manufacturing facilities and retail their own brands, such as Hart Schaffner & Marx, Cluett Peabody, and Phillips-Van Heusen.

Although the division that produces trousers and slacks had a phenomenal growth from 1960 to 1977, the latest figures show that work clothing has become the fast-growing sector. Whether the growth factor will continue is a matter for conjecture. There has been a recent softening in the price of jeans, even for those that were in high demand and sometimes in short supply.

In the face of the decreased demand for tailored clothing, some manufacturers have turned to selling directly to ultimate consumers. Radio and television are frequently used to publicize the value of buying directly from the maker. In practically all instances, the showroom is the retail location and open to the public during the workweek.

Boys' wear

The men's industry also includes clothing for older boys and youths. (Boys up to the age of five are served by the children's market.) Sizing is dependent on age and weight and includes the ranges of 7 to 14, cadets, and chubbies. Clothing for boys consists largely of carbon copies of adult attire, although the categories of concentration are those of casual wear. The trends of importance have been jeans, T-shirts, sweatshirts, sneakers, jackets, and leisure suits.

TABLE 7–4 Production and Value of Shipments of Men's and Boys' Apparel, 1980 and 1979 (value in million dollars)

	Unit of measure	1980		1979	
		Production	Value	Production	Value
Men's and boys' suits and coats, total	1000 units	46,443	$2,282.5	52,012	$2,260.2
Men's suits, including leisure and uniform	"	14,816	1,128.4	17,008	1,197.0
Men's overcoats and topcoats, including uniform	"	3,260	142.7	3,496	150.7
Men's tailored dress and sport coats, including leisure and uniform	"	17,692	831.5	17,017	705.6
Boys' suits, coats, tailored jackets, vests	"	6,281	133.6	9,781	159.5
Men's vests	"	4,394	46.3	4,710	47.4
Men's and boys' shirts:					
Knit sport shirts, including sweatshirts	1000 dozens	45,740	1,688.1	40,141	1,381.0
Dress and sport shirts, excluding knit sport shirts	"	16,718	1,318.1	18,297	1,307.2
Men's, youths', boys' dress and sport trousers, including short pants	1000 units	152,414	1,491.0	156,511	1,398.6
Men's, youths', boys' work clothing:					
Work shirts	1000 dozens	3,560	225.6	3,785	223.8
Jeans, dungarees, jean-cut casual slacks	1000 units	357,253	2,615.8	312,712	2,119.6
Other work clothing	1000 dozens	6,514	575.0	6,953	571.7
Heavy outerwear coats and jackets	1000 dozens	1,974	451.9	2,153	451.1
Light outerwear jackets	"	2,249	249.7	2,195	218.8
Swimwear	"	1,739	95.0	1,806	87.1
Sweaters	"	3,272	318.5	3,313	268.7
Skiwear	"	244	87.4	262	84.8
Athletic shorts and warmup or jogging suits	"	4,537	214.9	3,595	154.3
Men's and boys' raincoats	1000 units	3,706	120.6	3,722	108.8

SOURCE: U.S. Bureau of the Census

Table 7–4 from the Apparel Survey by the U.S. Bureau of the Census shows the production and value of shipments of apparel for men and boys for 1980 and 1979.

SUMMARY

The production of apparel takes place in diverse parts of the country, with the Northeast and California in the forefront of number of firms and employees. However, the

South is the region of fastest current growth. The number of apparel plants has decreased, but larger organizations with 250 or more employees have increased.

New York City is the world capital of mass-produced apparel for men, women, and children, with a market concentration in an area approximately seventeen blocks long and three streets wide. This "compound" is reputed to generate more sales volume of manufactured goods than any other area of the United States. Although most accessory production concentration is outside of New York, its marketplace, too, is New York.

Apparel markets are specialized by product, size range, age group, and sex. Although sellers of finished apparel are referred to as manufacturers, the fact is most use contractors on a full- or part-time basis. The marketing process to place goods in retail inventories is uncomplicated; most firms employ salespeople or sales agents (commission sellers) who sell goods "on the road." Most manufacturers maintain showrooms in New York City; however, there are manufacturers who service regions in which they are located. For example, one located in California sells western stores. It is not uncommon for a manufacturer to maintain several showrooms, one in New York and offices in regional markets. Manufacturers sell goods with some system of distribution, the selection of certain types of stores most suitable for consumers for whom their styles were intended when designed. Branding, licensing, "going public," and conglomerate ownership are relatively recent trends.

United States couture designers of women's apparel came into prominence in the 1960s and have assumed international stature. Men's ready-to-wear, established earlier than women's wear, originally in staid styles, made a turnabout as a development caused by two major influences: mass migration to the suburbs in the 1950s and new social and cultural values of the 1960s; hence, the "peacock revolution" in the 1960s. Despite a new attitude about clothing, however, men's apparel purchases are substantially below those of women. The ratio is approximately 65 percent to 35 percent in favor of women's apparel.

The proportion of larger firms in the men's field is greater than in the women's industry; twelve firms account for almost 60 percent of the total value of the industry's shipments. A unique feature of the men's wear industry is the dual ownership of some firms, manufacturing and retailing under one "umbrella."

One of the substantial differences between the marketing of men's wear and women's wear is the matter of market weeks. Women's apparel shows new lines up to six times a year. The men's market shows up to three times a year. Another difference is that this industry produces two major apparel classifications: men's wear and boys' wear. The women's industry has narrower specialization. Children's wear is a separate sector.

QUESTIONS FOR DISCUSSION

1. Why did New York City become the capital of mass-produced apparel?
2. What is the economic significance of the fashion industry?
3. Of what importance are regional markets?
4. Why are outside shops more numerous in the women's apparel sector than its men's counterpart?

5. Advertising expenditures by apparel manufacturers are low compared with those of other large industries. Why?

6. Nationally known brand houses are more numerous in the men's apparel business than in the women's industry. What led to the difference?

7. What are the advantages of licensing arrangements between manufacturers and well-known designers?

8. Why do some giant firms that produce unrelated products buy or merge with apparel-producing companies?

9. Describe three ways in which the techniques of marketing of women's and men's attire differ.

10. What are your thoughts about the continuance of the sportswear influence in men's apparel? Explain.

8

THE GLOBAL MARKET

Imports are an important consideration of all current and future marketers since they affect the range of stock assortments, intensify the degree of market competition, and add up to billions of dollars. At present, the United States has incurred huge trade imbalances that have had an adverse effect on our economy. Makers of many products complain about the market penetration of foreign producers and demand congressional action to combat what they call unfair competition. But the problems of setting equitable trade terms are as diverse as the number of countries involved in trading.

We will examine here the background of our national philosophy and current conditions and then the imports of fashion originators, a special situation that is not controversial.

International trade goes back to the beginning of civilization. No one country has a perfect balance of raw materials and productive capabilities, so nations have always sought the raw materials they need and the foreign markets necessary to sustain and expand their economies. The fundamental workings of international trade illustrate the theory of comparative advantage: a country specializes in producing those goods it makes most efficiently, exports these items, and imports those products which it makes least efficiently.

The United States, blessed with abundant resources for practically its entire history, was a creditor nation for many years, exporting more goods than it imported. But in the 1970s, the export-import balance changed and we began to incur trade imbalances. In 1977 our trade deficit was $26.7 billion, the largest in our history; in 1978 it increased to $28.5 billion. In 1981 it was up to $39.7 billion, and it was predicted to be even larger in 1982. There is indeed cause for national concern. In 1950 our share of international trade was 18 percent; by 1979 it had eroded to about 12 percent.

The United States has generally adhered to the philosophy that high tariffs and/or the exclusion of foreign goods lower the standard of living because (1) domestic firms with lowered competition can charge higher prices and thereby reduce consumer buying power and (2) marginal firms, those barely able to make ends meet but kept in business by government protection, may pay lower salaries. The further implication is that producers incapable of meeting competition are not entitled to special consideration.

The United States does, however, protect domestic manufacturers from foreign producers who "dump" goods. Dumping occurs when a government subsidizes exportation by lowered taxes and other incentives or when a company uses a foreign market to sell off excess goods at prices lower than can be commanded domestically.

A high rate of unemployment causes strong pressure for **protectionism—** the reduction, limitation, or exclusion of foreign goods, which can be exercised in three commonly used ways:

1. Tariffs may be imposed on goods as they enter a country, raising the cost so that domestic production has a comparative advantage.

2. Specific restrictions may either exclude certain products or limit them by a quota system.

3. "Buy Domestic" restrictions may require the government and sometimes private organizations to purchase products made domestically rather than imports. We have such a law that gives domestic bidders at least a 6 percent advantage over foreign suppliers.

The simplistic response to the problem is to have Congress pass laws that would favor domestic industries currently in difficulty, notably those that produce shoes, steel, textiles, electronics, automobiles, and apparel. But how would we be affected by the retaliatory acts of exporting nations upon whom we depend for such requirements as oil (one of the main causes of our huge deficits), sugar, coffee, manganese, tin, and sheet mica—which help sustain the level of our economy? It is held that of the twenty-four raw materials necessary to maintain our current economy, we have self-sufficiency in only four.

Possible economic punitive measures by other countries are one facet of the issue; the additional and perhaps even more important contingency is the probable political antagonism of affected nations. Historically, national economic limitations are in the forefront of the causes of war. Every nation of the world is dedicated to the economic betterment of its citizens, and other countries that cause a negative economic effect are hardly considered suitable allies. The international trade policies of the United States are the responsibility of the State Department, and for good reason.

Since World War II the complexities of international trade have multiplied. Many newly developed countries offer cheap labor for production; countries with political structures of economic command, and those entering the industrial age, have established trade barriers that inhibit free exchange; and the world monetary system has not been able to provide sufficient stability for the monetary values of trading nations.

INTERNATIONAL TRADE AND THE UNITED STATES

The United States is in a quandary about the way it can meet the energy shortage. An industrial nation is dependent on fuel to power the machinery of industry and to maintain the mobility and comfort of its citizens. The continued importation of oil adds to already burgeoning annual trade deficits. Continued trade deficits cause groups to demand protection against imports.

The emergence of new nations with available cheap labor threatens some of our industries, particularly those that are labor-intensive and require low levels of technical skills.

The international scene has players of unequal strength and different objectives. Japan, for example, continues to harvest the benefits of its industrial advances since World War II. It seeks to limit foreign imports and maintain a high level of exports. Some European countries have not recovered sufficiently from the current recession and are in a protectionist mood, particularly those grappling with high unemployment levels. The United States, despite trade deficits, is a fertile market for foreign goods.

The year 1979 was a landmark in international trade. That July President Carter signed a trade liberalization pact intended to bring a new order to the world trading system. The agreement was the culmination of multilateral trading negotiations that had extended over more than five years. Although ninety-eight nations participated in the talks, forty-one—representing 90 percent of world trade—agreed to the final terms. The pact is the most far-reaching since world trade rules were first codified by the General Agreement on Tariffs and Trade (GATT) in 1947.

The agreement provided for average tariff cuts on specific items of about one-third phased in over the next decade. Tariff rates on some items will eventually be reduced up to 60 percent, though on some other items considered sensitive they will not be reduced. In apparel, for example, cotton trousers and denim jeans are sensitive, and the tariff rates on them will remain virtually the same.

Despite the agreement many questions remain unanswered. Kurt Bernard, executive director of the Federation of Apparel Manufacturers, told the Senate Finance Committee on July 11, 1979, that the new tariff rates would "destroy what remains of the industry and the jobs it provides." Also, developing countries refused to sign the agreement because they felt it did not provide enough concessions. In addition, there remains the need to negotiate separate trade agreements between nations for specific products. Nevertheless, the agreement will benefit all concerned parties by the elimination of hidden payoffs to spur exports.

Our current stand on international trade and its comparative freedom is uncertain. Our course of action will depend on the condition of our own economy, especially the rates of unemployment and of business failures or dislocations. It appeared, in mid-1982, that the continuing worldwide recession was motivating most trading nations to establish trade barriers against imports and to subsidize exports. In February, 1982, U.S. trade representative Bill Brock said, "Around the globe, calls for protectionism are louder and more shrill than they have been in fifty years."

In Congress and within the Reagan administration, in mid-1982, there was talk of reciprocity—putting up import barriers to countries that were closing their markets to the United States. Behind this talk was the huge trade deficit with the rest of the world. As already noted, in 1981 the United States imported goods worth $39.7 billion more than the goods it exported, and the deficit was expected to be even larger in 1982.

United States dissatisfaction is directed mostly at Japan, which is a major supplier of automobiles, television sets, motorcycles, stereos, steel, and hundreds of other products. In 1982, our trade deficit with Japan was expected to exceed $20 billion, and some experts predicted that it would be $25 billion in 1983. Although he promised no punitive actions against foreign nations, President Reagan did place a quota on the importation of cars from Japan. This was a limited restraint that had no real significance for domestic manufacturers. However, a number of legislators, in mid-1982, were threatening to try to erect trade barriers unless Japan made its market more accessible to United States products. The developed nations of Western Europe were in a similar position. In April, 1982, Secretary of Commerce Malcolm Baldrige urged Japan to open its markets to U.S. products to balance trading between the two countries. "Our products are at least as good as Japan's," he said. "The problem is we can't get our products into their markets to compete." He said that Reagan administration officials hoped to end the trade deficit with Japan by negotiating with the Japanese, rather than by resorting to reciprocity legislation.

As a matter of fact, though Western Europe and Canada in mid-1982 were adopting nationalistic and inward-looking policies, Japan was slowly and reluctantly acting to internationalize its economy by opening up its market accessibility—to a degree. On June 6, 1982, in a televised message, Prime Minister Zenko Suzuki called on the Japanese people to "extend a welcoming hand to foreign goods." Responding, Secretary of Commerce Baldrige said: "We welcome this strong indication of Japan's intent to encourage foreign participation in its market."

The most current figures on U.S. jobs that depend on manufactured exports show that in the United States there are 4.8 million of these jobs—5 percent of total employment. The jobs are in all states, but 2.8 million of them are in only ten states, in order: California, New York, Ohio, Illinois, Pennsylvania, Texas, Michigan, New Jersey, Massachusetts, North Carolina.

In Washington the hope was widespread in mid-1982 that business recovery toward the end of 1982 would reduce the pressure for protection. As trade representative Brock put it, "The choices we make in 1982 are pivotal for the future of the world economic order."

FASHION APPAREL IMPORTS

The United States was an importer of textiles and apparel from its beginnings. Early in our history, before the American Revolution, we did not have the capability to produce our own cloth. At that time, English law prohibited textile craft or machinery from reaching these shores. Textiles had to be imported until Americans learned how to make machines in the late eighteenth century. Until the end of World War II we were complacent about the importation of many categories of apparel: styles from Paris, cashmere sweaters from Scotland, sweaters that reflect the art of Norway and Ireland, and leather goods from Italy. These were high-priced fashions considered status symbols for those who could afford them. The apparel industry was not concerned, since there was no serious inroad into the core of its business. The United States fashion industry's strength has always been as a mass producer for mass acceptance, and the importation of nominal amounts of high-styled merchandise was really a positive factor, since some of the styles could be copied and sold at moderate or popular prices.

After World War II the picture changed. The jet airplane brought easy and fast access to world markets, and retailers started to explore the capabilities of foreign makers. At first their approach was cautious. American retailers traveled to Europe and purchased principally shoes and sportswear. This merchandise was not exactly trouble-free, despite newness of styling and a willingness on the part of consumers to accept it. The difficulties were that foreign specifications were not always suitable for American customers, the delivery periods were extended, goods were not usually received in time for seasonal retail selling, and the stock composition was frequently out of balance—for instance, too many jackets for the number of skirts in outfits that were designed as **inseparables** (coordinates designed to go together, not sold as separate units). But, in the main, the results were sufficiently satisfactory for retailers to continue the practice.

Foreign apparel purchases were not a new experience for some high-priced stores; in one way or another they had had import stock in varied quantities before World War II. What was new was the interest of additional groups.

Among the first groups were moderate-price department stores who pooled orders. One of the leaders, the Associated Merchandising Corp., a powerful resident buying office, worked out a multimillion-dollar deal with a European sweater manufacturer for full-fashioned (all components knitted; no cutting needed) sweaters that could not be produced in this country as well as classically styled versions priced well below the domestic market. The retail result was successful. The combination of exciting styles and favorable prices gave the member stores of the resident buying office a competitive edge, which they used effectively. One of the terms of the arrangement was that purchasers set garment specifications—a well-conceived plan, as Americans are not physically built precisely like Europeans. A pattern was set for other retailers.

148   Early interest was also shown by retailers whose operations were founded on the importance of merchandise at a price—essentially, discounters. For years, despite mass purchasing power, they had been unable to penetrate the moderate-price market. Manufacturers would not sell them for fear of losing the heart of their business, price-maintaining stores. When a manufacturer sold a discount operation, it was considered an infraction of the rules by his regular customers, and more often than not the culprit was classified as a negative resource, one whose merchandise was being used as a weapon by discount competition. Discount stores saw in Europe a market that used the guidelines of depth of order and ability to pay for it. A United States prestige retailer of limited budgetary power today negotiates in Europe from a weak position, and a discounter with a big budget trades from strength.

At the same time that buying offices and discounters were discovering European resources, some American manufacturers recognized the comparative price and style advantages that Europe offered; they established facilities or partial ownership of plants in areas that gave advantages that could be used in the domestic market. The European market importance grew rapidly, and American fashion buyers were on the way to becoming well-traveled. The next trade area was the Orient, to complete the cycle and the establishment of the global market.

It did not take long for buyers to realize that although Europe offered style ingenuity and favorable prices, the market source of lowest priced production, particularly sportswear, was the Orient. Hong Kong and Japan were among the first countries explored. Whether the need was for woven or knitted styles, Japanese or Hong Kong production could be obtained at a fraction of domestic cost. The material for apparel was no problem—Japan is the knitting and weaving center of Asia. Somewhat later other Oriental countries developed textile plants for domestic and export output.

For many United States buyers, buying trips became circuitous—a stay in Europe to place nominal quantity orders and for exposure to style trends and then travel to the Orient to place orders in depth. As in any economic situation, the demand-supply factor began to operate. Japan became even more industrialized and its cost of living rose to the point at which the surrounding markets became more competitive. Hong Kong was similarly affected, although in some classifications it held its own (and is now concentrating on higher-priced apparel). Buyers from the United States concentrated on business dealings with firms in Korea, Taiwan, and Malaysia.

Stores of all size and price offerings were now involved. Large retail syndicates opened offices in the Orient and were represented in both the West and the East. Offices were staffed with people who handled necessary forms of the export-import business, followed through on letters of credit from stores, and checked the production of manufacturers for quality level and delivery of merchandise. Agents who either represent Oriental makers or purchase their merchandise for resale also established themselves.

The final completion of the global market came with the increased importance of the Mexican, Central American, and South American apparel manufacturing industries. Brazil, for example, has become a leather-producing market of sufficient significance to attract many major retail syndicates. **149**

Table 8–1 shows the results of all this quite graphically. Here the import penetration of selected items of apparel in 1979 is contrasted with the penetration in 1961.

ARGUMENTS ABOUT IMPORTS

The total factory dollar value of apparel imports for 1981, according to Department of Commerce figures, was about $6 billion. In order to arrive at a total retail value, this figure is multiplied by 4, 5, or 6, depending on who is

**TABLE 8–1 Import Penetration, Selected Women's and
Children's Garments, United States, 1961 and 1979
(in millions of units)**

	1961	1979
Coats and jackets		
U.S. production	54.2	51.3
Imports	.6	32.6
Import penetration[a]	1.1%	63.5%
Blouses		
U.S. production	232.2	388.5
Imports	29.4	222.4
Import penetration[a]	12.7%	57.2%
Knit sport shirts		
U.S. production	110.4	274.6
Imports	6.5	182.4
Import penetration[a]	5.9%	66.4%
Sweaters		
U.S. production	120.2	73.4
Imports	6.1	91.2
Import penetration[a]	5.1%	124.3%
Slacks and shorts[b]		
U.S. production	120.4	304.8
Imports	31.1	153.9
Import penetration[a]	25.8%	50.5%
Rainwear		
U.S. production	11.0	7.0
Imports	.6	6.9
Import penetration[a]	5.5%	98.6%
Brassieres		
U.S. production	207.6	209.9
Imports	31.5	133.7
Import penetration[a]	15.2%	63.7%

[a]Import penetration measured as a percentage of U.S. production
[b]Includes dungarees, jeans, and similar garments

SOURCE: U.S. Bureau of the Census and Research Department, International Ladies' Garment Workers' Union

TABLE 8–2 Imports, Selected Women's and Children's Garments, United States, 1975–1980 (in millions of units)

	1975	1976	1977	1978	1979	1980
Coats and jackets	18.2	27.0	32.7	36.7	32.6	42.9
Suits	4.3	3.8	3.4	3.5	2.2	1.7
Dresses	19.3	19.4	17.0	20.5	18.2	24.5
Blouses	117.2	143.0	147.6	208.7	226.2	211.0
Knit shirts[a]	194.4	220.0	221.2	222.8	182.4	168.2
Sweaters[b]	128.0	141.8	142.6	141.1	120.7	149.9
Skirts	6.1	9.4	7.9	12.4	14.1	14.8
Slacks and shorts	120.5	132.5	139.5	172.3	153.9	168.0
Playsuits	14.4	18.2	20.5	20.9	20.1	26.5
Raincoats[b]	5.4	8.5	7.2	9.9	9.5	6.7
Dressing gowns and robes	1.4	2.3	2.9	3.2	2.7	3.5
Nightwear and pajamas	4.5	6.5	7.9	9.3	8.2	8.5
Underwear	17.4	22.3	29.6	35.7	39.7	53.5
Brassieres	83.0	105.0	114.1	128.4	133.7	144.1
Girdles and corsets	1.6	2.8	3.2	4.3	5.1	6.8
Swimwear	5.8	9.4	9.9	14.0	13.9	11.4
Tops and vests	20.1	22.0	10.4	11.7	13.3	17.4
Body suits and shirts	2.5	1.6	1.1	3.6	3.1	.7

[a]Excludes knit tops
[b]Men's, women's, and children's

SOURCE: U.S. Bureau of the Census (imports for consumption)

making the evaluation. The apparel unions claim that the total retail value was more than $36 billion. Retailers contend that the cost should be increased only four times and that they achieved a lesser retail volume. The American Textile Manufacturers Institute claims that textile imports in 1981 amounted to 22 percent of domestic poundage and accounted for around 30 percent of apparel sold at retail.

In any case, as Table 8–2 shows, huge numbers of garments are imported each year.

Free market positions

The term *free market* would seem to imply that there are no tariffs on goods entering the country. The fact is that all imported goods are subject to an increase in value by the levying of an import tax; in fact, as a percentage of the factory cost, apparel import taxes are relatively higher than those for many other products. However, even with the addition of taxes and other shipping costs, the final cost to United States retailers is considerably lower than for domestically produced apparel. Once a tax is levied on our imports, there are no other restraints or additional taxes. This is not the case with our exports. A number of countries impose additional excise taxes and other penalties that make our goods economically unsuitable for sale abroad.

In favor of free trade

Consumers The American consumer has been a most willing customer for foreign-made goods. A case in point occurred three years after World War

II. A resident buying office pooled the orders of 200 client stores and bought more than 10,000 dozen cotton string gloves from a Japanese maker to retail profitably at $1 a pair. A carefully conceived plan took into account all possible causes of delay to ensure timely delivery for scheduled retail promotions. But a West Coast dock strike delayed delivery and receipt of goods in stock was long out of season. After deliberation, the stores agreed that the best alternative was to run their planned advertisements on the premises that consumers might buy a bargain and that merchandise held over for the next season ties up capital.

The result: the promotions were a complete sellout. The conclusions of 200 retailers were that customers are always in the market to purchase a value, frequently based on price, and that the origin of goods is a matter of small concern. After years of adverse propaganda and combat with the United States, Japan was, surprisingly, not in a position of commercial disadvantage with our consumers.

Americans have continued to give their purchasing support to products of all nations. Purchase decisions hinge on one consideration: whether the value is equal to or better than the offered price.

Ralph Nader, the consumer advocate, holds that import restrictions are espoused only by those who seek self-interest with no regard for consumer pocketbooks. Import restrictions, he holds, eliminate market competition.

Retail stores Fashion merchandisers are wholeheartedly in favor of foreign purchases. The obvious value to them is in consumer acceptance; that is what retailing is about.

That foreign markets can produce more cheaply in face of the comparative advantage of cheaper labor must be readily admitted. Lower prices feed the need of a large cross-section of American retailers, discounters, popular-price stores, moderate-price operators, and even some departments of better-priced establishments. The balance of cost versus value operates at every level.

The open distribution method of foreign makers is a distinct advantage for chains, discounters, and others who would be otherwise restrained from offering higher quality and style standards on the moderate- and higher-price domestic markets. Free trade allows them to throw off the imposed shackles of manufacturers and other retailers and gives the ability to be deeply in the fashion business, even to the extent of internationalizing their stores, an opportunity that did not exist previously.

United States retailers agree that consumers are the beneficiaries of widened style assortments. There are some goods that the American market either cannot produce at all or cannot produce as well as foreign makers. A few examples are cashmere sweaters, mitered knitted shirts, soft-as-butter leather products, and some better-priced garments that require handwork. In 1981, two representatives of one of the largest buying offices in the world said: "We had $500,000,000 at retail to spend for the current year. A study of world fashions by a team of experts collected what we considered best for our customers, and then offered American firms the opportunity to compete with foreign makers.

We were forced to make commitments abroad; American makers were outpriced and incapable of meeting the values offered by manufacturers of other countries."

Retailing is a highly competitive world in which stock sameness is a pitfall. Foreign purchases, many retailers hold, give the retailer an opportunity to express creativity in fashion merchandising, with the added incentive of stimulating sales with lower prices for comparable quality.

One factor not yet discussed is the fact that foreign purchases are made on the basis of specification buying. Contrary to the practice of the American market, the buyer does the product planning for styles that are not necessarily part of the manufacturer's line, with the buyer either suggesting the style or the actual garment or designating the details. In effect, the store, through the buyer's efforts, is the jobber, and the manufacturer is the contractor (although title to goods does not pass until the exchange of goods for payment). This purchase method provides a way for retailers to obtain goods that often have some degree of uniqueness.

The status value of imports no longer has great meaning. "Made in ——" labels, which once had snob appeal, are now considered commonplace. Some of the lowest-priced goods carry the woven gold-thread label "Made in the Crown Colony of Hong Kong." Customers care little.

American fashion merchandisers are now veterans of foreign travel in search of markets that offer better comparative values—sometimes styling, often price, and sometimes both.

Importers Importers are, of course, marketers who favor free competition. Their stand is summarized in a pamphlet entitled *Who's Right?* obtainable at no cost from American Importers Association, 420 Lexington Avenue, New York, NY 10017. This quotation gives a clear idea of their position: "The American economy has been suffering from the fever of inflation and a few other complications. But it is by no means senile and powerless. With a little more vigor and self-discipline, it can be again the youngest, strongest and most competitive economy in the world." It is the importers' opinion that United States industry should be more creative and promotional and make greater use of available technology.

Against free trade

Two groups that oppose increased imports and lowering of tariffs are the unions and the manufacturers. Cheaper foreign merchandise, they hold, eliminates jobs and makes for unfair competition.

There are several issues that unions and manufacturers want government to resolve in their favor. The first issue is concerned with orderly marketing agreements. During the 1970s the United States entered into bilateral arrangements with eighteen apparel-exporting nations. In essence, the exporting nations are permitted to increase their yearly exports of units 6 percent per year. The agreement is based on the exports of a given year, usually the year preceding the first year of the agreement, with the increase on a cumulative basis. For example, an arrangement could be based on 1975, when the exporting nation shipped a million units. The level of units for 1976 would be 1,060,000, with 6 percent added for each ensuing year.

153

The unions and manufacturers are unhappy because the foreign market penetration is already deep and a 6 percent rate of increase is in excess of projected domestic market growth, estimated at 2 percent or 3 percent, and therefore establishes conditions for further foreign-market penetration. Moreover, they hold, with an arrangement in units foreign makers can change material or price and make even greater inroads into our market. In addition, some foreign countries encourage their producers by extending benefits not available to domestic manufacturers, like subsidies in the form of low-cost loans, lower tax rates, and promotional money. These are sometimes covert acts known only to the participants.

Unions also point out that Americans subsidize foreign makers who are not required to pay taxes, unemployment insurance, and other levies that are part of the cost of doing business at home.

The handbill reproduced here was distributed in 1980 to pedestrians on Seventh Avenue in New York City. The unions, in addition to exerting strong

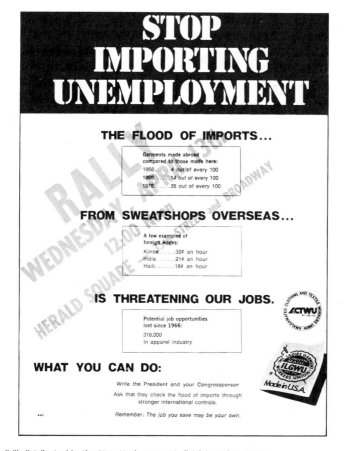

ILGWU handbill distributed in the New York garment district, spring 1980.

pressures to limit increasing imports, are also appealing to Congress to repeal item 807 of the tariff schedules, which permits manufacturers to use foreign labor as part of the manufacturing process, a procedure that permits lowered tariffs on apparel made essentially out of the country.

154

The International Ladies' Garment Workers' Union issued the following report in June 1981:

Imports

Imports of women's and children's apparel made of cotton, wool and man-made fibers (measured in terms of square yards of material used in their manufacture) rose 12.0 percent in 1980, following a brief respite in 1979 when shipments of foreign-made apparel dropped 9.7 percent. Even though economic conditions were uncertain during 1980 and retailers tried to keep inventories lean, they extended their commitments for imports at the expense of domestic apparel. The reason, obviously, was to secure larger profits through the higher markups available on imports.

The situation continued into 1981. In the first four months of the year, imports of women's and children's wear increased by 5.2 percent over 1980, with woven goods ahead 28.0 percent, while knits were down 13.1 percent. The largest 1981 increase, 32.8 percent, took place in wool garments. Running counter to the overall shift to woven goods, knit wool garments were 36.4 percent higher and wovens were up 17.8 percent. Imports of cotton women's and children's wear rose 11.3 percent, with woven goods up 26.4 percent and knit garments down 21.0 percent. In man-made fiber garments, a similar pattern emerged, with wovens increasing 30.1 percent, knits declining 12.1 percent and the overall gain being limited to 1.3 percent. Except for wool garments, where less expensive garments were imported in 1981, the trend was toward higher-priced merchandise. Average unit values for the three fibers combined were up 15.0 percent.

Imports of specific garments in 1981 ranged from sharp increases to steep declines. Robes and dressing gowns were ahead by 71 percent. Imports of skirts, coats, girdles, underwear, and nightwear rose between 25 and 45 percent. Suits, dresses and bodysuits were ahead 10 to 20 percent, while blouses, rainwear, knit shirts, infants' sets, playsuits, and slacks and shorts rose less than 10 percent. Showing declines in 1981 were brassieres, judo and karate suits, sweaters, and coveralls, all of which dropped by less than 20 percent, tops and vests, which were off by 33 percent, and swimwear and culottes, where imports were down by around 50 percent.

Renewed growth of apparel imports continues to pose a serious threat to the domestic industry. In 1979, the ratio of imports to domestic production had eased somewhat. However, heightened import flows in 1980 and 1981, coupled with declines in domestic production, indicate that import penetration is once again on the rise. This situation, requiring firm action to prevent further job erosion, must be dealt with when the Multifiber Textile Arrangement, now due to expire at the end of 1981, is renewed.

The Arrangement should provide controls in line with domestic production in the importing countries. Total imports of specific products should be regulated. Within such total levels, due regard should be given to the needs of developing nations as against those of the newly industrialized countries. Flexibility provisions must be tightened, undue surges in imports prevented, and the coverage of the Arrangement broadened to include all textile and apparel products. Only in this manner can our industry and that in other importing countries be safeguarded against further job erosion.

The unions recognize that imports are a way of life and that the reasonable position is to try to hold them to present levels of market penetration. If there is 2 percent growth in domestic sales, that should be the limit of foreign increase.

Our standard of living is high and workers enjoys wage scales far beyond those of emerging countries. Apparel production requires low technology and a high degree of labor, which makes it vulnerable to competition from the products of any country with an abundance of workers. The United States, with a combination of unprecedented total disposable income, shortened workweeks, widely held means of immediate communication, television, and free trade, is a most fertile market for apparel products of exporting nations.

Initially the concern over competitive imports was confined to the affected manufacturers and workers, but the problem has become wider. Higher oil import prices forced us to run up the deepest trade deficit in our history. The dollar position in international markets has been erratic. Our apparel trade imbalance problem, first an industrial concern, became part of the anxieties of those who guide our economic well-being.

Manufacturers and representatives of workers are exhorting legislators and the public with strong statements supported by governmental statistics to prove the high degree of foreign-goods penetration and its adverse effect on our economy. It is impossible, they say, to remain competitive when the cards are stacked in the form of the comparative advantages of cheap and plentiful foreign labor and a willingness to work on short profit margins. We are left with no weapons, they contend, because present technology cannot counteract the onslaught. Foreign markets, they say, copy our developed fashions and leave the fringe areas for domestic producers.

Retailers respond to the issue with an opposite point of view. They are charged with the responsibility of stocking the most consumer-wanted products of the world. These wants are characterized by price, quality, and styling. The lower prices of import goods improve the purchasing power of consumers, and the producing market, retailers claim, is shifting its competitive weakness to them. They hold that it is the responsibility of a market to respond to pressure and be sufficiently creative and professional to find the means to exceed the values of foreign makers. In the final analysis, it is claimed, when it recaptures the lead, the United States market will make for a healthier atmosphere for all concerned: the consumer will be the recipient of improved values; the retailer will enjoy a high level of sales with shorter merchandise pipelines; the market will brim with vitality; the workers will receive wages commensurate with their rate of production; and the manufacturers will be in an environment of high profit potential.

The cases of all concerned are rational and can be defended by industrial statistics. How the situation will be resolved is uncertain at this point. One

thing is certain: the problem will not be "cured" by time alone; it will take a great deal of compromise to satisfy both consumers and U.S. and foreign manufacturers.

The government is concerned but must take into consideration the fact that one American employee in six produces for foreign consumption and that we are the largest exporter in the world, vulnerable to retaliatory barriers by our present foreign consumers. (Exports of apparel, however, are a minor factor, about $8 million in 1982.) The Department of Commerce is exploring new programs in financing, export development and promotion, government regulations, and research and development.

Government measures

In response to the shoe industry's decline and unemployment due to foreign competition, President Carter issued a directive to the Department of Commerce on April 1, 1977, to set up a Footwear Industry Revitalization program. The following excerpts from the First Annual Progress Report, issued in 1978, give the aims and purposes of the program.

> The program was initiated in conjunction with the negotiation of orderly marketing agreements with Korea and Taiwan as part of a two-pronged Presidential effort to aid the U.S. footwear industry.
>
> • • •
>
> During its first year, the program included the following elements:
> An aggressive effort to inform all footwear manufacturing firms injured by imports about the benefits available under the trade adjustment assistance provisions of the Trade Act of 1974 and about other elements of this special program.
> Revamping the adjustment assistance program to speed the Department's certification procedures and to make loans and loan guarantees more attractive to certified firms.
> Organizing teams of specialists from consulting firms with expertise in shoe manufacturing to help certified companies deal with problems in operations, marketing, technology and management.
> Recruiting domestic shoe retailers to help manufacturing firms with their revitalization efforts.
> An intensive study of possible foreign markets for U.S. shoes, and an integrated Government-industry program to promote exports.
> A program to identify and develop new technologies which could significantly improve the competitive position of the entire domestic shoe industry.
> Working with the industry to establish a Footwear Center that would provide continuing educational and technical assistance to shoe manufacturing companies.

The Department of Commerce has also granted several million dollars to the Amalgamated Clothing and Textile Union to coordinate efforts by labor and management of the Men's Tailored Clothing Industry. They are attempting to build a more productive and competitive industry through an integrated program of technical assistance across the spectrum of production, marketing, and management needs. Additional research grants have also been given to several universities and a private research organization to study ways to overcome foreign advantages through technological applications.

On February 15, 1979, the Carter administration and the textile and apparel industry agreed on a package of measures to protect the industry against "import surges"* and provide other assistance aimed at reducing the industry's opposition to a new international trade pact. In return for greater import shelters and other aids, the industry pledged to support the national trade policy and adhere to President Carter's voluntary anti-inflation program.

Another governmental response concerns our possible trade relations with China. This country, with its 900 million-plus population and its regimented state-controlled work force, could become a textile and apparel colossus. Unions and manufacturers view the apparel trade possibilities with alarm. In mid-1982 our government was negotiating with China for a trade agreement that would include our importation of apparel.

The textile industry's largest import threat has been from Hong Kong, Korea, and Taiwan. In March, 1982, U.S. officials signed a six-year agreement with Hong Kong that limited to 2 percent the annual growth rate in textile exports from Hong Kong to the United States. The Hong Kong negotiators were persuaded that a larger growth rate would disrupt the U.S. market. At the same time, trade negotiations aimed at similar growth limitations were underway with Korea and Taiwan.

THE GLOBAL MARKET OF FASHION CREATORS

The market in the United States, the world capital of mass-produced fashion, is nurtured by ideas from other countries. From the turn of the twentieth century until World War II, the most important source of information was Paris, where ideas were purchased, copied, or mutated. The war brought an abrupt halt to this pre-eminence. After the war, there was rekindled interest in Parisian fashion, highlighted by the 1947 New Look of Christian Dior. The United States and the rest of the world became intrigued by the designs of creative members of the French **haute couture** (literally, finest needlework) trade association, Chambre Syndicale de la Couture Parisienne, a limited number of talented designers recognized then, as now, as master couturiers.

The following selected couturiers and looks had a strong influence on what Americans made and accepted during the period 1950 to 1960, when we had greatest interest in the couture capital. Christian Dior introduced a succession of silhouettes, the most popular of which were the New Look, the A line, and the free line. The A line was a flared skirt with the hemline just below the knee, popularized by Jacqueline Kennedy. The free line was a straight chemise dress with a shortened skirt. Jacques Heim emphasized the *jeune fille* look in

---

*Surges occur when foreign countries do not ship all allowable units in a given year, accumulating the units for export in a year when the market is fertile for merchandise acceptance by consumers.

clothes for younger women. Jacques Fath created elegant clothes for younger women and ready-made versions for boutiques.

158   In the 1960s the influence of Paris began to diminish. Perhaps one reason was the chemise look that was strongly sponsored by couturiers, accepted by American fashion makers, but rejected by American women, who neither liked nor bought the look. Paris was caught off-guard. Also, in the 1960s ready-to-wear began to assume importance in Europe. Europeans realized that ready-to-wear could be well-made and less expensive than dressmaker styles. Ready-to-wear clothing achieved greater prestige and was available at prices to suit every pocketbook. Couturiers recognized the opportunity to make **prêt-à-porter** (literally, ready-to-wear) garments gave them volume potential in excess of whatever couture clothes they could possibly sell to a highly limited market.

During the 1960s and 1970s American designers came into greater prominence, and designers like Bill Blass, Pauline Trigère, Donald Brooks, Norman Norell, Betsey Johnson, and Rudi Gernreich became familiar names and had a strong influence on customers of higher-priced apparel, but the new life style of the 1960s was not one that encouraged the growth or maintenance of a fashion customer enclave reserved for the few.

Although the institution of high-fashion French designers still gives a platform for a small group that receives worldwide press coverage, the commercial value of their apparel has lessened considerably. Many couturiers, however, are reaping gains by creating styles for ready-to-wear and by selling their names for licensing of a host of products, as do Pierre Cardin, Yves Saint Laurent, and Hubert Givenchy, as well as the American designers.

Paris' emergence as the fashion capital

Rose Bertin was the first couturier to achieve fame. As an employee of Mademoiselle Pagelle, a well-known Parisian dressmaker, she made contacts with influential ladies of royalty and in the early 1770s became dressmaker for Queen Marie Antoinette and French aristocrats, the queens of Sweden and Spain, the Duchess of Devonshire, and the Czarina of Russia.

The second designer of renown during the late eighteenth and nineteenth centuries was Louis Hippolyte LeRoy, the official dressmaker of Napoleon's wife Josephine. He served customers throughout the courts of Europe.

Following LeRoy, four Parisian designers, three women and one man, achieved fame during the early to middle nineteenth century, the last achieving international recognition. Palmyre, Vignon, and Victorine received wide acclaim in France for their designs but did not attain the fame of the two designers who preceded them or the one man who followed.

Charles Worth (1825–1895), an Englishman who migrated to Paris at the age of twenty, arrived when there was no established couturier or designer. He obtained employment with a small draper's shop and later with Gagelin and Opigez, then one of the most fashionable shops in Paris. He approached his employers at Maison Gagelin with the idea of setting up a small dressmaking department. Although the idea was ridiculed at first, a successful department was established. The operation became famous, and at the Great Exhibition in

London in 1851 the Maison Gagelin won the only gold medal awarded to France for fashion ingenuity.

Worth conceived the idea of selling models of his garments to foreign buyers **159** with permission to copy them, a practice that is still part of the couture method of operation. His other innovation was a department that sold ready-made apparel, the forerunner of couturier boutiques, another current practice.

Worth became the dressmaker for Empress Eugénie and other wealthy and often beautiful women of Europe. Financed by a Swedish businessman, he opened his own business in 1858, a shop at 7 Rue de la Paix, which was not a fashion district. Soon after, the Opéra was built nearby and attracted the people of high fashion to the area, plus other couturiers and business establishments. The high fashion market of Paris had developed.

Charles Worth is credited with being the founder of modern haute couture. His innovations included the draping of his own designs on live models, the selling of fashion ideas for copying, and production of apparel for both wholesale and retail sales. Up to the time of Worth, customers of high fashion dictated the design of garments to a great degree, with the designer asking and receiving customer acceptance of sketches before starting the dressmaking process on dummies.

The idea that couturiers could concentrate on their own creations, instead of following the dictates of their customers, was readily accepted by Worth's peers. In 1868, they established the **Chambre Syndicale de la Couture Parisienne,** the association already mentioned. The group performs the following functions for its membership of about twenty houses:

1. Coordinates the showing dates of collections so that buyers and reporters can visit several houses in one day.
2. Regulates shipping and press releases. All orders placed during the opening week are shipped on a uniform date, about thirty days after the first showings. Press releases and photographs are held up until approximately six weeks after showings. This gives the trade buyers the advantage of having copies made before the information reaches the knock-off levels of industry.
3. Regulates conditions for copying. A trade buyer purchases and signs an agreement to produce the garment only in his own country and is forbidden to sell paper patterns to other manufacturers.
4. Registers new designs of its members. Garment designs can be registered in France to inhibit style piracy. (The United States has no such laws.)
5. Issues press cards. Couture openings are of international interest; they attract the press from many nations and sometimes interested outsiders. The Chambre has complete control over the invitations to the media and ensures attendance of verified press representatives.

What led to the emergence of Paris as the couture capital is a moot question. One could say April in Paris, the elegance of the royal court and the apparel it demanded, its central location in Western Europe, the early international acceptance of French as the language of diplomacy, and whatever other factors that are especially "French." Regardless of the reasons, France became the undisputed center of elegant clothing designed by a series of fashion originators who built international reputations. In recent years these originators have capitalized on their fashion reputations by letting their names be used on items as diverse as perfume, shower sheets, eyeglasses, towels, and a host of others.

The business of haute couture

The market location of the French couturiers is unlike that of the American firms which are clustered in a few tall office buildings in one area of New York City. Each French firm is located in an elegant house in a residential neighborhood. The head of the organization, as a rule, is the designer whose name the firm carries. All couture houses show two collections a year, during the latter parts of January and July. The collections are first shown to American and European manufacturers and store buyers, who are interested in buying them for reproduction or selling them in their own countries. After these shows, the collections are viewed by private customers for their own wear. When such a customer purchases a garment, it is made to measurement.

The majority of houses charge trade buyers a fee, called a **caution,** which can range from $500 to several thousand dollars. If a purchase is made, the caution is deducted from the purchase sum. The reason is that a trade buyer is shown the designer's creation and can translate it for a domestic manufacturer into a copy. As a corollary, the cost of a garment is higher for a trade buyer than for a private customer for the same reason—the professionals may use the designer's new ideas for commercial purpose.

Two groups of trade buyers patronize the Paris couture, manufacturers and store buyers. Manufacturers buy original styles to have the right to produce them domestically, either as exact American-made versions (**line-for-line** copies) or as adaptations. Store buyers purchase them to have the right to have domestic manufacturers produce them for their stores. The garments are then imported into the United States tax-free as goods serving a purpose other than resale. Once the garments have served their purpose as models, they are shipped to Canada, to firms that specialize in buying and selling apparel brought into the United States under bond. By shipping original styles out after the copying process, manufacturers and stores effect considerable savings.

An interesting aspect of French couture is that styles are sold with no exclusivity, so there is always the probability of two fashion stores of the same trading area having the same styles. It is difficult to assess the dollar figure of French sales to the United States, but it is fair to say that the romance is currently far greater than the volume.

French ready-to-wear (prêt-à-porter)

The initial resistance to ready-made clothing was perhaps stronger in France than in any other country in the world. French pride in the institutions of the couture and the dressmaker was not easy to overcome.

Little by little in the 1960s, however, new design names became important. Daniel Hechter, one of the first, was recognized for his youthful, beautifully styled tailored suits and coats. Within ten years Hechter's firm was licensing his designs to countries all over the world, including the United States. Em-

A model shows one of the gowns in the Yves Saint Laurent spring/summer collection in Paris, January 1982. (Photo Pierre Vauthey/Sygma)

manuelle Khanh, a former model, burst on the fashion scene with styles appropriate for the new generation, featuring loose and soft silhouettes. Sonia Rykiel developed stardom with one look, the body sweater. She has since added cardigans, unusual pants and skirts, and crêpe de chine dresses that go back to the thirties. Her designs have been copied by fashion producers of all countries. Cacharel, another leading fashion firm, created a shirt without darts that hugs the body. These prêt-à-porter designs have captured a large part of the international fashion audience.

The biannual prêt-à-porter show, held in October and April just outside

Paris, started in 1961, with a thousand buyers. Current shows are attended by nearly a thousand manufacturers and about 30,000 buyers.

Although modern ready-to-wear was born in 1920 in the United States, it took nearly fifty years to break through into the last stronghold of tailoring: France. Ready-to-wear has now gained the support of the entire fashion world.

England

Although the fashion prominence of England is not so striking as France's, its couturiers and other fashion creators have assumed considerable recent fame. The British fashion output, once considered staid and traditional and hardly suitable for American taste, is now a vital and major contributor to the fashion world.

Up to World War II, fashion designers in England were well below the stature of the French couture group. Famous designers formed the association **The Fashion Group of Great Britain** in 1925 and listed such members as Norman Hartnell, Peter Russell, Worth, Madame Mosca Morton, Victor Steibel, and Hardy Amies. A little later, Molyneux, an Englishman, attained fame in France and was added to the roster.

When World War II broke out the English fashion industry went into a decline. The average consumer had to get along with one or two new garments for the duration of the war, adding only a few accessory items.

Immediately after the war, one or two designers tried to franchise their designs in America, with no success. Norman Hartnell, a dressmaker for the Queen, actually entered into an arrangement with a well-known popular-price maker of cotton dresses, McKettrick-Williams, but his name carried no weight with consumers.

But then things began to happen. England's "angry young men"—intellectuals, authors, and playwrights—emphasized themes about the lost generation, the victims of those who held power. Artists caught the spirit, and London became a beehive of intellectual activity. All art forms began to flourish. The rebellious spirit filtered down to youth, who expressed their feelings in various ways, one of which was to lampoon the attire that symbolized the ruling class. Young men began wearing Edwardian clothes, complete with canes and high hats, and the spoof received worldwide attention.

Then a band was formed that epitomized the new philosophy in music, apparel, and hair styles. The group was The Beatles. When they appeared on the Ed Sullivan Sunday night program, people ridiculed them but finally accepted them.

English fashion creators began to thrive in the postwar atmosphere, as an exciting stream of new ideas entered the marketplace and captured the imagination of the world for its freshness and sensitivity to the "now" world. Among the first was Mary Quant, who entered the field in a roundabout way. In the late 1950s, she and her husband opened a boutique in London's King Road and started selling ready-made clothes. She soon discovered that her customers were not satisfied with the offered styles. Quant then started to produce her own merchandise by using commercial patterns. Her selling was successful but the operation was not profitable. Accordingly, she visited American plants and learned how to produce goods profitably. Her clothing was a smash hit in Europe, North America, and Japan.

What gave her apparel appeal was its spirit of youth. Her clothes were well made, popularly priced, gay, and—most important of all—revealing. She took the stuffiness out of English styles. Eventually she made some designs exclusively for J. C. Penney, gave up the retail business, and extended her operation to include the sale of perfume, handbags, cosmetics, and sundry other items.

Another important English designer is Jean Muir, who arrived on the fashion scene in the early 1960s. This young designer of Scottish descent started as a sketcher in a London store, joined Jaeger as a designer, and finally founded her own firm. Considered one of the most exciting designers of the world, she features junior styles of the finest fabrics and workmanship. Henri Bendel, a fashionable New York store, uses an entire department to feature her garments. Her styles are admired in all fashion-conscious cities of the world.

Among other English designers who rose to fame are Sally Tuffin, Marian Foale, James Wedge, George McCann, Roger Nelson, Ossie Clark, Alice Pollack, Zandra Rhodes, and Bill Gibb. Cecil Beaton's designs influenced apparel, particularly evening wear. His costumes for *My Fair Lady*, *Coco*, and other Broadway hits received international acclaim.

Thus an industry that was considered traditional and slow-moving became a substantial contributor to its country's economy by the millions of dollars obtained from exports. English designers are now highly respected and are supported in their export efforts by the Board of Trade's Export Service Division, which maintains representatives in major cities in the United States.

Other countries

Italy has a couture group that has had a continuous degree of importance in American fashions. Its list of couturiers includes Emilio Pucci, Fabiani, deBerentzen, Fontana, Galitzine, Mila Schoen, Simonetta, Veniziana of Milan, and Valentino. Among its categories of interest are dresses, men's suits, coats, sportswear, and shoes.

Some Italian couture houses are headed by members of the nobility who run the business from ancestral palaces in scattered locations. There is no marketplace as such, but trade shows are held on a scheduled basis. The Pitti Palace in Florence is the glamorous setting at which ready-to-wear showings take place. The Strozzi Palace, also in Florence, is the mart where business—the actual buying and selling—is transacted. And Milan has become one of the foremost international fashion markets in the world.

Valentino has had great fashion-market acceptance in the United States. Pucci has won wide acclaim for his dresses with unusual fabric and style designs. He was trained as an architect in the United States.

Our Italian imports add up to multimillions of dollars, with greatest concentration on shoes, followed by sportswear.

The other countries of Europe attract some United States buyers for indigenous ready-made products. The most important fair is the exhibition of Eu-

Swimwear by Italian designer Salvatore Ferragamo being introduced to the public in the Sala Bianca of the Pitti Palace in Florence, March 1982. (Salvatore Ferragamo, Inc.)

ropean ready-to-wear held each season in Düsseldorf, Germany. Hundreds of firms display their lines there to thousands of buyers from around the world.

The Orient's main interest is the production of apparel for export, although on occasion a particular designer becomes well-known on the international

The Hanae Mori boutique, Tokyo. (*WWD*/The Fairchild Syndicate)

scene. Hanae Mori of Tokyo captured the imagination of the United States several years ago and was front-covered by *Vogue* magazine and window-displayed on Fifth Avenue by a leading fashion store. She too has franchised her name for various products sold in this country, including bedsheets and pillow cases.

SUMMARY

Trade among nations goes back in history thousands of years. As an economic principle, a country exports products it has in abundance or that it can produce with some advantage. In an effort to establish equitable terms, trading nations hold periodic conferences to establish exporting and importing guidelines.

During the 1970s, the United States, the most powerful trading nation, began to incur huge annual trading deficits, averaging about $25 billion. Our unfavorable balance of trade, according to experts, will probably continue to increase. Manufacturers and workers are in favor of legislation to curb foreign producer access to our market. On the other hand, importers and retailers are in favor of a continued free market in which products are purchased on the basis of value. Consumers are not concerned with product origin; they purchase to obtain value. The government favors free trade because protectionism lowers the standard of living, causes unfavorable relations with other countries, sets in motion retaliatory measures in countries on which we depend for products essential to our economic well-being, and jeopardizes the jobs of the one in six workers engaged in producing our exports. How and when a favorable balance of trade can be re-established is a matter of conjecture.

The importation of fashion apparel at prestige price levels has never been a concern because total dollar purchases are relatively insignificant, and the products create little or no competition in our domestic market. Moreover, some prestige foreign merchandise is of value for the purpose of producing in lower-priced versions.

From the time our nation was founded, we have imported apparel from Europe. When, however, mass production was established, we assumed the position as the world capital of ready-to-wear. After World War II, imports of ready-to-wear began to swell, and in a matter of a few years the market penetration reached flood level. We import tremendous quantities of fashion apparel from the Orient, Europe, and South America. Many types of moderate- and popular-priced fashion merchandise are of greater significance to retailers and ultimate consumers than those that are produced domestically.

At the start of the twentieth century, Americans became fascinated by high fashions created by French couturiers. Paris was the home of high fashion, and Americans held designers of haute couture houses in highest esteem. Better-priced retail stores and manufacturers expressed their admiration by buying the right to copy selected styles for either line-for-line copying or production of lower-priced versions. By 1960, however, Paris' prestige had begun to wane, at a time when American designers emerged as international fashion leaders. Concurrently with these developments, French couturiers and those of other countries entered the ready-to-wear business with considerable success. Obviously, ready-to-wear offered a broader audience and greater financial return.

Every country has its leading couturiers, some of whom have an international reputation. There is hardly anyone with any interest in fashion who is not familiar with the well-publicized names of, for example, Mary Quant, Cecil Beaton, Hubert Givenchy, Pierre Cardin, Yves Saint Laurent, Valentino, and Simonetta.

Apparel is a basic need, and the fashion of clothing has international interest—for trade, for art, for national prestige.

QUESTIONS FOR DISCUSSION

1. Should the United States increase import duties and thereby safeguard jobs for American employees? Why or why not?
2. Do you have feelings of guilt when buying a foreign-made product in preference to an American version? Why or why not?
3. To what extent would you be willing to give up convenience and pay higher costs for U.S.-made products to increase the United States' share of domestically produced products—including apparel, of course?
4. Trace the declining importance of haute couture.
5. Compare the practices of the haute couture of Paris and the couture houses of America.

CAREER OPPORTUNITIES IN APPAREL MANUFACTURING

Apparel-industry job opportunities are numerous and diverse, a condition that tends to bewilder an applicant with no background for specialization or relationship that guarantees an entry job. An astute applicant without family or friendship ties to the industry will realize that it is necessary to review the structure, practices, products, locations, job levels, and job descriptions of the market.

From the broadest point of view, there are about 25,000 firms that could be solicited, far too many for practical purposes. Hence, you should establish an order of priority.

The first realization, perhaps, is that the market is separated into three wide segments—apparel for men, women, and children.

Your choice of segment narrows the number of firms considerably, possibly offering quickly an area in which the products have greatest relevance for you. Further narrowing can be based on merchandising categories (coats and suits, dresses, sportswear, and so on), size ranges, and price ranges.

By taking into account the market segmentation and making a choice, you will have chosen an area based on some predisposition, talent, or calculation. Why not? Although to many people the most important reason for being in

168   business is to make a profit or to earn a maximum salary, why not work where there is the greatest chance to be employed most enjoyably? This option requires an analysis of the firms of a given division of the apparel producers—the type of merchandise handled, comparative size of the organizations, location of the main and subsidiary operations, and the manner in which the products are marketed.

Once having completed these initial steps, you need to make an incisive review of your personal attributes and assess how they measure up to job specifications. A self-evaluation for entry-job purposes is important.

If your training has been in an area that requires specialized skills, designing, for instance, or patternmaking, your job choice is easily evaluated. Even here, the entry job does not have to be specific. A formally trained designer may very well seek and accept a position as a sample hand, sample cutter, or pattern-maker to get a foot in the door of an organization. The objective is to obtain a beginning position that is related to and can eventually lead to a career position of your ambition. Many people do not remain in the discipline studied in school. Job experience and opportunities often cause careers to take paths not earlier considered.

JOB PROSPECTING

The easiest task, research, seems to confound some students: finding names, business locations, personnel, and organization specialties. No industry offers more books, pamphlets, and listings than the apparel manufacturing industry. An industry that is both opportunistic and highly competitive does not hide in the dark, and the more listings, publicity, and name-bandying the better.

Who makes what can be learned through such industrial publications as the *Fairchild Market Directory of Women's and Children's Apparel*, *Buyer's Guide*, and *Buyer's Blue Book: Apparel, Accessory and Textile Directory*.

The leading buildings that house apparel-manufacturer headquarters issue lists of their tenants' names. And since similar manufacturers cluster, it is easy to obtain the names of, for example, moderate-price junior dressmakers at 1400 Broadway in New York City.

Fairchild's *Textile and Apparel Industries* lists conglomerate ownership, volume of individual corporations, names of officers, and profit results.

Another excellent source of information is a local stockbroker, who will have or can obtain organizational facts about firms with publicly held stock.

For those who are not in or near New York and might have difficulty in finding these publications, the simplest method is to visit the nearest large store and see a buyer or assistant buyer. Either of them will have pamphlets or listings of the manufacturers of assigned merchandise classifications. A cooperative buyer (and buyers usually are) can offer specific resources and suggest contact names in firms of high reputation.

Other sources of valuable information are the unions and trade associations, which have lists of every firm in the business. Here are a few:

- International Ladies' Garment Workers' Union
  1710 Broadway, New York, NY 10019

- Amalgamated Clothing & Textile Workers Union
  15 Union Square, New York, NY 10003
- NAWCAS (National Association of Women's & Children's Apparel Salesmen)
  Hotel Statler Hilton, New York, NY 10001
- National Association of Men's Sportswear Buyers
  535 Fifth Avenue, New York, NY 10017

Compiling a target list will take the least effort of your whole operation.

THE JOB

Positions with apparel makers fall into five general categories: (1) production, (2) administration, (3) design, (4) selling, and (5) communication.

A fashion coordination specialty can be part of the areas of styling the line, conducting fashion shows (including store events), and selecting fashion colors. The duties can be varied and dependent upon a firm's particular job interpretation.

To illustrate the varied entry opportunities, selected jobs are listed for each general classification.

1. *Production*
Assistant plant manager
Engineer
Junior engineer
Costing engineer
Production assistant
Assistant production manager
Management trainee
Cost analyst
Assistant piece goods buyer

2. *Administration*
Accountant or bookkeeper
Cost controller
Order processor
Production control clerk
(Many other positions in administration are generic to firms in any business.)

3. *Design*
Assistant designer
Designer trainee
Assistant stylist
Assistant pattern maker
Assistant merchandiser (helps put the line in selling form)
Sketcher
Sample cutter
Sample hand
Draper
Assistant cutter

4. *Selling*
Showroom salesperson

Road salesperson trainee
Chain and resident buyer sales trainee

5. *Communication*
Public relations assistant (large firms only)
Copywriter (large firms only)
Fashion director or coordinator
Assistant to advertising manager

Review the tables of organizations and trace these jobs to see the positions to which they could lead.

APPLYING

Your list of selected firms should number about 100 to 150 and can contain the two sectors you have selected as highest-priority. A short letter of introduction and a complete resume, preferably professionally printed, should be mailed. One word of caution. All resume information should be accurate and relevant. (If you note that you like to cook and swim, the potential interviewer may get the impression that you indulge in healthful and useful hobbies, but they will not be the reasons you will be hired.) For a first job, a candidate should have a meaningful background of school training and, if possible, a part-time employment record. Do not list school courses in great detail or be too wordy. A potential employer is not interested in every course you have taken or the particulars of a part-time job. Get down to basics and statements of facts.

Make sure your resume includes times you are available for an interview and how you can be reached by telephone. (See Appendix B.)

SUMMARY

In preparation for your interviews, remember that there are sources of information about every firm. Background information will prepare you for the response to "Why do you want to work here?" Interviews should not be used for questions like "Why don't you try ———" or "Why do you not make more profit?" Be yourself, be truthful, and try to be relaxed.

QUESTIONS FOR DISCUSSION

1. What are the important career advantages of the apparel manufacturing sector?
2. Compare the advantages and disadvantages of employment by a big organization ($50 million per year) as compared to a small one ($2 million per year).
3. What are the restrictions on where you can reside when employed by a manufacturer?
4. List the steps of your own plan to obtain a position in the manufacturing sector.
5. What sector of the industry do you think has the greatest viability for your career? Explain.

Retailing is a marketing activity with which people are most familiar, since we are all consumers. In this part we will look at the history of retailing in different periods and the sequence of retail changes, then examine fashion-related data and their implications. Chapter 12 will deal with career opportunities in fashion retailing.

According to the latest United States Bureau of the Census survey, there are 1.5 million single units and over 34,000 multiunit retail firms, both together employing from 10 to 12 million people (10 percent with interest in fashion merchandising). This gigantic employment figure becomes more meaningful,

PART IV

THE RETAILERS OF FASHION APPAREL

perhaps, with the realization that it is three to four times the total population of Israel.

The objectives of Part IV are these:

1. To relate to the size, importance, and background of American retailing
2. To help the reader interested in professional retailing select a particular career area
3. To identify the problems and rewards of owning one's own store
4. To develop understanding of and ability to relate to the importance of consumers to retailers

Photo Bruce Paulson/*DNR*/The Fairchild Syndicate

10

RETAILING

In simplest terms, **retailing** is the sale of goods and services to final consumers. Others might add the activities of buying at wholesale and selling in retail quantities, plus the additional functions of placing the goods in the hands of the final users. Whatever the definition, consumers are the main focus of retail stores. In the economic process a retailer is a middleman between the producer and the purchaser.

Retailing is exciting and fascinating because it is in a state of perpetual change, with a continuous array of new products and new methods of merchandising them. The lifetime of someone now over sixty has witnessed the following partial list of market innovations:

- The development of:
  supermarkets
  discount stores
  boutiques
  nonstore retailers
  franchise retailers
  department stores as chains
  nationalization of department stores

membership discounters
apparel chains
- Introduction of electronic data processing, including point-of-sale computer terminals
- The use of cashiers instead of sales personnel

This list of changes could be much longer, especially if the retail innovations of the fast-food industry were included.

Tables 10–1 and 10–2 identify the giant retailers of America: the top 100 companies and the Billion Dollar Club.

The history of American retailing can be divided into five distinct periods, during which stores reflected different concentrations on location, size, ambience, types of ownership, lines of merchandise, and improved methods of operation. The last includes the use of electronic data-processing, a technological breakthrough that has strongly affected the ability of larger organizations to function efficiently.

The periods can be summarized:

- 17th century: the barter system
- 18th century: trading post and general store
- 19th century: variety store, specialty store, chain store, department store, mail-order firm
- 20th century (1900–1950): franchise and convenience stores, apparel chains, supermarkets, discount stores
- 20th century (since 1950): multiunits of branch stores, shopping centers, catalogue stores, warehouse showrooms

THE SEVENTEENTH AND EIGHTEENTH CENTURIES

Selling in North America was initially carried on by traders under the direction of ships' captains who were often more than master mariners. They were merchants of high caliber who were able to dispose of goods purchased abroad and sold at port stops.

The American Indians had a commodity of great importance to the European market—furs. Hence, the barter system was the first method of retailing: the Indians exchanged furs for food, liquor, and jewelry. And, of course, one of the most famous barter transactions was the exchange of the island of Manhattan for twenty-four dollars' worth of jewelry. Not a bad deal—for the colonists.

Gradually, during the colonial period the population began to expand into other commercially fertile regions, and the settlers who did not have easy access to established trading posts required merchandise. Peddlers became retailers of importance. They carried goods inland by backpack, horse, boat, and wagon. They were also among the trail-blazing settlers. The peddlers' stock assortment contained the essentials of frontier life: cloth, tinware, flints, bullets, household

TABLE 10–1   The Top 100 Department Stores, 1980

Company/division	Affil.	Units	Sq. ft. (thousands)	Volume (millions)
1. Macy's New York	RHM	15	5,998	$775
2. Bamberger's New Jersey	RHM	20	5,656	725
3. May Co. California	May	31	7,181	650
4. Hudson's, Detroit	DH	18	5,832	641.5
5. Broadway-So. California	CHH	40	7,058	625
6. Macy's California	RHM	19	4,221	600
7. Bloomingdale's, New York	Fed	15	3,397	566.8
8. Marshall Field, Chicago	MF	18	5,764	550
9. Abraham & Straus, Brooklyn	Fed	12	4,907	547.6
10. Burdine's Florida	Fed	21	3,980	498.8
11. Dillard's, Little Rock	Ind	50	6,342	470.7
12. Lord & Taylor, New York	ADG	35	4,902	460
13. Foley's, Houston	Fed	10	3,006	453.0
14. Bullock's, Los Angeles	Fed	22	4,726	447.4
15. Emporium-Capwell, No. California	CHH	19	4,746	415
16. Dayton's, Minneapolis	DH	16	3,149	382.1
17. Hecht's, Balt.-Washington	May	21	4,225	365
18. Jordan Marsh, New England	All	14	3,595	360
19. Rich's, Atlanta	Fed	17	4,076	351.7
20. Wanamaker's, Philadelphia	CHH	16	4,356	335
21. Lazarus, Columbus	Fed	15	3,607	332.8
22. Joske's, Texas	All	27	4,832	315
Famous-Barr, St. Louis	May	12	3,439	315
24. The Bon, Northwest	All	32	3,983	310
25. Woodward & Lothrop, Washington	Ind	15	2,965	308.4
26. Robinson's, Los Angeles	ADG	19	3,309	295
27. Filene's, Boston	Fed	15	2,017	288.7
28. Goldblatt's, Chicago	Ind	22	3,192	265.9
29. Sanger-Harris, Dallas	Fed	12	3,358	262.1
30. Carson, Pirie, Scott, Chicago	Ind	25	3,842	255
31. Gimbels New York	BAT	11	2,930	240
32. Strawbridge & Clothier, Philadelphia	Ind	11	2,300	225
Maas Bros., Tampa	All	19	2,521	225
34. Shillito's, Cincinnati	Fed	9	2,330	215.1
35. May Co., Cleveland	May	10	2,938	215
Kaufmann's, Pittsburgh	May	10	2,589	215
Jordan Marsh, Miami	All	13	2,487	215
38. B. Altman & Co., New York	Ind	6	1,953	210
39. H. C. Prange Co., Sheboygan	Ind	31	3,183	209.7
40. D. H. Holmes, New Orleans	Ind	13	1,790	197.3
41. L. S. Ayres, Indianapolis	ADG	12	2,286	190
Higbee's Cleveland	Ind	12	3,134	190
43. Hess, Allentown (ending 4/30/81)	CAC	21	1,995	189.9
44. Frederick & Nelson, Seattle	MF	13	2,009	185
45. Elder-Beerman, Dayton	Ind	20	N/A	180
46. Davison's, Atlanta	RHM	12	2,091	175
Thalhimer's, Richmond	CHH	24	2,252	175
Macy's-Midwest (incl. LaSalle's)	RHM	—	—	175
49. Gimbels-Philadelphia	BAT	10	2,219	170
50. P. A. Bergner, Peoria	Ind	24	1,500	165
G. Fox, Hartford	May	8	1,910	165
J. B. Ivey, Charlotte	MF	23	2,425	165
53. Wieboldt's, Chicago	Ind	14	N/A	164.9

TABLE 10-1 (continued)   The Top 100 Department Stores, 1980

Company/division	Affil.	Units	Sq. ft. (thousands)	Volume (millions)
54. Gimbels-Midwest, Milwaukee	BAT	11	2,471	$160
55. Younker's, Des Moines	EI	29	2,200	152.1
56. Stern's, Paramus	All	7	1,254	150
Liberty House, Honolulu	Amfac	12	N/A	150
58. Joseph Horne, Pittsburgh	ADG	13	2,474	145
59. Meier & Frank, Portland	May	7	1,826	135
Weinstock's, Sacramento	CHH	12	1,929	135
Stix, Baer, Fuller, St. Louis	ADG	13	3,022	135
Gimbels-Pittsburgh	BAT	7	1,500	135
Howland-Steinbach, White Plains	SG	28	N/A	135
64. Broadway-Southwest	CHH	9	1,472	130
Miller & Rhoads, Richmond	GBB	21	1,605	130
66. ZCMI, Salt Lake City	Ind	7	1,118	127.0
67. Gayfer's, Mobile	MS	11	1,537	125
68. Diamond's, Phoenix	DH	10	1,242	123.1
69. Rike's, Dayton	Fed	5	1,672	115.5
70. Pomeroy's Pennsylvania	All	14	2,201	115
May-D&F, Denver	May	9	1,409	115
72. Goldsmith's, Memphis	Fed	4	1,107	110.9
73. Sibley, Lindsay, Curr, Rochester	ADG	9	1,684	110
74. Halle's, Cleveland	MF	9	1,438	105
75. McRae's, Jackson	Ind	14	906	104
76. Boston Store, Milwaukee	Fed	6	1,343	101.3
77. McAlpin's, Cincinnati	MS	9	1,394	100
M. O'Neil, Akron	May	10	1,791	100
Denver Dry Goods	ADG	13	1,478	100
Boscov's	Ind	8	N/A	100
81. Donaldson's, Minneapolis	All	10	1,733	95
82. Jones Store, Kansas City	MS	6	1,273	90
Hahne & Co., Newark	ADG	8	1,466	90
J. L. Brandeis, Omaha	Ind	14	1,273	90
85. Gertz, Long Island	All	4	942	85
Goudchaux, Baton Rouge	Ind	3	300	85
87. Block's, Indianapolis	All	8	1,199	80
Strouss, Youngstown	May	9	1,056	80
McCurdy's	Ind	12	1,200	80
90. Bullock-No. California	Fed	5	872	75.7
91. Hutzler's, Baltimore	Ind	6	1,000	75
Gottschalk's, Fresno	Ind	6	N/A	75
93. Goldwater's, Phoenix	ADG	7	809	70
94. Adam, Meldrum, Anderson, Buffalo	Ind	8	1,000	65
H & S Pogue, Cincinnati	ADG	5	1,041	65
Read's, Bridgeport	All	5	753	65
Pizitz, Birmingham	Ind	10	850	65
Robinson's, Florida	ADG	7	998	65
Joslin's, Denver	MS	7	816	65
Miller's, Tennessee	GBB	11	1,222	65

Note: Figures ending in "5" or "0" are estimates; others are exact sales as reported.
Affiliation Code: All, Allied; ADG, Associated Dry Goods; BAT (BATUS, Inc. Retail Division);
CHH, Carter Hawley Hale; CS, City Stores; DH, Dayton-Hudson; EI, Equitable of Iowa; Fed,
Federated; GBB, Garfinckel, Brooks Bros.; Ind, Independent; MF, Marshall Field; MS,
Mercantile Stores; RHM, R. H. Macy; SG, Supermarkets General.

SOURCE: *Stores*, July 1981

TABLE 10–2 The Billion Dollar Club of Department Stores and Mass Merchandisers, 1980

	Sales	
	1980	1979
Department stores		
Federated Department Stores	$ 6,301,000,000	$ 5,806,000,000
Dayton-Hudson Corp.	4,033,000,000	3,385,000,000
The May Department Stores	3,150,000,000	2,957,000,000
Carter Hawley Hale Stores	2,632,921,000	2,408,028,000
R. H. Macy	2,484,522,000	2,266,954,000
Allied Stores Corp.	2,268,711,000	2,210,301,000
Associated Dry Goods Corp.	1,952,200,000	1,783,200,000
Mercantile Stores Co., Inc.	1,108,076,000	1,067,937,000
Marshall Field & Co.	1,012,501,000	904,296,000
Mass merchandisers		
Sears, Roebuck & Co.	18,707,000,000	18,549,000,000
K Mart Corp.	14,204,381,000	12,731,145,000
J. C. Penney Co.	11,353,000,000	10,856,000,000
F. W. Woolworth Co.	7,218,000,000	6,785,000,000
Montgomery Ward & Co.	5,916,000,000	5,652,000,000

SOURCE: *Women's Wear Daily*, July 16, 1981

necessities, and minor luxuries. Some remained at central points along the westward trail, and opened a trading post or general store.

The general store was an outgrowth of the need for wider assortments of merchandise in settlements. It is a retail axiom that wherever people settle in sufficient numbers, stores will follow. The American general store is an example that can be related to current retail opportunities. The first general stores were small and carried a variety of products ranging from flour to guns and including fabrics for home sewing. The Western movies and television horse operas depict replicas that are sometimes accurate. Interestingly enough, the general store and the saloon were always places of town activity. This is further evidence of another retail principle: retailing success is dependent on traffic, and traffic is the result of consumer need and convenience.

THE NINETEENTH CENTURY

Specialty stores

The size and population of the United States virtually exploded during the nineteenth century. In 1800 the population was 5,308,483, and the occupied land area was 864,746 square miles. By 1900 the resident population had grown to 75,994,575 and the land area to 2,969,834 square miles, astounding increases in the most fundamental needs of retailing—people and locations.

When the industrial revolution reached North America in the mid-nineteenth century, we entered the industrial phase of our history, and the pattern of our life style changed radically; where we lived, worked, dressed, socialized, and shopped were affected. Cities were becoming more heavily populated and prod-

ucts more numerous. Since retailing is predicated on these factors, a new series
of stores came into being. The recognition that certain classifications of merchandise were sufficiently varied and needed retail concentration led to the **179**
founding of **specialty stores,** among the first of which were those that stocked
food, an elementary requirement in the hierarchy of need. Gradually, shops
that had other kinds of merchandise were opened. Among the earliest specialty
shops that had relevance to fashion were jewelry and shoe stores.

Chains

Specialty stores, established as individual units, expanded into other cities,
and the **chain store** became part of the American retail scene. The A&P was
founded in 1859, and the first Kinney shoe store opened in Waverly, New York,
in 1894. Kinney is now owned by a conglomerate, F. W. Woolworth Co., part
of another retail type that evolved in the same period.

Variety stores

The **variety store,** a late-nineteenth-century innovation originally known as
a 5 & 10 cent store, was conceived to sell a broad assortment of merchandise
at low retail levels.

One of the leaders of the movement was Woolworth's, now a conglomerate
that owns stores in Canada, Germany, Mexico, and England as well as the
Richman Bros. Company in Cleveland, Ohio. Woolworth's established its first
unit in Utica, New York, in 1879. The 5-&-10-cent-idea inspired chains founded
by S. H. Kress, S. S. Kresge, and W. T. Grant.

These retail outlets operated on the theory that as the tempo of life speeded
up during the country's expansion, people would be interested in seeking fast
service on pick-up items on a cash-and-carry basis. As part of the retail strategy,

The F. W. Woolworth 5 & 10 cent store in Kenosha, Wisconsin, about 1928. (L. Pelaez Collection)

180

the merchandise was sold on one floor for greatest consumer convenience. Later, basements were added when new classifications of merchandise were added to the retail mix.

In the twentieth century, 5-and-10-cent stores were restructured with the addition of higher-priced products and became known as variety stores; relatively recently, some were restructured the other way to become mass-priced operations. Kresge's, K-Mart, and Woolworth's Woolco are examples.

Mail-order retailers

Although the industrial revolution caused population movement to cities, the 1800s were a period in which the United States was still largely rural. An interesting note is that 68 percent of the population now lives on 1½ percent of the acreage of the country; 1920 was the year the population used the greatest percentage of land for living purposes. The farm population for 1920 was 31.9 percent; in 1978 it was in the neighborhood of 5 percent. In 1800, 93.9 percent of the population was rural; in 1979 approximately 5 percent.

These statistics reveal the reason for many national changes, of interest to us chiefly because they led to another retail type of business. The farm and rural population were scattered geographically but were accessible to major centers after the completion of the transcontinental railroad in 1869. Available transportation plus the postal system of rural free delivery created a great opportunity: the possibility of selling goods by mail. Accordingly, in 1872, the first general merchandise mail-order firm was founded: Montgomery Ward. Chicago, the railroad center of the nation, became the headquarters of the mail-order business; the main offices of Montgomery Ward; Sears, Roebuck; and Spiegel are still there.

From the beginning, the large mail-order business was successful. As a result of the developments of the first third of the twentieth century, which saw the coming of age of the automobile, the shift of population, the birth of modern ready-to-wear, and newer methods of retailing, the big three—Ward, Sears, and J. C. Penney—became deeply involved in a race to open new retail stores and develop the highest level of chain-store merchandising. And they have set some record! Their total retail volume for 1980 was more than $35 billion.

Students of retailing who live in large cities are often unfamiliar with the size and importance of the mail-order sector. To help understand their proper relationship to retailing and the economy, here are data of interest.

Sears, Roebuck

1. Operates the largest retail organization in the world.
2. Advertises more than any local advertiser (approximately half a billion dollars yearly).
3. Maintains 36,000 selling locations, including 1100 independent catalogue stores in fifty states; stores in Puerto Rico, Central America, and Spain; and catalogue desks in seventeen Japanese retail stores.
4. Merchandises 854 retail stores in the U.S., twelve catalogue-order plants, and more than 2600 catalogue and telephone sales offices.
5. Services 20 million credit customers.

6. Operates nine regional shopping centers.
7. Employs 440,000 people.
8. Owns the nation's largest real-estate brokerage firm (Coldwell, Banker & Co.). **181**
9. Operates the nation's fifth-largest securities firm (Dean Witter Reynolds).
10. Insures over 20 million policyholders (Allstate Insurance Co.)
11. Mails more than 85 million catalogues a year.
12. Occupies the Sears Tower in Chicago, the world's tallest building, with total space second only to the Pentagon.
13. Operates two other major subsidiary enterprises: Homart Development Company (develops and operates shopping centers) and Allstate Enterprises (registered savings and loan holding company).

Figure 10–1 shows the many offshoots that indicate Sears' importance to retailing, banking, insurance, and real estate. In terms of retailing alone, one-third of all Americans shop at Sears at least once a year.

J. C. Penney
1. Operates second largest retail organization in the world.
2. Runs 1686 Penney stores, 37 Treasury stores, 1506 Thrift catalogue centers, and 299 Thrift drug stores, and the Treasury Drug centers.
3. Owns the 87-store Belgian chain Surma and stores in Italy.
4. Has as subsidiaries: J. C. Penney Insurance Company, Great American Reserve Insurance Company, J. C. Penney International Financial Corporation, J. C. Penney International, Inc.
5. With Wendy's International, Inc., developed and operates Wendy's hamburger restaurants in Belgium and Luxembourg.

Montgomery Ward
1. Operates 411 full-line department stores in 43 states, 246 limited-line catalogue retail stores, and 296 catalogue centers.
2. Owns the Miami-based seven-store Jefferson chain.
3. Is owned by Marcor Inc., a wholly-owned subsidiary of Mobil Oil Company.

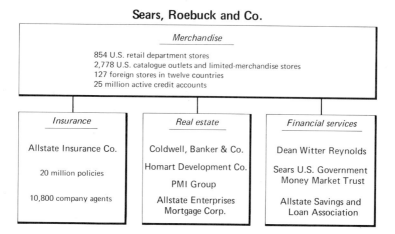

Sears, Roebuck and Co.

Merchandise

854 U.S. retail department stores
2,778 U.S. catalogue outlets and limited-merchandise stores
127 foreign stores in twelve countries
25 million active credit accounts

Insurance	*Real estate*	*Financial services*
Allstate Insurance Co.	Coldwell, Banker & Co.	Dean Witter Reynolds
20 million policies	Homart Development Co.	Sears U.S. Government Money Market Trust
	PMI Group	
10,800 company agents	Allstate Enterprises Mortgage Corp.	Allstate Savings and Loan Association

Figure 10–1 Sears, Roebuck and Co.: scope of retailing and subsidiary enterprises.

4. Among its subsidiaries are: Golden Bear Family Restaurants, Inc., Montgomery Ward Development Corporation, Montgomery Ward Realty Corporation, Montgomery Ward Life Insurance Company.

The mail-order chain organizations have captured a large wedge of the retail business, which may make one wonder how the mail-order business, about 20 percent of their operations, can still flourish in a day when stores are everywhere and consumers have great mobility. But customers appreciate important factors:

1. This is a time-saving method of shopping.
2. The mail-order companies have built a reputation for integrity, excellent merchandise specifications, and value.
3. The scope of merchandise assortments is vast.
4. The prices often reflect the savings of huge purchasing power.

Department stores

The clustering of people in cities, with the industrial revolution as the strongest influence, was the stimulus for the founding of the **department store.** As cities became more populated, consumers' needs could be most conveniently accommodated by a store somewhat larger than the already established general store. The general store, at best, had limited product availability and was not geared for servicing large groups. It was, however, the last step in the evolution of a more sophisticated retail type—a collection of specialty shops under one roof. And in the last half of the nineteenth century the department store was born.

In this organization the merchandise was decentralized into specific departments, each of which operated as a separate unit to obtain sales goals and contribute a share of profit to the total organization. To put it in another form, each department was defined as a separate entity and, in essence, a profit center. The stores' total merchandise included everything from food to furniture and appliances. Hence, the definition that a department store is an organization that employs at least twenty-five people and handles a wide variety of merchandise that includes home furnishings, apparel, and household linens or dry goods.

Nearly all American cities have one or more department stores that are part of their history, with many dating back to the 1850s and the following years of the nineteenth century.

As the years went by, organizational structures became more sophisticated, particularly in response to the growing population, increased competition from other types of retailers, and the broadening of consumer expectations. In the first half of the twentieth century, stores became even more decentralized with the addition of departments of a more specialized nature; for example, junior, petite (5′4″ and under), misses, and half-size dress departments. Formerly, a woman visited a dress department and went to an appropriate rack or case. The newer method was the department specialization by size, price, and, later, life style.

As department stores became larger, there was a need to assign responsibility for the many activities of the operation. Accordingly, stores developed organization charts and job descriptions for the fulfillment of the assigned **183** tasks. Many department stores became mammoth, with a hierarchy of personnel with different levels of responsibility.

Figure 10–2 is a typical organization chart that shows the different functions and/or positions of a large department store or specialty store organization.

1900–1950

Apparel chains

In 1920, as we know, modern ready-to-wear was born. Women were offered clothing that was inexpensive, although its quality left much to be desired. City population growth was among the influences for a new retail form: the women's apparel chain.

The combination of an increased city population that always included sufficient numbers of people with common taste and the availability of modestly priced garments resulted in a golden opportunity. Entrepreneurs formed organizations principally to sell dresses at popular prices—$5.00 to $25.00 and during promotional events often two for the price of one. These organizations used aggressive selling methods.

The chain store age, 1920–1930, was the period during which chain organizations came into their own. Perhaps the best example is Lerner Shops, which has remained a significant member of the institution of retailing.

Brooks Brothers, so important to the history of men's clothing, is a chain operation and was the progenitor organization of men's apparel chains. Chain retailing of men's apparel was already an established retail form by 1920. Figure 10–3 shows the structure of a modern chain organization.

Discount stores

For twenty-five years, starting in 1920, department stores became synonymous with integrity and success and enjoyed unprecedented growth and prosperity.

In 1945 the entrenched retail leaders, the department stores, started to receive a series of jolts from an upstart sector that caused concern and strong competition, and finally influenced many department stores to add the new method to their corporate operations.

When World War II ended, the United States went about establishing a peacetime economy. The return of war veterans to civilian life, the changeover of production to civilian products, and the opportunity to buy products that had disappeared from the market during the war years added up to a vigorous economic outlook for the period ahead.

People, particularly the young married couples, wanted to establish a "good life" and forget the immediate past with its horrors of war. What was the ambience most suitable to put this dream into reality? Suburbia, where homes were lower-priced and where the air lent itself to a new living style that in-

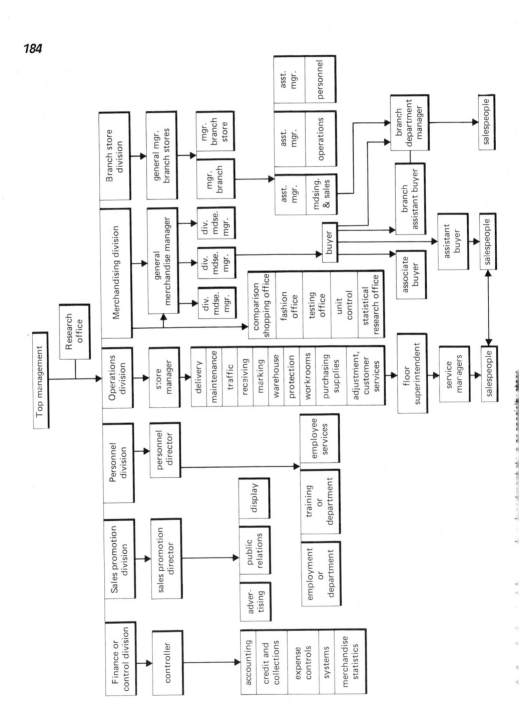

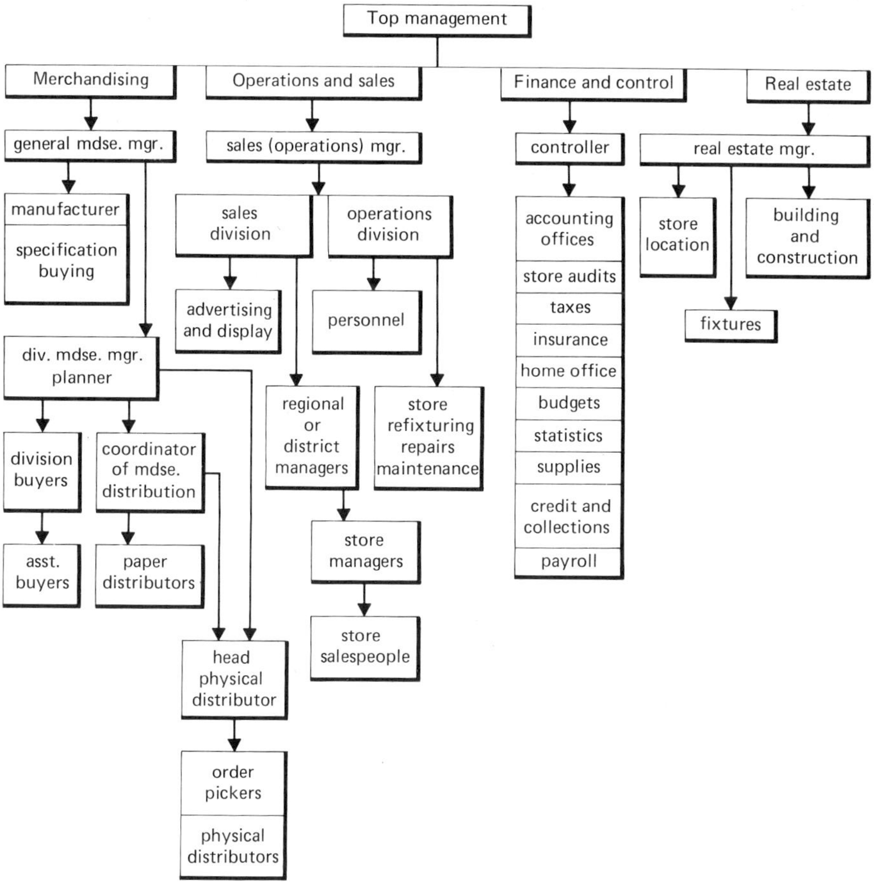

Figure 10–3 Organization chart: apparel chain.

cluded comfort and breathing space: an ideal place to bring up a family and establish roots. There followed a mass exodus from the cities to the suburbs. America was on the move again, following the earlier move to the cities, to surrounding areas twenty to fifty miles outside the urban centers.

Many of the new homeowners had little money left after making their monthly house payments. Budgets were strained by the purchase of home appliances, furniture, garden equipment, and lawn and shrubbery maintenance. Consumers were budget-conscious and highly selective in their purchases. Discount operations had a strong appeal to many.

Again, a new environment required new retailing methods.

The groundwork was laid for discount operations. By definition, a **discount store** offers a variety of merchandise at less-than-normal retail prices and with fewer than usual conventional retail services.

In order to retail goods below conventional retail prices, it is necessary to reduce the cost of doing business, to effect savings by reducing (1) the cost of location and ambience, (2) the cost of sales help, and (3) markup.

In California larger food markets had evolved self-service as a marketing strategy to reduce the cost of doing business and offer customers goods at reduced prices. In San Francisco, for example, the Crystal Palace—with 68,000 square feet of selling area, parking space for 4350 cars, and one-hour free parking—reported huge selling results.

Filene's in Boston has a long history of success with its basement store, which is famous for its bargains and operates with virtually no customer service, but this is not strictly a separate discount store.

The highest cost of conventional retail stores except the cost of merchandise is personnel, but cutting back on it was not exactly a new idea. Supermarkets of the 1930s took to the self-service method on a national scale, led by King Cullen, a supermarket chain that held to the philosophy of "A kind of cut-rate chain of wholesale direct-to-the-public." Two elements of cutting the cost of operation were inherent in the supermarket method: self-service and low markup.

And then a third element was introduced by retailers: locations that offered low rent and low-cost interiors. The first of these were mill-outlet operations. One of them was Ethan Ames Factory (Monarch Mills) outlet in New Bedford, Massachusetts, an operation that had extraordinary success. The three elements for discount operations had come together.

Monarch's success inspired imitation, and in the early 1950s mill operations got underway. Among them were Ann Hope in Cumberland, Rhode Island; Atlantic Mills in New Bedford, Massachusetts; Coatsfield Shoppers World, Pawtucket, Rhode Island; J. M. Fields, Salem, Massachusetts; Mammoth Mart, Framingham, Massachusetts; Aaron Cohen's Store, Brockton, Massachusetts; Rockdale Stores, Turner, Massachusetts; Kerr Mill Bargain Centers, Fall River, Massachusetts. All were established between 1950 and 1953.

By the late 1950s, traditional specialty store chains, junior department stores, variety chains, and some department stores were losing sales to discount stores. Adding to their problems was the decaying of main store locations as a result of the exodus to the suburbs. The entrenched joined the new movement. Here is a selected list of those that added discount stores to their operations:

Virginia Dare	Atlantic Thrift Stores
Mangel's	Shoppers Fairs
Hartfield	Zody Stores
Allied Stores	Almart Stores
Federated Department Stores	Gold Circle Discount Stores

The Wheel of Retailing, as explained by Professor Malcolm McNair of Harvard, was clearly evidenced by the retail inroads of discounters. The theory is that newcomers improve on the retail methods of success, gain success, and then join the establishment with all the high costs of operations. They are followed by a new group that again creates operations at a saving and becomes the competition of the newly entrenched.

Franchise and convenience stores

Franchise stores are independently owned and feature merchandise of a franchiser. Convenience stores are often franchised. These stores, however, are of minor significance to our discussion.

Franchising is a business that exceeds $180 billion a year with about 400,000 franchised operations, principally concerned with gasoline stations, nonfood retailers, automotive products and services, and fast-food operations.

Convenience stores, as the term suggests, are located close to customers' homes and remain open longer hours than other retail outlets.

Branch stores

With the migration to the suburbs and the increasing intensity of competition, beginning in the late 1940s, department-store growth began to slow. The large single stores were located in the hearts of urban centers, and retail viability pointed to a move to the new centers of population. Department stores soon opened branches in the suburbs. The experience was unique. Pipelines of merchandise and communications were created, along with the problems of

The 263,000-square-foot Bloomingdale's branch store in the White Flint mall at Kensington, Maryland, opened in 1977. (David Whitcomb/RTKL Associates, Inc.)

maintaining store character in new locations and servicing customers whose expectations were not so definable as those of the group previously served. Some of the specific questions were these:

- How large should a branch store be?
- To what degree should merchandise assortments and depth vary between the main store and branch stores?
- How does management communicate effectively with the branch store?
- Who handles the liaison?

Operating a branch store was a big step from the traditional retail structure of one store in which a buyer was the department manager of a specialty shop with personal relations with the merchandise suppliers and the personnel.

Starting in the 1940s, branches were established in the outer rims of the cities, some ten to twenty miles from the anchor store, within the established but extended trading area and still close enough to be under the scrutiny of the "hen" store. The "chick" was fairly easy to control with frequent main-store buyer visits and telephone calls. The pattern of store size was not set, and some customers complained about inadequate stock assortments and depths found in some "junior-sized" branches. The main store still contributed the greatest volume and had the widest assortments of merchandise. J. L. Hudson of Detroit, an early leader of the new movement, founded a branch the size of its main store in Northland, about ten miles out, with great success.

And another direction was taken using the rationale that large units could conceivably produce greater sales than a main store and that the addition of a series of stores could generate even higher sales results. Department store corporate goals were widened and there was a new interpretation of potential trading areas. Bloomingdale's in New York no longer restricted its thinking to New York City; Abraham and Straus in Brooklyn saw "foreign" market potential; Neiman-Marcus in Dallas looked beyond the horizon of Texas; Marshall Field in Chicago began to realize the restraints of the city; and every department store in the country faced the eventual demise of the single unit. In due course the individual department store as an institution was past history.

SINCE 1950

The race for more units

The years between 1950 and 1960 can be considered the era of the Revolution of Retailing. Discount operations were opened everywhere, department stores merged and opened new branches, chain stores raced for locations for new stores and catalogue centers, and big became mammoth. Department stores became conglomerates. Here are a few examples:

- Allied Stores, New York, owns 26 anchor-store corporations with each store having its own branches, a total of 175 units.
- Associated Dry Goods Corporation, New York, has 19 main-store corporations and branches totaling 146 stores.
- Federated Department Stores, Cincinnati, owns 193 department stores, 96 super-

markets, and 69 discount operations, with a total store ownership of 358 units, plus four shopping malls.

- R. H. Macy, New York, owns 6 major stores with a total ownership of 76 units.
- Dayton Hudson, Detroit, has 10 anchor operations (including bookstores, jewelry stores, franchise and discount operations) that total 474 units.

And the proliferation of ownership is indeed bewildering. Here are a few examples:

- Carter Hawley Hale owns Bergdorf Goodman, Neiman-Marcus, Broadway Stores, and others.
- BATUS, the U.S. arm of B.A.T. Industries of London, owns Saks Fifth Avenue, fashion-specialty chain, Gimbels, department-store chain, Kohl's, department stores and food stores (Wisconsin) and the Marshall Field complex of department stores.
- Marcor owns Montgomery Ward, as we have seen.
- Associated Dry Goods, New York, owns Lord & Taylor, Goldwater's (Phoenix, Arizona), Joseph Horne Co. (Pittsburgh), J. W. Robinson (Los Angeles), among others.

There is much more ownership information in *Fairchild's Financial Manual of Retail Stores*, which gives details on ownership, volume, and other financial data.

A breakdown here of one of these conglomerates gives a good example of this kind of organization—see the list of divisions of Federated Department Stores as of 1980 (with planned 1981 additions) that follows. There is much of interest in it. For instance, note that almost all of the branch stores were opened after World War II. Also note that some individual stores have expanded into other states, for example, Bloomingdale's into Connecticut, New Jersey, Virginia, and Maryland; and Abraham and Straus into New Jersey.

Divisions of Federated Department Stores, Inc.
and Federated Stores Realty, Inc., an Unconsolidated Wholly Owned Subsidiary

Note: The figure in parentheses following each store location indicates gross floor space in thousands of square feet.
*Denotes headquarters store.

Abraham and Straus, established 1865
*Brooklyn, NY (1638)
Garden City, NY, 1950 (80)
Hempstead, NY, 1952 (546)
Babylon, NY, 1957 (257)
Huntington, NY, 1962 (315)
Manhasset, NY, 1965 (329)
Smith Haven, NY, 1969 (242)
Woodbridge, NJ, 1971 (286)
Rego Park, NY, 1973 (307)
Paramus, NJ, 1974 (302)
Monmouth Mall, Eatontown, NJ, 1978 (278)
White Plains, NY, 1980 (327)

Short Hills, NJ, Spring 1981 (278)
King of Prussia, PA, Fall 1981 (235)
Massapequa, NY, Fall 1981, replacement of Babylon store (135)

Bloomingdale's, established 1872
*Manhattan, NY (908)
Fresh Meadows, NY, 1949 (149)
Stamford, CT, 1954 (228)
Riverside Square, Hackensack, NJ, 1959 (274)
Short Hills, NJ, 1967 (240)
Garden City, NY, 1972 (260)

White Plains, NY, 1975 (263)
Tyson's Corner, McLean, VA, 1976 (235)
White Flint, Kensington, MD, 1977 (263)
Chestnut Hill, MA, 1978 (125)
King of Prussia, PA, Fall 1981 (234)
Home Furnishings Specialty Stores:
New Rochelle, NY, 1947 (110)
Manhasset, NY, 1971 (119)
Scarsdale, NY, 1971 (27)
Jenkintown, PA, 1972 (110)
Chestnut Hill, MA, 1973 (86)

Boston Store, established 1900
*Milwaukee, WI (516)
Bay Shore, Glendale, WI, 1958 (141)
Boston Village, Milwaukee, 1962 (89)
Brookfield, WI, 1967 (221)
Southridge, Greendale, WI, 1969 (221)
Northridge, Milwaukee, 1972 (155)
Racine, WI, Fall 1981 (106)
Capitol Court Milwaukee, Fall 1981, re-
placement of Boston Village store (87)

Bullock's, established 1906
*Los Angeles, CA (806)
Pasadena, CA, 1947 (314)
Westwood, L.A., 1951 (233)
Santa Ana, CA, 1958 (336)
Sherman Oaks, L.A., 1962 (310)
Lakewood, CA, 1965 (262)
Del Amo, Torrance, CA, 1966 (262)
La Habra, CA, 1968 (271)
Northridge, L.A., 1971 (190)
South Coast Plaza, Costa Mesa, CA, 1973
(187)
Mission Valley, San Diego, CA, 1975 (188)
West Covina, CA, 1975 (150)
Century City, L.A., 1976 (138)
Camel View, Scottsdale, AZ, 1977 (159)
Christown, Phoenix, AZ, 1977 (162)
Mission Viejo, CA, 1980 (138)
Carlsbad, CA, 1980 (115)
Las Vegas, NV, Spring 1981 (138)
Beverly Center, L.A., Fall 1981 (161)
Bullock's Wilshire Stores:
Wilshire, L.A., 1929 (230)
Palm Springs, CA, 1930 (47)
Woodland Hills, L.A., 1973 (84)
Newport Beach, CA, 1977 (80)
La Jolla, CA, 1979 (64)
Rolling Hills, CA, Fall 1981 (70)

Bullock's Northern California,
established 1971
*Stanford, Palo Alto, CA, 1972 (180)
Walnut Creek, CA, 1973 (188)
Vallco, San Jose, CA, 1975 (180)
Stonestown, San Francisco, CA, 1977 (176)
Oakridge, San Jose, CA, 1978 (148)
Fashion Island, San Mateo, CA, Fall 1981
(131)

Burdines, established 1898
*Miami, FL (502)
Ft. Lauderdale, FL, 1947, 1980 replace-
ment (217)
Miami Beach, FL, 1953 (98)
West Palm Beach, FL, 1954, 1979 replace-
ment (190)
163rd Street, Miami, 1956 (258)
Dadeland, Miami, 1962, 1981 expansion
(426)
Westland, Hialeah, FL, 1967 (220)
Pompano Beach, FL, 1969 (153)
Hollywood, FL, 1970 (151)
Colonial Fashion Square, Orlando, FL, 1973
(206)
Altamonte, Orlando, 1974 (153)
Clearwater, FL, 1975 (160)
Tampa, FL, 1976 (181)
Sarasota, FL, 1976, 1981 expansion (144)
Furniture Clearance Center, Ft. Lauder-
dale, 1978 (45)
Broward Mall, Plantation, FL, 1978 (202)
Boca Raton, FL, 1979 (169)
South Dade Furniture Clearance Center,
Miami, 1979 (73)
Edison Mall, Ft. Myers, FL, 1979 (169)
St. Petersburg, FL, 1980 (172)
Cutler Ridge, FL, 1980 (123)

Filene's established 1852
*Boston, MA (656)
Hyannis, MA, 1923, 1970 replacement (81)
Wellesley, MA, 1924 (53)
Worcester, MA, 1928, 1971 replacement
(106)
Belmont, MA, 1941 (56)
Chestnut Hill, MA, 1950, 1974 replace-
ment (186)
North Shore, Peabody, MA, 1957 (141)
South Shore, Braintree, MA, 1961 (195)
Natick, MA, 1965 (110)

Burlington, MA, 1968 (151)
Warwick, Providence, RI, 1970 (119)
Manchester, NH, 1977 (60)
Basement Store Branches:
Saugus, MA, 1978 (32)
Framingham, MA, 1978 (36)
Worcester, 1979 (35)

Foley's, established 1900
*Houston, TX, (788)
Sharpstown, Houston, 1961 (376)
Pasadena, TX, 1962 (212)
Almeda Mall, Houston, 1966 (308)
Northwest Mall, Houston, 1967 (308)
Home Furnishings Store, Houston, 1972 (67)
Memorial City, Houston, 1974 (263)
Greenspoint Mall, Houston, 1976 (317)
Highland Mall, Austin, Tx, 1979 (210)
San Jacinto, Baytown, TX, 1980 (157)
North Star, San Antonio, TX, Spring 1981 (200)
Willowbrook, Houston, Fall 1981 (250)

Gold Circle, established 1967
Columbus, OH, Morse Road, 1968 (122)
Columbus, Hamilton Road, 1968 (122)
Columbus, Olentangy, 1969 (133)
Dayton, OH, Salem Avenue, 1969 (128)
Dayton, Centerville, 1969 (128)
Dayton, Kettering, 1969 (127)
Columbus, West Broad Street, 1970 (138)
Cleveland, OH, Elyria, 1971 (107)
Cleveland, Middleburg Heights, 1971 (107)
Cleveland, Chardon Road, 1971 (138)
Cleveland, Memphis Avenue, 1971 (138)
Cincinnati, OH, Ridge Road, 1973 (134)
Cincinnati, Colerain Avenue, 1973 (134)
Cleveland, N. Olmstead, 1973 (103)
Cincinnati, Glenway Avenue, 1973 (135)
Springfield, OH, 1973 (139)
Cleveland, Mentor, 1973 (136)
Akron, OH, West Market Street, 1974 (133)
Akron, Talmadge Avenue, 1974 (133)
Cincinnati, Tri-County, 1974 (105)
Cleveland, Bedford, 1974 (138)
Canton, OH, 1974 (101)
Columbus, Westerville, 1974 (144)
Rochester, NY, Irondequoit, 1975 (105)
Rochester, Henrietta, 1975 (104)
Rochester, West Gates, 1975 (104)
Columbus, South High Street, 1975 (105)

Sacramento, CA, Arden Way, 1976 (103)
Sacramento, Florin Road, 1976 (103)
Sacramento, San Juan Road, 1976 (103)   **191**
Lexington, KY, 1976 (105)
Florence, KY, 1976 (108)
Akron, Romig Road, 1976 (152)
San Jose, CA, Sunnyvale, 1977 (105)
San Jose, Camden and Leigh, 1977 (106)
San Jose, Blossom Hill, 1977 (101)
San Jose, Capital and McKee, 1977 (105)
Pittsburgh, PA, Penn Hills, 1977 (117)
Pittsburgh, Pleasant Hills, 1977 (121)
Pittsburgh, Braddock Hills, 1977 (118)
Pittsburgh, New Kensington, 1978 (106)
Parma, OH, 1979 (99)
Cleveland, Severance Center, Fall 1981 (85)

Goldsmith's, established 1870
*Memphis, TN (496)
Oak Court, Memphis, 1961 (289)
Southland Mall, Memphis, 1966 (150)
Raleigh Springs, Memphis, 1971 (172)
Jackson, TN, Spring 1981 (85)
Hickory Ridge Mall, Memphis, Fall 1981 (150)

Gold Triangle, established 1968
Plantation, FL, 1970 (76)
Skylake, Miami, FL, 1970 (76)
Dadeland, Miami, 1970 (76)
Orlando, FL, 1973 (86)
Tampa, FL, 1973 (86)
Hialeah, FL, 1976 (85)

Lazarus, established 1851
*Columbus, OH (1309)
Westland, Columbus, 1962 (214)
Northland, Columbus, 1964 (321)
Eastland, Columbus, 1967 (255)
Richland, Mansfield, OH, 1969 (195)
Kingsdale, Upper Arlington, OH, 1970 (105)
Lima, OH, 1971 (195)
Home Store East, Columbus, 1972 (73)
Town and Country, Columbus, 1973 (34)
Castleton, Indianapolis, IN, 1973 (320)
Lafayette, Indianapolis, 1974 (144)
Washington Square, Indianapolis, 1978 (140)
Henderson, Columbus, 1978 (87)
Westerville, Columbus, 1978 (55)
Greenwood, Indianapolis, 1980 (160)
Huntington, WV, Spring 1981 (160

Levy's, established 1903
*Tucson, AZ (298)

192 **I. Magnin,** established 1876
*San Francisco, CA, (249)
Oakland, CA, 1931 (65)
Los Angeles, CA, 1939 (141)
Beverly Hills, CA, 1945 (99)
Santa Barbara, CA, 1945 (24)
Pasadena, CA, 1949 (41)
Seattle, WA, 1954 (80)
La Jolla, CA, 1954 (29)
Palo Alto, CA, 1955 (100)
Santa Ana, CA, 1958 (42)
Carmel, CA, 1960 (19)
Sherman Oaks, L.A., 1962 (55)
Portland, OR, 1962 (32)
Phoenix, AZ, 1963 (33)
Santa Clara, CA, 1964 (32)
San Mateo, CA, 1965 (29)
Del Amo, Torrance, CA, 1967 (22)
Palm Springs, CA, 1967 (27)
Walnut Creek, CA, 1967 (56)
Chicago, IL, 1971 (138)
Vallco, San Jose, CA, 1976 (56)
South Coast Plaza, Costa Mesa, CA, 1977 (78)
White Flint, Kensington, MD, 1978 (81)
Northbrook, Chicago, 1979 (107)
Oakbrook, Chicago, Fall 1981 (85)

Ralphs, established 1873
96 supermarkets, with floor space of 3,239,000 square feet, located in southern California. Nine additional supermarkets, with floor space of 316,000 square feet, are planned for 1981.

Rich's, established 1867
*Atlanta, GA, (1260)
Lenox Square, Atlanta, 1959 (336)
Belvedere, Atlanta, 1959 (84)
Cobb Center, Atlanta, 1963 (171)
North DeKalb, Atlanta, 1965 (174)
Greenbriar, Atlanta, 1965 (197)
South DeKalb, Atlanta, 1969 (192)
Perimeter Mall, Atlanta, 1971 (266)
Outlet Home Store, Atlanta, 1971 (37)
Cumberland Mall, Atlanta, 1973 (282)
Brookwood Village, Birmingham, AL, 1974 (206)

Century Plaza, Birmingham, 1975 (60)
Southlake Mall, Atlanta, 1976 (204)
Columbia Mall, Columbia, SC, 1978 (192)
Augusta Mall, Augusta, GA, 1978 (157)
Haywood Mall, Greenville, SC, 1980 (133)
Shannon Mall, Atlanta, 1980 (125)

Richway, established 1970
Atlanta, GA, Covington Highway, 1970 (157)
Atlanta, Cobb Parkway, 1970 (157)
Atlanta, Old National Highway, 1971 (157)
Atlanta, Jonesboro Road, 1971 (157)
Atlanta, North Druid Hills Road, 1972 (110)
Charlotte, NC, Freedom Drive, 1973 (118)
Charlotte, Independence Blvd., 1973 (118)
Atlanta, Holcombe Bridge Road, 1974 (115)
Atlanta, Tara Blvd., 1974 (115)
Atlanta, Buford Highway, 1976 (86)
Columbia, SC, Decker Blvd., 1977 (92)
Columbia, Bush River Road, 1977 (92)
Columbia, Garner's Ferry Road, 1977 (92)
Charlotte, Eastway Drive, 1977 (92)
Charlotte, Tyvola Road, 1977 (92)
Gastonia, NC, 1978 (90)
Atlanta, Sandy Springs, 1978 (90)
Atlanta, Tucker, 1979 (93)
Atlanta, Austell, 1980 (94)
Atlanta, Sandy Plains Road, 1980 (94)
Athens, GA, 1980 (74)
Chattanooga, TN, Northgate Park, Spring 1981 (85)
Chattanooga, Lee Highway, Spring 1981 (85)

Rike's, established 1853
*Dayton, OH (939)
Kettering, OH, 1961 (156)
Salem Mall, Dayton, 1963 (209)
Dayton Mall, Dayton, 1969 (191)
Springfield, OH, 1971 (177)

Sanger Harris, established 1857
*Dallas, TX (460)
Highland Park, Dallas, 1949 (33)
Preston Center, Dallas, 1957 (231)
Big Town, Dallas, 1959 (107)
Plymouth Park, Irving, TX, 1963 (139)
Six Flags Mall, Arlington, TX, 1970 (164)
Town East, Dallas, 1972 (168)
Valley View, Dallas, 1973 (300)

Red Bird Mall, Dallas, 1975 (152)
Hulen Mall, Fort Worth, TX, 1977 (199)
North Hills Mall, Fort Worth, 1978 (199)
Collin Creek Mall, Plano, TX, 1980 (206)
Tyler, TX, Fall 1981 (100)

Shillito's, established 1830
*Cincinnati, OH (840)
Tri-County, Cincinnati, 1960 (230)
Western Woods, Cincinnati, 1963 (189)
Kenwood Mall, Cincinnati, 1966 (209)
Beechmont Mall, Cincinnati, 1969 (114)
Oxmoor Center, Louisville, KY, 1970 (281)
Fayette Mall, Lexington, KY, 1971 (185)
Florence Mall, Florence, KY, 1977 (125)
Jefferson Mall, Louisville, KY, 1979 (157)

Federated Stores Realty, Inc.,
established 1973

Enclosed regional shopping malls
Wholly owned and operated:
Riverside Square, Hackensack, NJ, 1977 **193**
(600)
North Hills Mall, Fort Worth, TX, 1979 (435)
Town Center, Boca Raton, FL, 1980 (800)
Collin Creek Mall, Plano, TX, Fall 1981
(1200)
Joint ventures with other developers:
Hulen Mall, Fort Worth, 1977 (545)
Hickory Ridge Mall, Memphis, TN, Fall 1981
(600)
Fashion Island, San Mateo, CA, Fall 1981
(845)
Developed and managed:
Greenspoint Mall, Houston, TX, 1976 (1541)
Broward Mall, Ft. Lauderdale, FL, 1978
(1200)

Shopping centers

There are more than 19,000 shopping centers and/or malls in the United States, a development since World War II. This subject deserves an in-depth study that would include history and present-day relationships. For our purposes, however, we can say that the centers have mushroomed and created shopping marketplaces that include a mix of different types of retailers (as well as amusement emporiums) and offer one-stop shopping convenience. Over the years some have deteriorated while others are elegant architectural prize winners. With an eye to demographic projections, real-estate developers and larger retailers will continue to establish new centers and create retail environments appropriate to segmented markets.

The shopping center is certainly a major part of the retailing revolution of the second half of the twentieth century.

Warehouse showrooms

Warehouse showrooms follow the general recent trend but have little present relevance to our subject. They are an innovation of recent years with greatest concentration on furniture. The Miami-based leader, Levitz Furniture Corporation, with 70 stores, had a sales volume of more than $500 million in 1981. This is a retail method to watch.

Additional mergers and government interest

During the past several years many mergers have taken place as a result of eroding profit and the continuing recession. In 1981, Associated Dry Goods Corporation bought Caldor, a discount chain; Allied Stores bought Garfinkel, Brooks Brothers, and Miller and Rhoads, Inc.; and Wal-Mart Stores took over Kuhn's Big K. In early 1982, BATUS, a U.S. unit of London-based B.A.T Industries, acquired Marshall Field & Company, and Best Products was bidding for Basco, Inc., catalogue showrooms.

194   In March, 1982, the Bureau of Competition of the Federal Trade Commission sent a questionnaire to twenty-five giant retail organizations, including discount and mass merchandising chains and department stores with multiple operations. The purpose of this investigation was to determine whether recent mergers had violated the Clayton Act, which prohibits acquisitions that may substantially lessen competition or tend to create a monopoly. Among the organizations contacted were Sears, Roebuck; Montgomery Ward; May Department Stores; and Allied Stores. In the questionnaire the FTC asked for information about the sale and acquisition of other retail operations since January 1, 1980. The FTC also asked the retail organizations to supply information about plans for new stores or conversions of stores to other types, consumer studies, their methods of monitoring competitors' prices, and their expenditures on advertising.

SUMMARY

The institution of retailing that started out as a simple barter system has become incredibly complex and the major component of the marketing system of the United States. Methods of doing business, ownership, size, location, and other subjects are often controversial. But what is safely predictable is that they will continue to change.

The changes have been so rapid that they have outdated their definitions. A chain is usually defined as an organization of at least four centrally owned stores, an office in a major market, and stores carrying similar goods in stores of similar architecture and ambience. Discount operations, founded as organizations offering goods at reduced prices, low markups, and fewer services than conventional stores, now say they are promotional department stores. Some have charge accounts and offer some services. Some department stores have eliminated sales help in favor of central cashier desks. Chain/mail-order organizations operate stores that are in reality department stores and the leading retail organization of many cities. And to add to the complexity of the retail operation:

- Not all discounters sell close-outs.
- Some discounters open a new season with structured stocks (assortment and depth); many do not.
- Many department stores sell appliances on shorter mark-up; some sell at full mark-up.
- Consumers are sometimes confused as to where the best values may be obtained—department store, discount store, or chain.

One overriding characteristic of current retailing is the trend to the continuous expansion of operations. Whether this condition spells opportunity for a small retailer is probably to a great extent a matter of creativity.

One present department store consideration is that the yearly volume of branch stores far exceeds that of main stores. The branch store numbers would, of course, be the basic reason; but in many instances one branch generates greater volume than the anchor store. One problem for some retailers is the economic value of continuing main store operations.

Retailing is the largest segment of our economy and is highly responsive to new **195** environmental conditions. In the near future, retailing should include the growth of nonstore retailing, with greater concentration on mail and telephone promotions, national and regional catalogues, and telecommunication by cable television.

QUESTIONS FOR DISCUSSION

1. Successful retailing is dependent on traffic. Can a large store operate successfully today in an area of limited population? Explain.
2. Explain two major problems of operating branch stores.
3. Despite the loss of rural population, catalogue operations flourish. Why?
4. Select an era and show how the environment influenced a new retail method.
5. Explain the difference between a chain and multiunit department-store organization.
6. With examples, prove that the Wheel of Retailing can be considered a retail principle.
7. What functions do retailers perform in the economic system? What are the benefits consumers derive?
8. What was the period of the Revolution of Retailing? Discuss it in detail.
9. Identify five conglomerates that operate multiunit department stores and branches. Describe the operation.
10. What has happened to the family or privately owned department store in America?

THE W.H.K & S.
ELLEN TERRY CORSET.

11

FASHION RETAILING

The retailing of ready-made clothing has a relatively short history that had its beginnings in the nineteenth century, as we have seen. The production of apparel during the latter part of that century was essentially confined to European couture houses, custom tailoring and dressmaking firms for the well-to-do, and the neighborhood dressmaker for those in modest circumstances who could not sew.

EARLY RETAILING OF FASHION APPAREL

The period from 1870 to 1880 saw the beginning of the rise of the great department and specialty stores that became the main sources of retail distribution for clothing manufacturers. Ready-to-wear in this period was largely for men and children. Women's items were available in the form of cloaks and mantillas. Some fashion-oriented stores, among them John Wanamaker in Philadelphia, Marshall Field in Chicago, and B. Altman in New York, maintained clothing salons that featured merchandise from abroad and models of styles that could be custom-made. In New York City, in the 1870s and 1880s, the "ladies' mile" was the district from Madison Square down Broadway to 8th Street and included Lord & Taylor and Arnold Constable.

During the 1880–1890 period, although the industry continued to grow, factory-made clothes were perceived as for the lower class. The only ready-to-wear available for women consisted of man-tailored jackets with skirts and shirtwaists. Few stores carried them, although Marshall Field did note in its 1896 catalogue that it could furnish ready-made man-tailored garments (skirt, jacket, and waist) for $65, $75, and $85. Since women's clothing was very decorative and not suitable for street wear, women who were employed needed the man-tailored "uniform" as a practical way of dressing. This garment was the foundation for the ready-to-wear business, since it included a waist that had wide customer appeal and could be worn as part of a three-piece ensemble or a two-piece outfit when the weather was warm. In a sense, too, it laid the groundwork for both the ladies' sportswear and dress business. The blouse was a salable item that could be featured by department stores, mail-order firms, variety stores, and general stores.

When the resources of labor, management, innovators, and textile breakthroughs coalesced in the early twentieth century, women's clothing joined men's and children's wear as products for retail selling.

At the beginning, ready-made women's apparel held no interest for many retail stores, even the largest. The potential customers were not in the upper-income brackets, the prices were modest, and sales volume was limited, with the bottom line of profit-and-loss statements often showing a red figure for this merchandise classification. As a consequence, another institution developed: organizations that leased space and ran department store ready-to-wear operations. This worked fairly well; the stores received approximately 15 percent of the net sales, and the operators were able to feed merchandise into stock from their New York base of operations. Indeed, such arrangements, necessarily based on the same percentage, exist today in such areas as cosmetics, shoes, hats, furs, and other specialties.

In 1920, with the beginning of modern ready-to-wear, a new retail institution came into being: the apparel chain store. The idea of joining a shirtwaist and a skirt into a dress gave the chain operators a product that could sell in widespread metropolitan areas because urban consumers tended to have similar taste. The New York-based chains placed large orders and were able to obtain the advantages of lower prices, fast delivery, and constant style newness. The department stores with leased operations as well as those that did their own merchandising began to realize that they were being outdistanced by the invaders. They started to merchandise aggressively—and successfully. Once modern ready-to-wear was developed, it did not take long for different types of retailers to recognize its profit potential.

MODERN RETAILERS OF FASHION APPAREL

Department and specialty stores

The sides have been drawn in the matter of where the sexes prefer to shop. Traditionally, the department store has been a feminine institution. Without women, it would never have flourished. Patronage motives are easily discerned in the matter of specialty stores, men's shops for men, women's shops for women.

The modern department store's success is based on its ability to sell fashion apparel and related items, and statistics show that fashion apparel sales are approximately 53 percent of its total yearly volume. Indeed, ready-to-wear has come a long way from the time it was considered an insignificant product for the lower class. Ready-to-wear went through a period of democratization. So did stores.

On the average, a department store obtains a contribution to its total sales from apparel and accessories as follows:

women's apparel	17%
women's accessories	19%
men's apparel and furnishings	10%
infants', boys' and girls' wear	7%
	53%

Sales distribution figures give further evidence of men's preference for their own specialty shops. Men's clothing and furnishing stores account for over 50 percent of reported sales of men's suits and outerwear. Department stores account for about 27 percent of the total sales. The mail-order chains (Sears, Ward, and Penney) control the largest share of the sale of men's sport coats in terms of units, but specialty shops are ahead on a dollar basis. Specialty stores also hold the largest share of dollar volume in men's separate trousers.

It is well to remember that a specialty shop is a store that specializes in certain categories of merchandise, usually in a narrow range of prices. Apparel and accessory specialty stores are the most numerous type of retail outlet, numbering about 120,000 and doing an annual volume in excess of 50 percent of the total fashion sales volume of the United States.

Discount stores

Discount stores, as we know, are stores that are able to sell merchandise below the retail market average because of reduced operational costs. During the past twenty years, discount operators have multiplied and now present a rather complicated maze of contradictions for the fashion consumer.

In a recent informal survey conducted at the Fashion Institute of Technology, 100 students were asked, "If you were going to buy a dress or man's jacket at $200, would you consider the ——— store, one that is part of a major discount chain?" The stated condition was, "You know that the same type of garment will cost $20 to $25 more at a conventional store." The response was unanimous: "No!" On the other hand, men and women flock to specialty discount chains that offer better goods at lower prices. Loehmann's, specializing in women's clothes, has gone national and public and does an annual retail volume of more than $150 million.

Initially, discount retailers were divided into two classes, low-rental-area mill stores that featured apparel and departmentalized stores that featured hard lines as well as soft goods (appliances as well as apparel). The latter were miniature department stores with limited or no customer service that in most cases sold branded appliances for less than normal retail prices.

The mill stores continued operations. Although some went out of business, some are highly successful and are presently most visible in New England, where they got their impetus.

One of the later developments is the medium- to better-priced discount store featuring apparel that includes some brand styles. The ability to obtain imported goods has helped them, and their mass purchasing power gives them a position of power with moderate- and better-priced manufacturers. The departmentalized discounter was originally cut off from these manufacturers and was given two alternatives: buy popular-priced apparel from popular-priced makers with an open distribution system or use foreign apparel-manufacturers.

Hence, the importance of price as a strong motivation for consumer apparel purchases has influenced the creation of a cross section of discount operations. To say that apparel at a lower price was the only reason for discount stores in general would be an overstatement. However, the importance of apparel to a discount operation has often spelled the difference between success and failure. A considerable number of promotional department stores are presently under severe pressure because of inability to develop strong apparel appeal. Clothing sales yield a higher markup than hard lines, and without apparel success there could be failures. Discounters have had greater consumer support in children's wear than in adult clothing (the exceptions are the specialty discount chains like Loehmann's).

Discount operations that sell apparel can be classified as follows:

		Example
1.	Mill outlets (including manufacturers who sell goods at regular prices from their showrooms)	Ann Hope Factory Outlet (Rhode Island-based)
2.	Promotional department store	Magic Mart Discount Department Stores (Little Rock, AR)
3.	Traditional stores that have added discount operations	Federated Department Stores Gold Circle Discount Stores (Cincinnati-based)
4.	Specialty discounters	Loehmann's (New York-based)
5.	Closed-door approach (membership customers)	Gemco (California-based)
6.	Leased departments	Winnie Lee (New York-based)

Getting a bargain has almost universal appeal. Even though some people do not admit that they patronize discount stores, these operations move tremendous quantities of apparel, and the range of customers is not confined to lower-income levels. There is a discounter type for almost every pocketbook. But the term *discount prices* is suspect; are they sometimes cheaper goods for cheaper prices? Another moot question to pose is whether discounters offer better values than traditional stores.

Chain and variety stores

The term *chain store* has become increasingly difficult to define. In our context it includes those corporations that own and operate multiunit operations from a central base and excludes department stores and branches, which are referred to as ownership groups.

From the apparel chain-store era, the specialty-shop chain obviously had an interest in fashion. But the large mail-order chains, and many stores that sold a variety of goods, had little or no investment in clothing. Organizations like Sears, Penney's, Montgomery Ward, and Woolworth did not consider fashion apparel an important part of the retail merchandise mix. But these organizations have always enjoyed the inherent advantages of professional management and strong capital positions. As giant operations they featured standardized business procedures, centralized policymaking, and excellent physical facilities. To these advantages they add the ability, through mass purchasing power, to obtain lower prices, exclusivity of merchandise, and delivery as wanted. They thus enjoyed the opportunity to deal with a product that is part of the life of every one of their customers—a business that offers a high return for successful practitioners. Following World War II, a new dimension was added to the chain-store business: the serious intent of the big three and variety stores to enter fashion merchandising.

These operations were able to offer consumers a high level of quality control, the introduction of national television commercials for apparel, and mail-order fashion assortments never available before. Chain-store merchandising of apparel reached new volume heights and has become a force to be reckoned with. Although their first interest was principally popular-priced merchandise (and still is for variety stores), chains began to enter the moderate levels. Some experts claim that within the foreseeable future Sears, Montgomery Ward, and Penney will dominate the number of units of apparel sold in the country.

Market share chain-store selling of clothing is approximately 60 percent for shoes, 48 percent for women's apparel, and 35 percent for men's and boys'.

Nonstore retailers

The profit-making opportunities of fashion have attracted organizations that sell without the benefit of a store—by mail or sometimes in the homes of potential customers.

Beeline, a party-plan operation, took a leaf from the books of Avon cosmetics and Fuller Brush and was able to produce a volume of over $60 million within ten years of the start of operations. Avon itself has established a fashion division. Thus, the party plan has become an accepted apparel-selling technique.

As a selling principle, consumer contact enhances the probability of selling related or unrelated products. Any holder of oil-company credit cards knows that monthly statements contain merchandise offerings, including items of fashion. Illustrated is an example from an Amoco spring catalogue that features both men's and women's clothing and accessories.

One of the largest mail-order apparel firms is New Process of Warren, Pennsylvania, which sells shoes, dresses, jackets, and the like—all by mail. The illustrated flyers (page 202) suggest the ease of selection. New Process is one of the country's most successful nonstore apparel retailers.

Spiegel, one of the early and famous mail-order firms, has already been mentioned in passing.

Another mail-order organization, United States Purchasing Exchange, "a

These items, shown on one page of an Amoco spring catalogue, can be charged to the oil company's credit-card revolving charge account.

private stock corporation, not connected or affiliated with the U.S. Government," features apparel items as part of its Christmas flyer.

The many mail-order organizations include such outlets as Hollywood Fashions of California, which has received national publicity. The widened scope of the sellers of fashion now includes many retailers without stores.

Boutiques

During the 1960s the **boutique** (a small store that features unique merchandise in a unique ambience for those who want and can afford "different" merchandise and full service) sprang into prominence. The boutique caused excitement at every level, from the small independent store to giants like R. H. Macy. Independent stores were set up in unlikely areas for the selling of fashion, larger stores set up boutique sections, and some manufacturers set up franchise stores.

Two New Process mailing pieces—for Western-influenced men's suits and for shoes—suggest the range of clothing and accessories that can be ordered by mail from one of the country's highly successful nonstore apparel retailers. (New Process, Warren, PA)

It was certainly easy to create ambience, often with unusual lighting, specific kinds of recorded music, and fancy wrappings. What was difficult was the maintenance of a store with unique merchandise. In the course of time most independents failed, and the large-store trends went into new directions, among them merchandising by life style. This was an era of fun and excitement that may one day return in reaction to sameness and bigness.

Bijan's, said to be the most expensive men's wear shop in the world, Beverly Hills, California. (Bijan)

The Galleria, children's boutique in Burdines, Fort Lauderdale, Florida. (Retail Reporting Bureau)

SUMMARY

The approximately $115 billion a year spent by Americans for apparel goes to a mixed bag of final distributors. In a day of "scrambled merchandising" the following are examples:

- An oil company that owns one of the largest retailers of fashion (Mobil—Montgomery Ward)
- A British-based tobacco company that owns one of the leading and oldest department-store chains of the country (B.A.T Industries through BATUS—Gimbels) as well as Marshall Field
- Oil companies with general merchandising divisions that sell fashion
- Party-plan companies
- Leased operations
- Mail-order companies
- Original 5- and 10-cent stores with large retail units that sell fashion
- Manufacturers who are apparel-chain-store operators
- Department stores that are in reality chains, owned in turn by parent companies

There is no shortage of stores that sell fashion merchandise, and the range of prices is as diverse as the customers. It is difficult to segment consumer wants with precision: the discount-store consumer of hard goods may turn up her nose at its fashion offerings and a high-fashion-store patron may use only the toiletries of a variety store.

QUESTIONS FOR DISCUSSION

1. What is the importance of fashion apparel to a department store?
2. Why is it difficult for promotional department stores, which are discount operations, to achieve a position of fashion importance?
3. Who are the fashion-apparel customers of promotional department stores?
4. What is the appeal of specialty discounters?
5. Why have the mail-order chains been able to obtain a fashion position of importance?
6. Would you buy fashion apparel from a mail-order house? Why or why not?
7. What type of store offers the best fashion apparel value? Explain.
8. Why did department stores originally lease out their ready-to-wear operations?
9. How did apparel chains of the 1920s affect the entrenched retailers?
10. What advantages do larger chains enjoy in the merchandising of fashion?

12

CAREER OPPORTUNITIES IN FASHION RETAILING

Although our main concern is with the planning, buying, and selling of fashion apparel, we must remember that the other activities of retailing are broad and require executives for the multiple functions of administration and operations. Regardless of the track of formal education, there are those who will enter the profession with a new point of view, a change of job option. Let us therefore examine three career approaches:

1. Retail opportunities—administration/operations
2. Fashion buying—merchandising
3. Small-store ownership—entrepreneurship

At this point it would be a good idea to list all the types of retailers and review the organization charts in Chapter 10. This step may help you relate your personal attributes to specific areas and lead you to research job descriptions and, eventually, a thought-out decision. Moreover, such a review of retail structure highlights both entry-level and career job opportunities.

The advantages of a career in retailing include these factors:

1. Retailing is the means by which products are brought to customers and serves a most fundamental economic need.

2. Retailing is unlike some careers or businesses that become obsolete by reason of new technology or economic changes. When new environmental factors occur, retailers change to accommodate them.
3. The retailing need is all-pervasive, so one can work for or establish a store wherever there are people.
4. Retail organizations are constantly in search of young people and willing to train and remunerate them consistent with responsibility and their contributions to organizational profit.
5. Large retail organizations offer continued job viability. Many, in fact, as policy offer job rotation for selected employees so that personnel may gain a widened understanding of the retail operation and sustain work enthusiasm.
6. Since retailing is an institution in a perpetual state of change to newer conditions, people with imagination have the opportunity to express their creativity.
7. Retailing is a completely people-oriented institution and therefore never dull for someone who relates to people. There are constant interrelations with other personnel and the customers who are being served. There is some variation for those in the impersonal selling sectors, but even there one must be a people-watcher who understands current life styles.

There is hardly any formal training that is not pertinent to some position in retailing. To use extreme examples, medical training is required for someone who heads the infirmary, and climatologists are employed by one of the largest retailers in the country for long-term planning. Larger retailers are in constant need of new applicants and conduct at least two executive training programs a year.

In reviewing the charts in Chapter 10 you can see that there are typically six divisions of a large retail organization and that the employees constitute a virtual army. Hence, the structure of an organization of size has six broad areas of interlocking responsibility that add up to a system that sustains it:

1. Merchandising and buying
2. Store operations
3. Control and credit
4. Sales promotion
5. Personnel and employee-customer relations
6. Store planning and development

If one analyzes the positions of management of a department store in layers, it can be done as follows:

1. Top management
   a. Board of directors
   b. President
   c. General merchandise manager
   d. Department heads of
      (1) sales
      (2) promotion
      (3) finance
2. Middle management
   a. Divisional merchandise managers
   b. Warehouse managers

3. Lower management (in descending order of importance)
   a. Buyers
   b. Section managers
   c. Department managers
   d. Associate buyers
   e. Assistant buyers
4. Operating management
   a. Assistant managers
   b. Stockroom managers
   c. Office managers
   d. Floor supervisors

High-level managers are largely responsible for developing objectives, establishing policies, controlling operations, and organizing and assembling the resources of a firm. Middle managers are responsible for carrying out the policies formulated by top management within narrow spheres of interest, usually on a divisional or departmental level.

Appendix A contains the job descriptions of major retail career opportunities. Our consideration here is the fact that the larger organization employs trainees for two executive tracks: (1) administration/operations and (2) merchandising. In many stores an applicant can select either of these major options.

EXECUTIVE TRAINING PROGRAMS

Most large organizations have management programs to give newly accepted employees executive training as well as in-service sessions for positioned employees to facilitate advancement. For the most part, programs last a matter of weeks and can be structured in one or all of the following ways: (1) formal training (in a school situation), (2) on-the-job training, or (3) job rotation.

A few companies maintain training programs for a longer period; Woolworth's complete term of new-employee schooling lasts two years. IBM (not a retailer, of course) probably has the most extended program, a regular return to school by all employees for at least two weeks a year. This could be a wave of the future for large retailers, who are always in a state of flux with new store openings, new tools of management, and new marketing techniques. Whatever the structure used, the training starts with an indoctrination in company policies, instruction in the required knowledge and skills of the selected track, and information about standards of performance.

The second step is assignment to various departments so that the trainee sees the flow of merchandise and the ultimate transaction of title change from company to customer. One assignment is selling on the floor to assure understanding of the most basic part of the total retail effort, a necessary step for all executive trainees, regardless of eventual career goal.

In the formal method, the third step includes both examinations and homework assignments. In some organizations, performance is rated and the top performers are given the first interviews with divisional merchandise managers and later with buyers, who select trainees for entrance to lower management as assistant buyers.

The interview may raise one problem. Suppose you want a position as an assistant buyer in a fashion department and there is no vacancy, a common occurrence. There is only one answer: Accept a post-trainee position in another division. In due course an opening will occur and a qualified assistant buyer can be shifted to an area of choice.

ADMINISTRATION/OPERATIONS

In a day of multiple units and long pipelines of merchandise, the functions of administration and operations have become more important and provide excellent opportunities for job advancement, not inconceivably to the top layer of the hierarchy.

There are far more types of positions in this broad area than in merchandising. Refer again to the organization chart; trace the way merchandise enters a store, the way it is shipped, and the control system by which merchandise is acccounted for. Note how credit is extended to customers, how good administration has an influence on the profit level, how employees are hired, and how the physical plant is designed and operated, among other necessary concerns of retail management. You should be able to realize that, as in a military organization, it takes eight staff members to support one combat soldier.

Managerial personnel advantages include tenure, transferability of skills and knowledge, job advancement, and opportunities to understand the management end of retailing, including the cost and financing of the marketing effort.

FASHION MERCHANDISING

Students with some experience in store selling often have strong feelings in favor of or against a buying career. What must be remembered is that although selling experience is desirable and an excellent credit when applying for an executive training program, it can lead to a false notion about the merchandising relationship. Unfortunately, many students with part-time store employment do not have the time or expend the effort to learn more about the buying executive's part of the retail function. A curious applicant can seek help in a store from an executive and obtain a frame of reference of the relations and responsibilities of the ladder of buying and merchandise, the rungs of which are these:

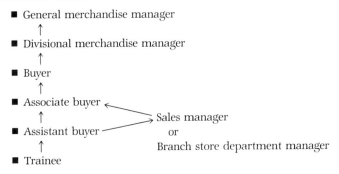

- General merchandise manager
  ↑
- Divisional merchandise manager
  ↑
- Buyer
  ↑
- Associate buyer
  ↑   → Sales manager
- Assistant buyer   or
  ↑   Branch store department manager
- Trainee

The position of *associate buyer* is a recent addition to the ladder. The term refers to a seasoned assistant ready for buyership, usually after having served as a department manager in a branch store for a year or two.

APPLYING FOR A JOB

The procedure that should be followed in applying for a position can be broken down into the following steps:

1. *Selection of a type of organization:* chain, department store, discount operation, mail order firm, etc. For size and complete financial data of organizations, for full research purposes, a financial report of any store can be obtained from a stockbroker or from *Fairchild's Financial Manual of Retail Stores*. The significance of this choice is that retail sectors differ in the methods of training and career responsibilities.

A department-store buyer is a complete merchant, one who plans, buys, and sells. Selling applies here in the broadest sense and does not refer to floor selling but to the promotional activities of moving goods.

A chain-store buyer is a market specialist who neither plans nor sells, since these are the responsibilities of a merchandise manager. There is no customer contact. It is a more impersonal aspect of retailing in which the buyer almost always works in an office building separate from the store.

A mail-order buyer is also a market specialist with no personal customer contacts.

One of the more recent career opportunities in chain-store merchandising is the distribution of merchandise to member stores. Employees in this operation are known as *paper distributors*. This is a vantage-point job because the distributor becomes familiar with the selling patterns of different regions and the manner in which trends develop, experience that can lead to a grasp of the inner workings of chain merchandising.

A resident buyer's responsibilities are described in Chapter 13, but for purposes of classification, this buyer is a market specialist involved in no planning and no buying without permission (actually a representative).

2. *Choice of location*—an important consideration, of course. Department stores are numerous, are located in diverse areas, and probably afford the widest choice, although chains and larger specialty shops are also strategically placed to serve populated areas. Once you target your chosen geographic area, the stores there can be easily found. Here are a few manuals that can help:

Sheldon's Retail Directory (32 Union Square, New York, NY 10011) lists department stores, women's specialty stores, chain stores, and resident buying offices. The Salesman's Guide (1140 Broadway, New York, NY 10001) also publishes nationwide and metropolitan New York directories listing stores and buyers in every fashion field.

Major Mass Market Merchandisers, a publication of the Salesman's Guide, 1140 Broadway, New York, NY 10001, lists discount stores, variety stores, drug chains, supermarket chains, rack jobbers, factory outlet stores, and leased department operators.

210 If you are ambitious to work in a foreign retail organization, refer to *Stores of the World Directory*, which lists department stores, supermarkets, chains, retail executives, trade buyers, and resident buyers worldwide. (The publisher is Newman Books, Ltd., 48 Poland Street, London, WIV 4 PP, England.)

Additional information can be obtained from the National Retail Merchants' Association, 100 West 31st Street, New York, NY 10001. A selected region's Chamber of Commerce can supply a local retail list. An aspirant need never be at a loss for information about store type or location and personnel of a retail organization; finding this is the least difficult step in the process of job hunting.

3. *Preparation of resume and the short covering letter of transmittal* (see Appendix B). The same terms already outlined should be followed: the resume must contain pertinent background; be professionally printed, if possible; and be mailed to as many potential employers as circumstances demand. The number could be twenty-five, fifty, or a hundred, depending on locale, width of your interest, and job market competition.

4. After responses are received but before interview dates, seek advice from someone in the industry, a teacher with industry experience, or anyone who can be depended upon for information about the responding firms.

In preparation for interviews, obtain general information about the firms and anticipate such probable questions as "Why do you want to become a buyer?" and "Why do you want to work here?" It should go without saying that if the interview is for a merchandising position, you will brush up on your arithmetic skills, particularly when you are told that a test is to be given. You may have a high level of skill, but the allotted time is usually short and a review adds security.

Realize that employment managers are seeking candidates with good and strong motivations for retailing, with sufficient skills to learn and carry out organizational policies for corporate goals. The cost of training each selected buying candidate runs into thousands of dollars, so the selection process is rigorous and very competitive.

Certain highly regarded stores with well-known training programs receive as many as five times more applications than there are openings. The result is a large labor pool for selection and high standards for applicants. This competitive race will vary with economic conditions, the popularity of the career option, and the pay scale. It is extremely difficult to discuss job opportunities and standards without over- or understatement. At the same time, a dedicated graduate of a community or four-year college program is almost always able to obtain a position as a merchandising trainee. This is not to say that everyone can attain the position of first choice or connect with the type of retailer that is his or her highest priority. Sometimes it takes some digging and imagination, sometimes it takes compromise, but always there is one job waiting for the qualified, dedicated graduate who perseveres.

The greatest obstacle may be the difficulty of targeting a specific job with a specific firm and getting the job as a result of the first interview.

This leads to the question of what employment managers look for in candidates. There is no precise answer, to be sure, but some combination of the following attributes is a realistic response.

1. Ability to express oneself clearly
2. Understanding of mathematical relationships
3. Ability to get along well with others
4. Enthusiasm
5. Alertness
6. Creativity
7. A good memory
8. Curiosity
9. Willingness to accept responsibility
10. Leadership
11. Stamina, emotional and physical

SMALL-STORE OWNERSHIP

Owning one's own store is an expression of individuality and independence. This is the dream of some students—and of some professionals who have attained high merchandising position.

To put small-store ownership into focus: the small, independent store represents about 88 percent of all retail units of the country, and about one-third of the total retail sales. These numbers would seem to favor the growth of small stores into bigger units that eventually add up to a group of independently owned department stores, which was the case earlier in our history. Small often becomes bigger, but present-day competition does not favor independently owned department stores, as we have seen earlier.

There are rich rewards for the intrepid and creative who are willing to learn and work hard. For those who have the ambition and drive, the following points should be studied:

An independent owner is a generalist and must fill a variety of roles to meet the requirements of buying, receiving, marking, and selling of merchandise; financing the operation; and maintaining the store.

Statistical records show that 95 percent of all small-store failures are due to two factors: lack of experience and undercapitalization. The latter is most obvious; when finances are limited, there is vulnerability to the unexpected. The former has a more complicated reason. Retail experience as a buyer or merchandise manager would seem to be adequate preparation. And that is true, to a point. But the ground rules change when you open a store: the specialist from a large organization becomes a generalist in a small operation. The new owner is faced with a series of important decisions:

- How should a store be acquired?
- What is the best source of the necessary capital?
- Can the population be segmented with sufficient precision so that there is proper merchandising direction?
- What degree of expertise is needed to buy, price, and sell merchandise in small quantities?

- What degree of acumen is needed to operate a business that demands proper allocation of funds to direct and indirect expenses that require record-keeping and other important operational functions?

The operation of a small, independent retail fashion business is intricate and calls for more than an affinity for or love of clothing.

There are no guaranteed steps for small-store success; far from it. However, the most complete background for success would probably include:

1. Several years of work experience in fashion merchandising with a company of moderate to large size.
2. Examination of a successful small-store operation, either by working in one for a period of time or by developing a close relationship with an operator, to learn particular problems and intricacies. One aspect of merchandising that should be clearly delineated is that buying mistakes are difficult to move. Limited traffic is a constraint and certainly a characteristic of a small-store operation. Former buyers are often surprised and chagrined when they become small-store victims of errors of merchandise selection, either in style or depth, that would be of no consequence in a larger store.
3. Careful study of the pamphlets available from the U.S. Department of Commerce, Small Business Administration, that enumerate all the steps that should be followed in opening a small store.
4. An in-depth discussion with a lawyer and/or accountant to assess potential profit, contingent liabilities, governmental forms (local, state, and federal), and the relationship of assets to liabilities.
5. A self-examination that reveals a motivation consistent with the demands of small-store success.

This is a brief outline only. Books that cover the subject in detail are noted in the bibliography. Success is a matter of the meshing of proper ingredients, some of which are the style or creativity of the merchant, the proper location, the personal touch, the proper financing, and a head for business.

SUMMARY

Fashion merchandising (as a buyer, merchandise manager, or store owner) is a career with high financial returns, and rightfully so. A merchandiser (in the broad sense) is a decision-maker in a fast-moving business and must be an expert in the numbers, opinions, wants, beliefs and lifestyles of customers as they pertain to apparel.

It is an activity that is measurable; a merchandiser knows the statistical values of success, works with goal figures, and tries to improve estimated results with creativity. Creativity must be an ever-present element in the life of a fashion professional. The identical merchandise in two different stores, for example, can have a different level of appeal, variety of use, and even sell at different retail prices. Merchandising, as we have seen, is more than just visiting the market and buying apparel; performance is selling at a profit and the repetition of that process with present and future customers. In a literal sense, the position of a merchandiser is that of an agent for the ultimate user, and its responsibility carries the requirement of studying the selected consumers, both demographically and psychographically. Could there be a more interesting problem than knowing what people want, what price they are willing to pay, how many items they will buy, and when they will buy them?

The various ways in which fashion apparel is merchandised present a wide range of opportunities for those who are interested in such a career. On the other hand, for those interested in the administration and operational functions of retailing, the range of opportunities is just as great, especially in a typical large organization.

Merchandising, or retailing, is a profession, and it demands motivation, knowledge, skill, and dedication for high-level attainment.

QUESTIONS FOR DISCUSSION

1. Which fashion merchandising career do you believe would bring you the greatest career satisfaction? In answering, include your thoughts about the type of organization, size of organization, entry job position, and career position.
2. Discuss the major sources of information for response to the four parts of Question 1.
3. Explain the considerations of small-store ownership.
4. Of what career significance would the personal and impersonal methods of fashion merchandising be in your selection of an organization for an entry job position?
5. Review the steps that should be followed to obtain an interview. Discuss them.

The critical nature of consumption in an abundant society demands a marketing system based neither on coincidence nor on chance. A business environment largely devoted to mass production for mass consumption must include a communications network that informs potential consumers and creates demand consistent with productive capacity, enables consumers to decide quickly what they want, provides consumer convenience in procuring goods, and enhances the value of goods to consumers. The fashion industry system of the United States includes a sophisticated and highly developed network of intelligence that assists the marketing effort of the largest fashion complex of the world. It relies on various types of information:

1. Messages of textile companies to manufacturers about what and why particular fabrics are produced and why they should be favored
2. Reports from manufacturers to stores to create demand for finished products
3. Communications from retailers to potential consumers who have a wide range of options to purchase products

PART V

THE AUXILIARIES OF FASHION MERCHANDISING

This part, therefore, will dwell on the communication part of the industry: the auxiliaries of fashion marketing, touching on historical background, the methods of relating information, by whom it is passed, and career opportunities in the communication of fashion information. The four chapters deal with resident buying; publications, advertising and public relations; fashion experts; and career opportunities in fashion communication.

Part V has three objectives:

1. To indicate the importance of fashion communication
2. To reinforce the understanding of where and how communications are developed
3. To suggest sources of information and other related data needed to seek an entry position in one of these areas

13
RESIDENT
BUYING

A **resident buying office** is an organization located in a major market to represent member stores that have their own complement of buyers. A resident buyer, therefore, is more accurately called a resident representative. The primary function of a resident buying office is to render a service; it has three major functions:

1. Researching
2. Buying with permission of member stores
3. Helping stores promote goods

The time and environment of the founding of the resident office have been mentioned in a different context. We noted earlier that modern ready-to-wear was born in 1920, a development that made the resident buying office necessary. When the chain-store era began, it was apparent that the already established department stores were weak in fashion marketing. They purchased merchandise, when the operation was not leased, for an entire season, often from jobbers. Ready-to-wear did not have a high degree of importance to volume or profit. The chains proved that apparel could be sold profitably to a wide consumer segment, and this was sufficient reason for department stores to show greater interest. But how were the advantages of the chains' main office location in the market and their mass purchasing power to be overcome? The answer was obvious: join offices that were set up by enterprising business- **217** people who recognized the need of stores to belong to an organization located in the main market, New York City. Such an organization could send out a constant stream of market information, represent the stores in dealings with manufacturers, and pool orders with other client stores to obtain mass purchasing benefits.

Resident buying and modern ready-to-wear therefore developed together, with 1920 recurring as the most significant year in the historical background of fashion marketing.

TYPES OF RESIDENT BUYING OFFICES

What is the difference between the resident buying office and a central merchandising office? Think of it this way: a chain operation *owns* a number of stores and merchandises them from one location, with the stores having little or no part in the functions of planning, buying, or promoting. Chain-store personnel concentrate efforts in one direction, the selling of goods bought and distributed by the central office. The resident buying office is a *service* arm; member stores do their own merchandising and use offices for service purposes only. Hence, a chain uses its stores to service the merchandising effort; member stores use the resident buying office to help service its merchandising goals.

Five types of resident offices serve the particular needs of different kinds of retail operations.

The salaried or independently owned office The most usual type of resident buying office is owned by a company or individual, not by a store. It receives remuneration from its member clients, usually based on store volume (a larger store pays a larger fee). Salaried offices represent both specialty and department stores.

The associated office A group of stores may cooperatively own and manage their own office, each paying a proportionate share of the cost of operation. Such an associated office ensures the particular type of market coverage the stores require; obviously, the joint ownership consists of stores that have common interests, a condition that is not always the case in an independently owned office.

The syndicated office In some cases, a corporation owns both the buying office and the stores it services. This type of office is described in the specific lists below.

The merchandise broker A merchandise broker was once called a commission buying office. Income is obtained from orders placed with cooperating manufacturers, who pay a commission. The store members, usually smaller retailers, do not pay any fee. There could be a conflict of interest when the choice of manufacturer is between a cooperative and a noncooperative one. However, as a matter of office policy, the market representative normally places the order where it serves the best interest of the client.

The private office   A special office for one retail organization is known as a private office. Usually such an office is physically located in the larger resident buying office of which the store is also a member. In a very few instances a store maintains a private office for itself, an extremely costly arrangement.

Some examples of types of resident buying organizations follow:

Independent or Salaried Offices

Independent Retailers Syndicate (IRS), Inc.
Felix Lilienthal & Co., Inc.
Retailers Representatives, Inc.

These offices all service client stores in noncompeting trading areas, including some foreign stores in Europe and the Orient.

Associated Offices (cooperatively owned)

Associated Merchandising Corp. (AMC)
Frederick Atkins, Inc.
Specialty Stores Association

These are offices owned by their member stores, among which are some of the largest and most prestigious in the United States. AMC, for example, is the office to which all Federated stores belong. AMC would appear to be, but is not quite, a corporately owned office. It has several major store organizations that are not Federated members (for example, Dayton-Hudson), so it functions as a mutually owned type.

Syndicated Offices (corporately owned)

The May Company Buying Office
The Macy Corporate Office
The Allied Purchasing Corporation
Associated Dry Goods Association, Buying Office

In these instances, the parent organization owns both the office and the stores it services. For instance, the Macy Corporate Office services R. H. Macy stores—Macy's New York, Bamberger's in New Jersey, Davison's in Georgia, Macy's Midwest in Kansas City, and Macy's California in San Francisco.

Merchandise Broker

Apparel Alliance

This office is the largest of its type and has hundreds of clients, none of which pays a fee. When a store member gives an order for placement, the broker representative receives from the cooperating manufacturer a percentage of the net delivered goods (invoice total less trade discounts) as payment for the office effort.

Private Offices

Marshall Field
Rich's of Atlanta

Marshall Field is a large, important store that has a private office in New York City. Rich's, an Atlanta-based store and branches, maintains a private office within AMC, the associated office to which it belongs.

Within the independent group are offices that specialize in infants', children's, and teen apparel and in men's wear.

SERVICES PERFORMED BY RESIDENT BUYING OFFICES

The resident office is the communication link between manufacturers and stores. Without it, neither stores' fashion operations nor manufacturers could maintain the pace demanded of modern fashion marketing. The most recent innovation of resident buying service is representation in foreign markets. Large organizations like Allied and AMC have offices in the major markets of the world— Tokyo, London, Paris, Milan, Florence, Vienna, and Zürich. Smaller offices maintain import buying divisions and pool store orders, visit foreign markets, and arrange for delivery of import merchandise.

A resident buying office:

1. *Reports on developments in wholesale markets.* The resident buying office provides market coverage in all classifications of fashion merchandise but also relates the value of the merchandise to store needs. The market coverage information saves the store buyers time, money, and effort when they come to the market. As the market eyes and ears of the store buyer, resident representatives collect market information (new and best-selling styles), edit the information, and then send it to the member store buyers. The illustrations show both sides of an IRS flyer that is representative of the type of information resident buyers send to their client stores. The information sent includes reports that concern top-level management, merchandise managers, buyers, fashion directors, and store supply buyers.

2. *Buys for stores at their request.* When a store buyer requires merchandise and feels that it would be handled best by the resident representative, an order is sent to the representative with instructions on where, how, and when to place the order. The degree of discretion the store buyer gives the representative depends on type of goods and time schedule.

3. *Follows up on deliveries.* Stores require merchandise delivery from manufacturers during specific periods. The resident representative makes periodic visits to manufacturers and reviews the orders placed by member stores and presses for order completion. This chore is usually handled by an assistant resident buyer or trainee follow-up person.

4. *Handles adjustments and complaints.* As a representative for many stores, a

220

RE-ORDER RECAP

DIVISION: HOME FURNISHINGS

THE FOLLOWING ITEMS ARE CURRENTLY RE-ORDERING AND HAVE
A CONTINUED SELLING LIFE IN MOST AREAS OF THE COUNTRY.

DEPT.	RESOURCE	STYLE # AND DESCRIPTION	COST	DELIVERY	COMMENT
Gifts	Maurice Duchin Inc. Net 10 EOM FOB: Shrewsburg, N.J.	FV1 – Bud vase, silverplate with silk rose.	$ 6.65 Each	2 wks ROO	These make fine bridal gifts. 22 stores reordered in 3 weeks.
Stationery	First American Flowers Net 30 FOB: Blauvelt, NY	12 Dozen of a style, assorted colors	1.60 D	2 wks	Silk flowers just keep growing in importance. Display them massed in vases, separated by color. Many reorders in last 7 weeks.
Notions	E. Mich...				his piece, because it has o many uses, has proved be quite popular – 15 rders noted in week.
					velty woven top or tom weight sportswear ic. Basic durable with tant reorders.
					This item should be featured on T-stand in all updated misses departments.... / ed mini prints selling or decorative quilts ats and general room Will continue strong ll.
					dly sells out after in toy and childrens ents. Great impulse
					(OVER PLEASE)
					IRS MEMBER TH.

SYNDICATE INC.

ACTION OPPORTUNITY

THE "PRAIRIE SKIRT"
FOR THE URBAN COWGIRL...

The prairie skirt is not new to the West. The re-emergence of the American way, the relaxed Western look is becoming apparent for Spring, Summer and will be a definite way of life for '81. The prairie skirt already reordering in the "Better" contemporary market in most major cities. This skirt incentively priced at $13.60, regular price $17.50 in 9½ oz. washed indigo denim.

DEPT.: UPDATED SPTS – Misses Moderate
MERCHANDISE: Skirt
RESOURCE: VIA WEST SPT BY DOWN SOUTH ENT.
TERMS: 8/10 EOM
DELIVERY: A/R 1/30 Complete
F.O.B.: New York City, N.Y.
DEPT. HEAD: BILL FRIEDMAN
BUYER: RITA CHILDS
NUMBER: 4-2-4405-4
DATE: 1/12/81
ck

Style #9113 –
9½ oz. pre-washed indigo denim prairie skirt. 84" sweep, 2 in-seam pockets, full flounce bottom. Back zip. 30" length.
$13.60 Less 8%, 6/16 in Indigo Denim.

© 1980 INDEPENDENT RETAILERS SYNDICATE INC.

Resident buying office bulletins. (Independent Retailers Syndicate, Inc.)

KID STUFF

DEPT.: CHILDRENS
MERCHANDISE: Girls Coats
RESOURCE: THE PHILADELPHIAN
TERMS: 8/10 EOM
DELIVERY: 9/15 A/R Oct 1 complete
F.O.B.: Phila, Pa.
DEPT. HEAD: James J. Cohn
BUYER: Pearl Atlas
NUMBER: 6-1-5536-0

```
*********************
* SPECIAL           *
* ATTENTION         *
*********************
```

<u>WOW - DO WE HAVE A DEAL FOR YOU! ALL</u>

<u>WOOL COATS -</u>

Create volume with these eye catching "Fashions" cosy styles from the Philadelphian

Quality - Fabric - Work————————————————————lling thru fall season - Promotion - All styles
equal in importance.

Style #
305 Girls Plaid Coa————————————————————all wool

205   same a

322 Girls Coa
     Lined -

222

316 G
    C

216

rk

SPORTSWEAR SCENE

DEPT.:
MERCHANDISE: JUNIOR SPORTSWEAR
Jump Suits

Jumpers are Jumping!

(OVER PLEASE)

RESOURCE: SPACE LEGS
TERMS: 8/10 EOM
DELIVERY: A/R October 30
F.O.B.: New York
DEPT. HEAD: D. Steinberg
BUYER: Ronnie Lazar
NUMBER: 4-1-6991-3

resident office has sufficient clout to represent stores effectively in any disputes between stores and manufacturers.

5. *Answers requests for information.* One of the staff functions of a resident office is to supply research information when required. Store requests can be directed to any level of the resident office chain of command, from president to buyer. The most common requests concern trend importance, most important manufacturers, fashion shows, and foreign markets.

6. *Provides office space and clerical help for visiting buyers.* When buyers visit the market they need a desk and telephone to write orders, contact manufacturers, and perform other market-visit functions. Offices maintain space for these purposes.

7. *Publishes arrivals of out-of-town buyers.* Some visiting buyers have their names published in trade papers to alert manufacturers of their presence. In this instance, an appropriate RBO person supplies the information for publication.

8. *Accompanies buyers to market.* Store buyers visit the market as often as there are merchandising needs. It is standard for a store buyer and representative to visit manufacturers together. The RBO buyer has research information, and a store buyer is often more comfortable in making decisions when accompanied by a market representative.

9. *Offers sales promotion aids.* One of the major resident buying services is helping stores promote goods, and accelerate selling. The following are some of the sales stimulants offered:
   a. Ad mat services, art and copy that can be used as newspaper advertisements
   b. Statement enclosures (sent with store customer bills)
   c. Catalogues geared to important seasonal events
   d. Displays, designs of window display, props, copy for window displays, and so on
   e. Sales promotion calendars, recommended long-range store sales promotion planning
   f. Fashion office services
      1. Fashion bulletins, prepared by the fashion director, which include seasonal themes and other important fashion information
      2. Fashion promotion kits for advertising, display, publicity, and public relations events
      3. Handling of store fashion shows by the fashion director
      4. In-office fashion shows

10. *Arranges personal services.* Although visiting store personnel often have their own favorite hotels, an office offers the services of personnel to make hotel reservations and other personal services such as obtaining theater tickets (at store cost) and arranging for reservations at restaurants.

11. *Collects merchandise samples for buyer viewing during market weeks.* In order to show new season themes or current reorder styles, a representative maintains a rack of sample merchandise to save the store buyer time and effort.

12. *Handles foreign market purchases.* Most large offices maintain a separate foreign department to facilitate the flow of merchandise from abroad. The office can be involved in all or any combination of the following services: soliciting and collecting store orders, then visiting a foreign market to place them; maintaining a resident buying office in a foreign country; holding periodic meetings with store buyers to develop ideas for foreign purchasing.

13. *Holds seasonal clinics.* To help stores in selecting the important fashion themes of a season, each department (men's department, fur department, dress de-

partment) holds a meeting and exhibits styles culled from the market. Clinics are usually held on the first day of market weeks, in the RBO office or at a hotel.

14. *Offers central merchandising services (at an extra fee).* Resident buying offices can only buy with the client's permission. However, some offices make available a service by which the office operates one or several popular-priced departments. All plans, buying, and sales promotion plans are performed by the office, and each participating store furnishes its daily selling records to the office so that a tally can be maintained. The fee is usually based on the sales volume of a department handled. This arrangement works precisely like a chain operation, with the merchandising performed in a central office located in a major market.

15. *Supervises group buying programs.* Most offices, large and small, arrange for the coordination of the purchasing of some merchandise so that member stores can benefit from mass purchasing power in one or all of the following ways:

a. Merchandise exclusivity
b. Preferred delivery
c. Lower price

Arrangements for stores to act in unison are usually initiated by a RBO merchandise manager who turns the details over to an appropriate buyer. A committee of store buyers (the steering committee) meets and then gives the RBO department such targeted programs as private brand development, foreign purchase, and exclusive styling.

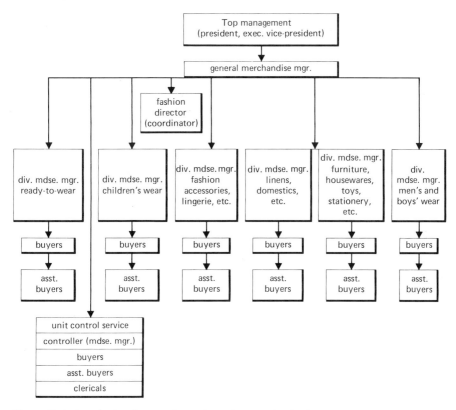

Figure 13–1 Organization chart: moderate-size or large resident buying office.

224 A resident buying organization is set up so that its personnel parallels those of the stores it services, so that visiting store people have an office counterpart. An office that specializes in servicing small fashion stores could have a merchandise manager and a few buyers; on the other hand, offices that represent giant retailers must have multiple divisions and large staffs and offer highly specialized research data, as shown in Figure 13–1.

SUMMARY

The resident buying office is an outgrowth of the need for fashion communication. The United States is the only country with a network that disseminates information almost as soon as it becomes available. Stores are always abreast of what is happening in the world of fashion, a world that has expanded from the domestic scene to the entire globe.

For every type of store there is a type of resident office. An office is part of the retail system of the country, but the resident representative is not a retailer in the qualitative sense; he or she is a staff person who works in a market—as a market specialist—and services the needs of the retailer.

Shown is the type of information culled from the market by a representative, prepared by the advertising department, and then sent to member stores.

QUESTIONS FOR DISCUSSION

1. Explain the difference between a CMO and an RBO.
2. What are the three broad functions of a resident buying office?
3. List and define the different types of resident buying offices.
4. What conditions led to the development of resident buying offices?
5. Which office serves a major store in your locale? What type of office is it?

14

PUBLICATIONS, ADVERTISING, AND PUBLIC RELATIONS

The modern fashion business, concerned with a product that changes each season, feeds on fashion news. In this constantly changing environment, there must be some means of communication that broadcasts the changes and makes evaluations of the fashion rightness of market offerings. One of the most important forms of this communication linkage between the market and the consumer is the fashion magazine. Fashion magazines help introduce and educate the consumer to the newest fashion ideas.

As early as the fourteenth century, the ladies of the courts of Europe were introduced to fashion newness through dolls, sometimes life-size. From 1750 until the start of the Civil War, such dolls were sent to America featuring the latest styles or fabrics.

MAGAZINES

In the nineteenth century, with the emergence of a strong middle class as a result of the industrial revolution, there was a growing interest in the proper manner of dress. Some 150 fashion publications appeared in Europe, in French,

Fashions from *Godey's Lady's Book* for April 1865. (Division of Costume, Smithsonian Institution)

English, German, Italian, and Spanish (most were published for only a few issues).

In the United States, three magazines remained popular for years. The first recognized fashion publication, *Graham's Magazine*, was considered a most important fashion source from 1826 until 1857. *Godey's Lady's Book*, established in 1830, became the most popular fashion magazine of the nineteenth century and continued publication until 1898. It was especially admired for the quality of its illustrations. *Peterson's Magazine* was first issued in 1842 and continued publication until 1898. The two reproductions here show the styles of fashion and artwork of the time.

These magazines were devoted to information of feminine interest, carrying instructions and drawings for needlework, knitting, and crocheting; architectural plans for homes; the latest fashions; advice on medicine and health and manners of the day, as well as fiction. Through them women were able to follow the social events of the larger cities of the Northeast—particularly New York, Philadelphia, and Boston.

In the late nineteenth century, eighteen women's magazines were being published in the United States, among them *The Woman's Home Companion*, started in 1897; *Pictorial Review*, 1897–1935; and *Queen of Fashion*, begun in 1873 and still being published under the name *McCall's*.

The Ladies' Home Journal, also a current publication, was started in 1883. *Harper's Bazaar*, originally brought out in tabloid newspaper form in 1867, was later called *Bazaar*. Another current popular magazine, *Vogue*, was started in 1892 and was essentially concerned with social activities of the day.

Although fashion magazines were predominantly for women, there were, and are, magazines devoted to men. The most notable nineteenth-century publication was *Burton's Gentlemen's Magazine*, a publication that had as its editor an illustrious literary figure, Edgar Allan Poe, in 1839 and 1840.

Gowns shown in *Demorest's Monthly Magazine,* January, 1874. Demorest patterns were available for these designs. (Division of Costume, Smithsonian Institution)

Magazine specialization

Magazines use approaches intended to interest a selected group. Each magazine therefore assumes a point of view and becomes characterized for its fashion position. Fashion magazines are, by definition, largely devoted to fashion information, although most of them today do carry some general-interest material. General or service magazines like *Cosmopolitan, Redbook, Ladies' Home Journal, Good Housekeeping,* and *McCall's* have extremely large readerships but limited interest in fashion apparel. Their circulation is so large that advertising space is too costly for most fashion manufacturers' purposes.

The advertising expenditure of the average fashion manufacturer is less than 1 percent of net sales, a very low level compared to most other industries. As we have already discussed, the very nature of fashion—the element of change— inhibits investment in the advertising of a specific style that may be out of popularity by the time it appears in print. A further deterrent is the cost. Since most ready-to-wear manufacturers are small businesses, the cost of national advertising is too heavy a burden to assume. Therefore, although fashion magazines offer the means for establishing brand name familiarity, only the larger organizations can afford to advertise well.

Even so, the fashion magazines of the United States offer a comparatively inexpensive means of reaching a national audience through a medium that has multiple readership: each copy generally has more than one reader.

Front cover of the October 1918 *Delineator*. (Butterick archives)

The following is a selected list of magazines, with a mention of their target audience:

Vogue and *Harper's Bazaar* are directed toward the sophisticated, higher-income consumer who is interested in the early trends of fashion; their readership is small and selected.

Glamour is a fashion publication for the widest audience: the homemaker and career woman interested in the middle range of fashion, in both prices and trends.

Mademoiselle is for the college student with sufficient concern and money to be interested in fashion and for the young married.

Seventeen and *Ingenue* are essentially addressed to high-school students and some college girls.

Brides and *Modern Bride* are structured for prospective brides who are interested in gowns for themselves and members of the bridal party and in home furnishings.

Men's magazines, particularly during the past ten to fifteen years, are show-ing livelier interest in fashions and feature articles about fashion news. *Esquire*, *Gentleman's Quarterly*, and to some degree *Playboy* all cater to a national audience that has an interest in current fashions.

Fashion magazine merchandising

The content of fashion magazines can be grouped into articles, advertising, and editorial credits. Articles are written by both staff and outside authors and focus on topics of current readership interest. Advertising forms approximately half the content. The cost of space is based solely on circulation: the greater the number of copies distributed, the higher the cost. In the fashion field, the major publications' circulations range from about 1 million to 3 million, of-fering a rather inexpensive means indeed to reach a segmented national au-dience. Manufacturers are assiduously solicited by space salesmen to become advertisers, the chief source of the magazines' revenue. The newsstand price often does not cover the magazine cost; in fact, some magazines limit the number of copies published because copies in excess of a certain figure lessen the profit margin.

The extent to which fashion magazines influence the movement of fashion through their merchandising efforts is not generally appreciated. These efforts, which include editorial credits, follow.

The magazines have merchandise staffs who are in constant contact with the market here and abroad. Whether their title is editor, assistant, or mer-chandiser, their activities add up to merchandising. In their shopping of the markets, they view better-priced collections, moderate-priced lines, and specific styles, sometimes during the early stages of line development. This gives them the opportunity to see trends in their earliest stages, analyze them, and come to conclusions as to the direction in which fashion is going. Their conclusions are their own points of view, usually a consensus arrived at in their home offices, in concert with the other members of the staffs concerned. These con-clusions are the fashion positions, those that will be espoused in the issues for proper seasonal timing. In order to support a position, a magazine frequently contacts a manufacturer and suggests the production of particular styles in line with its prognostication. (For example, an editor may be impressed with a look seen in Paris showings. When she returns home she relays its importance to cooperative manufacturers.) For further support, the magazine can work with stores to effect a retail promotion and complete the cycle, giving reader vali-dation of the magazine's fashion expertise. The availability of merchandise from particular manufacturers and specific stores where the merchandise can be purchased is an education for the reader interested in the new fashions of the season.

As part of the merchandising effort to support the styles selected as the winners, **editorial credits** are given. A representative sees a style that fits into the magazine's selected theme. The manufacturer is asked the cost, when it will be on the line, and other details, including whether the firm sells to certain stores that have meaning to the magazine readers. For example, a high-fashion

publication will be interested in Bergdorf Goodman, Saks, Marshall Field, and J. W. Robinson. Better-priced fashion stores of importance will not allow use of their names in a list that features other retailers of lesser prestige. If all information is positive, the style or styles are requested for delivery to the magazine's office, where they are reviewed by the editor and staff for possible inclusion as an editorial feature. When a style is selected, the manufacturer is advised, as are a selected group of stores located in diverse areas, possibly Lord and Taylor in New York; Jordan Marsh in Miami; Marshall Field in Chicago; and J. W. Robinson in Los Angeles. This publicity is free. It is hoped that the manufacturer will produce the style and that the stores will buy it.

Failure can occur in both cases: the manufacturer may not produce the style because of disagreement with the magazine's assessment of its importance; store acceptance of the credit may have been made by a publicity director who cannot buy anything or failed to notify the appropriate buyer—or the buyer may have had no confidence in the manufacturer or the style. Another problem is the possible conflict of interest. Since magazines must sell advertising, and manufacturers welcome free editorial credits, there are sometimes trade-offs— the purchase of advertising space for editorial credits. It is easy to understand a manufacturer's complaint to a space salesperson: "XYZ manufacturer had three editorial credits and does no advertising; I advertise and get nothing." The salesperson's response could be "Work with me and I'll get you a credit in a month or two."

In addition to researching the manufacturing sector, editors work with the textile and leather industries. The research efforts are often published and sometimes sold to stores at a nominal cost. Store buyers therefore have an additional source of fashion prediction that includes major fashion themes of silhouettes, colors, and the manufacturers in the vanguard of developments.

As part of their merchandising efforts, and to maintain influence with both manufacturers and retailers, magazines use a variety of other techniques. Manufacturer's ads are enlarged and made available to stores for window and floor display, usually at nominal cost to the manufacturer. For example, certain retailers are known as *Seventeen* stores. As a kick-off for the fall season, some will feature windows banked with magazine-advertised merchandise and blow-ups of the ads. Merchandise in stock will feature a hangtag "As advertised in *Seventeen*." These are made available at a small cost to the manufacturer, who hangs them on garments in the final stage of production.

During market weeks, particularly during the shopping period for fall, magazines run fashion shows, and some feature advertised styles in a special show-room.

Most magazines maintain a research department that makes available merchandising information and statistical data. *Seventeen*, for example, issues periodic reports based on surveys to determine current and future fashion preferences of teenage girls. Other reports are concerned with current shopping habits, clothing budgets, and other statistical values that can be used by both manufacturers and retailers for short- and long-range planning.

TRADE PUBLICATIONS

The fashion industry has a number of professional publications intended for the trade. Their purpose is to research the markets and keep those in the field aware of current business events.

There is no classification of fashion merchandise that is not covered by roving reporters who are in the markets daily and cover lines, business conditions, and national and international news as they affect the business. Editorial credits, often accompanied by photos or sketches, are given when merchandise is noteworthy. Feature writers express editorial comments on up-to-date subjects; personnel appointments and line opening dates are announced; and statistical information is given on a regular basis.

Trade newspapers and magazines concentrate either on one phase of the industry (*Boot and Shoe Recorder*) or cover the entire industry (*Women's Wear Daily*).

Since the media of the business world aim at a highly specialized audience, the number of readers is limited but it includes the middle and upper levels of management of their respective industry segments; thus they exert considerable influence. *Women's Wear Daily*, for instance, has a subscription list of approximately 100,000, but few fashion merchandise managers and manufacturers fail at least to scan the paper daily. One advantage to manufacturers is that this limited distribution makes for a comparatively inexpensive way to reach a pinpointed audience, so the influence far exceeds numbers.

Here is a selected list of trade publications:

Advertising Age	*Femme Line*
American Fabrics	*Footwear News*
American Textile Reporter	*Fur Age Weekly*
Apparel Manufacturer	*Handbag and Accessories*
Apparel World	*Hosiery and Underwear Review*
Body Fashions	*Intimate Fashion News*
Boot and Shoe Recorder	*Knitting Times*
Boutique Magazine	*Masculines*
California Apparel News	*Men's Wear*
California Men's Stylist	*Modern Textiles*
Chain Store Age	*Small World*
Clothes	*Stores Magazine*
Daily News Record (men's apparel)	*Style*
Department Store Management	*Teen and Boys Outfitter*
Discount Merchandiser	*Texas Fashions*
Display World	*Variety Department Stores*
Earnshaw's Review (children's apparel)	*W*
Fabricnews	*Western Apparel Industry*
Fashion Week	*Women's Wear Daily*

Special mention should be given to two of the Fairchild Publications fashion newspapers. *Women's Wear Daily* and the *Daily News Record* appear five times a week and are as much a part of the daily reading habit of fashion professionals as regular newspapers.

Women's Wear Daily, which covers the fashion news of the women's apparel industry, was founded in the nineteenth century by E. W. Fairchild and has its headquarters in New York City. Like a general newspaper, it has its own wire service and maintains offices in cities throughout the United States and in foreign countries. The men's counterpart is *Daily News Record.*

232   A newcomer to the fashion industry will be wise to get into the habit of reading the appropriate paper to get a sense of the industry and become conversant with events that affect fashion.

ADVERTISING

The overall advertising expenditure of the United States is about 2.1 percent of the gross national product, a yearly total of approximately $60 billion, including time and talent cost for television and radio and production cost of print media. The reason for being in business is to make a profit, and the way to make it is to sell goods. Advertising is an important influence on the purchase of goods.

Advertising is a paid, nonpersonal message by an identified sponsor that appears in media to influence the sale, service, or acceptance of an idea or item by a potential buyer. An **advertising agency** is an organization that renders advertising and marketing service to clients.

Advertising has had a phenomenal growth in America over the past 150 years due to certain identifiable forces:

1. With increased competition, ways had to be found to stimulate demand for individual firms' products.
2. New technology provided new products and methods of doing business and demanded more consumer education.
3. The increase of the middle class added to existing business opportunities and required sharpened marketing tools, one of which is advertising.
4. Greater mobility gave consumers wider choices—back to competition.
5. Increased education made people more attentive to messages about the "better life."
6. The decline in personal selling made for greater dependence on advertising as a nonpersonal means of communication.
7. The proliferation of brands required increased advertising.
8. Mass production required repeated advertising to generate mass acceptance and mass consumption.
9. The popularity of consumer credit made for a more consenting consumer.
10. The introduction of the computer and improved research methods helped advertising take more precise aim at consumer motivations, although the effectiveness of these techniques is not yet proved.

We are exposed to advertising in almost every place of our daily activities. It is a significant force in shaping our political leanings and a critical aspect of our economic life. The impact of Madison Avenue in helping to elect presidential candidates has been well-documented in the media. And without broad dissemination of information to influence consumer purchases, we could not have a society of mass production for mass consumption.

Marketing, the basis of all sales activities, has five "P's." Advertising is part of one of these, promotion, which involves personal selling, advertising, display, publicity, and special events. (The five "P's" are: planning, product, pricing, promotion, profit.)

Because of its strong impact on molding public opinion, advertising has its share of proponents and detractors. Here are some interesting points of view:

Sir Winston Churchill: Advertising nourishes the consuming power of men. It creates wants for a better standard of living. It sets up before a man the goal of a better home, better clothing, better food for himself and his family. It spurs individual exertion and greater production. It brings together in fertile union those things which otherwise would never have met.

Aldous Huxley: It is far easier to write ten passably effective sonnets, good enough to take in the not enquiring critic, than to write one effective advertisement that will take in a few thousand of the uncritical buying public.

***Sovetskaya Kultura* (Soviet culture magazine):** The purposes of advertising in Soviet Russia are the following: (1) to educate public taste, (2) to develop demand, (3) to help consumers quickly find what they want to buy, (4) to help them buy it easily, and (5) to tell them the price.

Advertising Agency Chairman Arthur E. Meyerhoff: The techniques of persuasion by which the Russians seek to subvert governments, win the allegiance of new countries, and turn every political situation to their own advantage, are fundamentally the same psychological devices that we apply daily in selling products to consumers, and selling ideas at home.

Sociologist David Riesman, in *The Lonely Crowd*: Academic and professional people are frequently only too pleased to be told that those horrid businessmen, those glad-handing advertisers, are manipulative. And, as we all know, the businessmen and the advertisers flock to plays and movies that tell them what miserable sinners they are.

Advertising Agency Chairman David Ogilvy: Every advertisement must be considered as a contribution to the complex symbol which is the brand image. . . . The manufacturers who dedicate their advertising to building the most favorable image, the most sharply defined personality for their brands are the ones who will get the largest share of these markets at the highest profit—in the long run.

At first all advertising was vocal. In ancient Greece, town criers sold slaves and cattle, made public announcements, and chanted advertising rhymes. The next form of advertising was the sign, a sort of brand name. In ancient and medieval Europe and Asia, the signs were symbolic because originally goods were used in the immediate area where they were produced, and there was no need for differentiating them. A boy being whipped indicated a school, a coat of arms designated an inn, a goat was a sign of a dairy, a mule driving a mill meant a bakery, and later, in the United States, a carved wooden Indian identified a cigar store.

In the seventeenth century, a new medium gave advertising a strong springboard—the first English newspaper. *The Weekly News* was first published in 1622 by Nicholas Bourne and Thomas Archer. Advertising in English papers became widespread and, finally, when the newspaper was introduced to the American colonies, the format of advertising was already established.

The first successful American newspaper, published in 1704, contained an advertisement promoting the newspaper as a medium for advertisers. In 1729, Benjamin Franklin, often considered the father of American advertising, began publishing the Philadelphia *Gazette,* the first issue of which contained a soap advertisement. Franklin was copywriter, advertising manager, salesman, publisher, and editor. He was possibly the first purveyor of a product to use the modern method of selling "the sizzle, not the steak." His famous copy for the Franklin stove was not about the features of the hardware but of rewards derived from the product—health and comfort.

Newspapers prospered in the nineteenth century, and most carried full inside pages of advertisements.

Magazine publishing began in the eighteenth century. Many early magazines were pamphlets or booklets designed to influence opinions or raise cultural standards, and up to 1860 about 60 percent failed during the first year of publication. The publishers of many magazines did not at first consider them an advertising medium; *Godey's Lady's Book* did not carry any advertising.

The idea of an agency to handle advertising for clients was first put into practice by Volney Palmer, who set himself up as an agent in Philadelphia in 1841. In 1845 he established a branch office in Boston and in 1849 another one in New York. Palmer prepared advertising for various advertisers and collected 25 percent of the cost of advertising from the newspapers in addition to a fee from his clients.

Following the Civil War, the great era of business began and the assortment of consumer goods widened tremendously. James Gordon Bennett, editor of the New York *Herald,* was the first to realize that people buy papers for advertisements as well as for their news items. In an expanding New York market Bennett took a firm grip on the demand for the medium's new use. The post-Civil War period saw the rise of a new ruling class—the middle class, the business people. Advertising became a necessary arm of selling. It paid to advertise.

An advertising man who recognized the need for the modern agency was Francis Waylard Ayer, who in 1869 founded N. W. Ayer & Son, still one of the largest agencies in the United States. The agency started advertising in eleven religious papers. Ayer bought the entire space allocated for advertising in them and sold it for what he could get and in so doing established the modern agency that supplies both service and space.

During the 1875-to-1905 period advertising was bold, vigorous, and often deceptive. The entrepreneur was in full command, laissez-faire was the philosophy of business, and businessmen went their ways unbridled. During this period John Wanamaker built the largest men's clothing establishment in the United States, in Philadelphia. As part of his promotional efforts, he had 100-foot-long signs posted along the Pennsylvania Railroad tracks leading into Philadelphia. Wanamaker was also completely sold on newspaper advertising.

During the first twenty years of the twentieth century, advertising continued its rapid growth, but not without problems. The public was disenchanted with advertising claims, including promises of patent-medicine cures for many diseases. In due course both the government and professional organizations set up industrial codes in an attempt to clean up the industry. Since the 1940s, television has become an important part of the activities of agencies, and again advertising practices have come under investigation from time to time. Many agencies have now added computer programming to their research efforts to obtain a more precise fix on their marketing efforts and, perhaps, give rise to a new era of advertising realism.

The discussion of advertising must be broken down for our purposes into the areas of textiles, manufacturing, and retailing because size, business methods, and corporate goals vary widely. Although generalizations cannot include the numerous small firms that are characteristic of all three, it can safely be said that few fashion firms do not advertise to some degree. Every firm establishes an advertising budget as part of its marketing effort. In the fashion industry the percentage ranges from somewhat less than 1 percent to 3 percent of net sales. The larger the firm, the greater the budget, and therefore the wider choice of the means to carry the message to potential users.

The breakdown of industry advertising expenditures is approximately as follows:

	% of sales
Textiles	2.0
Manufacturing	.8
Retailing	2.5

These figures are averages. The advertising rate for the manufacturing industry is low because most firms are small and cannot afford to advertise with the frequency required to attain a brand-name position.

Each sector has the following media to consider for its advertising efforts:

- Direct mail
- Trade newspapers and magazines
- Fashion magazines
- Service magazines
- Newspapers
- Television and radio

Place, frequency, and quality of advertising are naturally dependent on the size of the budget. However, regardless of size, a creative marketer can find one or some combination of media to support marketing plans.

The textile market

Many giant textile and chemical firms can afford to use the total availability of media. From the 1950s on we have seen a steady stream of brand-name advertisements identifying man-made as well as natural fibers, the latter sponsored by the trade associations dealing with wool and cotton. The concentration on a medium is a matter of product strategy, product life, stage of acceptance, and institutional goal. For example, on occasion Monsanto, Burlington, Du Pont, Collins and Aikman, and Eastman Chemical have used national television. Their messages to ultimate consumers also appear in fashion magazines, service magazines, and newspaper advertisements in the form of cooperative advertising.

The advertising of the giant firms is pervasive, but the moderate-size and small firms concentrate on direct mail, personal selling, and trade papers.

Manufacturers

Because manufacturing is the most volatile link in the fashion chain as well as an area with numerous small firms, the communications of most firms are confined to direct mail, personal selling, and sometimes cooperative advertising. The exception is the large firm that requires a national distribution and desires brand identification. These firms aggressively use fashion magazines, Sunday news supplements, sometimes service magazines, and—if large enough—television and radio. Television has been used, for example, by Manhattan Shirt and Warnaco, but these instances are far from the rule. Television is still in the future of fashion advertising.

Direct mail is an effective means of reaching ultimate consumers. The manufacturer most commonly cooperatively supports stores' direct-mail pieces, usually for a seasonal promotion—summer, spring, holidays, and so on.

One of the factors inhibiting cooperative advertising is the Robinson-Patman Act, a national law that sets the guidelines for manufacturers to extend proportionate sums of cooperation to all customers. The law also requires the manufacturer to have a plan that must be brought clearly to the attention of every retail customer.

Retail stores

Retail-store advertising puts its major effort into newspapers because they are the final link in the chain, in direct contact with the end user. This advertising is measurable when the advertisement features a product (some ads are institutional). Several days after the advertisement, the sales promotional value can be assessed by determining the difference between a normal rate of selling and the selling results following the promotion.

Retail efforts also make liberal use of direct mail (statement enclosures) and, of increasing importance, radio—an older standard medium that has once more been found an effective and inexpensive means of communication. Some large stores are presently allocating up to 20 percent of total advertising budgets for radio.

Television fashion advertising is increasing but is still in its infancy. New techniques are required to make the medium economically feasible for retailers, who have limited area audiences. The development of cable television and home computers should lead to interesting innovations in this field.

Small stores generally use the same media, although with less frequency and less powerful ads. In the larger cities the smaller stores cannot afford to use radio and may use the telephone to call customers. Individually owned stores in smaller cities and towns have the advantage of lower-cost newspaper space and local radio time.

Trade papers and magazines are rarely used for retail exposure. However, textile companies and manufacturers are often involved in retail advertising. For example, when larger stores make use of full-page color advertisements in Sunday supplements to general newspapers, these are usually prepared either by a cooperating textile company or manufacturer's advertising agency; sometimes they are prepared by the staff of the store.

Of all three sectors, the retailer maintains the most highly developed advertising department. In a typical large store, the advertising staff includes copywriters, artists, and production people.

Modern advertising agencies

According to the American Association of Advertising Agencies, the major trade organization of the industry, in April 1982 there were 547 member agencies with 1013 offices located in 238 cities in 48 states, the District of Columbia, and Puerto Rico; these member agencies also maintained 617 branch offices in 123 cities in 67 other countries.

Advertising agencies customarily obtain revenue from the placement of space in the media and receive a 15 percent commission from the media. They also charge a fee for the cost of preparation and placement of the advertisements. There are some who advocate a different working arrangement, but no changes have yet been made.

Agencies in the fashion business are used for the most part by the larger textile and manufacturing firms. National advertisement efficiency is predicated on advertising frequency, and the goal is usually to obtain brand-name identification. The retailer occasionally uses an outside consultant to work on a specific problem, such as the creation of a new logo or signature or a new thematic advertising approach. The smaller producers in textiles or finished goods also use advertising firms for specific opportunities or assignments.

Few advertising agencies specialize in fashion, although most have an interest in fashion because it enhances the products they advertise. Hence, most larger agencies have on staff fashion directors who select apparel for models or actors in promotions in all media, from magazine features to television commercials.

The giant firms use such large agencies as Doyle Dane Bernbach; Batten Barton Durstine & Osborne; McCann-Erickson Worldwide; and Ted Bates. At the other extreme is the use of the services of small companies that prepare ad mats and offer ad placement for such infrequent advertisers as small manufacturing firms that want an occasional promotion.

The organization chart in Figure 14–1 includes the functions of a large agency that handles the complete range of media.

PUBLIC RELATIONS

An advertisement is a controllable message since it is paid for by the sponsor. However, as part of the strategy of communication, some of the larger firms maintain public relations departments to obtain favorable free publicity. Smaller firms can make contacts with the media to obtain editorial credits, a form of publicity. The objective here is to submit newsworthy information about a product, a policy, personnel, service, event, or involvement that will be accepted by the media as a news event and lead to favorable reaction from customers, vendors, employees, or stockholders.

In a sense, every firm broadcasts affirmative statements about its products

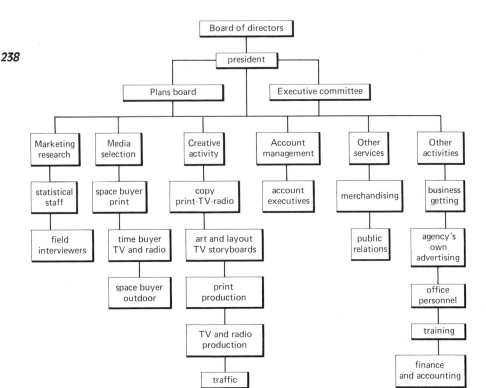

Figure 14–1 Organization chart: functions of a large advertising agency.

and how it does business. The degree of concentration is a matter of organization size and the ability to afford a plan and its implementation. Major American corporations issue yearly statements that are often pieces of art, and they do not happen by accident. Public relations staffs work long and hard to present an image of the company in its most favorable light. However, in the fashion business, the vast majority of firms are not public corporations and do not have special staffs for press releases or other public relations (although some of the larger textile firms can and do). Therefore, they must rely on their own initiative or employ experts who can create or direct news for the media.

The difference between publicity and public relations is more than semantic. Publicity can be obtained as a result of an event or events that have occurred or were created to obtain news value. Public relations is a sustained effort, a series of calculated programs or events to create an image or climate of feeling about a firm.

In the fashion business, being a leader has great value. If this is a fact of business life, why not flaunt it? An exclusive style or breakthrough is unusual. When a manufacturer is inundated with reorders, it is news, and, in this instance, an easy road to free publicity. All one has to do is contact resident buying offices with proof. The information will be disseminated nationally in a day or two.

A fashion-related firm can use many outlets to obtain publicity: newspapers, trade publications, magazines, radio, and even television.

The first step is to have news that has credibility, the second is to prepare **239** the information in proper fashion copy, and the last is to contact the proper media with good reasons for publication. Some specialists in the fields of publicity and public relations work exclusively for the fashion industry.

Department stores sponsor such events of public interest as art shows, cultural seminars, and children's shows to exhibit interest in the communities they serve and thereby gain favorable consumer opinions.

SUMMARY

The fashion magazine is a very important form of communication for the apparel industry. Magazines encourage product obsolescence, which is perhaps the most important factor motivating customers to buy new clothing. Fashion magazines influence a consumer's purchasing behavior. They also serve the industry by bringing together producer, retailer, and consumer.

Trade publications are about and for the people in the fashion business. They disseminate the news and research information that should be part of the knowledge of every fashion professional. (Applicants can find leads for positions in these publications. Some carry help wanted ads, but even those that do not contain information about companies that can be used in a job search.) Trade publications, as well as fashion magazines, help the movement of fashion through journalistic efforts.

Sales promotion is an important part of the strategy of a business firm. How skillfully fashion marketers create and place their message influences the ability of a business to attain corporate goals. The mix of advertising, personal selling, distribution, and pricing has to be carefully balanced. How much communication is needed is a matter of the nature of the business, the product, the competition, and other business variables.

Fashion advertising and communication must be different because the product is different. The advertising of fashion is certainly one of the more fascinating areas of business communication. It takes daring to be positive and both talent and awareness to strike a solid business ground.

QUESTIONS FOR DISCUSSION

1. Why is fashion communication different from that of other types of business information?
2. Can it be said that fashion merchandising takes place in the sector of magazines and trade publications? Explain.
3. Why is the yearly advertising expenditure of the finished apparel market low compared to other industries?
4. What are the major purposes of a trade publication?
5. What is the difference between a trade publication and a fashion magazine?

15
FASHION EXPERTS

The importance of fashion in the world of the educated consumer requires that fashion and fashion-related organizations demonstrate fashion know-how. Coordinated retail fashion stocks and other products sell best when they are properly displayed or arranged so that they reflect the guiding hand of a fashion expert.

Fashion director, *fashion coordinator*, and *fashion administrator* are titles that vary with firms but have the same meaning. Outside experts are referred to as *fashion consultants*. Unlike most professionals, fashion experts' responsibilities vary and depend on individual firms' job descriptions. In some organizations a fashion expert's responsibilities can center on the selection of colors; in others they can run the gamut of arranging and participating in fashion shows to being the house expert on fashion.

Fashion, as we have seen, requires acceptance by a substantial group. Since commercial success has a quantitative value, products beyond apparel depend upon how they relate to current fashion trends. Automobiles, for example, are not sold to the general public because of gear ratios or wheelbase dimensions. Color and upholstery play an important fashion role in the successful marketing of this high-priced product. Television performers and personalities must be dressed in fashions that are appropriate to the mood and setting of programs. Fashion in marketing is hardly left to chance; what is pleasing and effective is a matter of careful calculation. A fashion expert is one who has been educated **241** about the subject, knows its history, current events, its principles or dynamics, and can make estimations of what is likely to be accepted and why.

Fashion experts are employed by firms in many fields, including:

- Advertising agencies
- Buying offices
- Public relations offices
- Photographers
- Cosmetic companies
- Fragrance companies
- Pattern companies
- Home furnishings manufacturers
- Linens and domestics producers
- Fashion manufacturers
- Fiber producers
- Fabric mills
- Retailers
- Trade associations
  - Wool Bureau
  - National Cotton Council
  - Corduroy Council
  - Fur Fashion Information Council
  - Millinery Institute
  - American Wig Association
  - National Shoe Retailers Association

The list will continue to grow because the added dimension of product/service success includes the element of being in fashion. The fashion expert is an important person and, although the position sounds romantic, like any profession it takes career preparation and a talent for creativity.

TEXTILE MARKET

The textile market produces a myriad of fabrics, but what is successful must be proper for particular styles. The fashion director must be extremely sensitive and responsive to the market; fashion apparel starts with fabric. And fabric production is not measured in days or weeks, but rather as much as a year and a half. It is the fashion director who, through intensive research, predicts forthcoming trends that necessitate certain fabrics for best performance. When the fashion of a season is a soft silhouette, the fabrics must be soft and drapable, perhaps filmy. Miscalculation means being out of trend—the cardinal sin of fashion merchandising. In the textile business, once a commitment is made, there is no recourse for that season. The fashion director's role is of great importance. It can include:

- Working with mills a year in advance to develop suitable fabrics for upcoming trends

- Working with color experts to develop a color range for a new season
- Working with designers of garments to illustrate the importance of developed fabrics
- Working with retailers (fashion coordinators and buyers) to show market importance of the firm's fabric collection
- Working with resident buying offices, fashion magazines, and other media

The range of duties can also cover:

- Line presentation at internal and external sales meetings
- Research of foreign markets
- In-store fabric shows
- Advising the firm's advertising agency for proper trend presentation in advertisements, including the proper accessories

Man-made fibers, the result of man's ingenuity, of themselves perform no function. It takes fashion expertise to make a combination of fabric, color, silhouette, and details into garments that offer consumer satisfaction. It is the fashion expert who has the sensitivity and knowledge to recognize what consumers are likely to accept.

The term *fashion expert* may sound like a description of one person who has divine power and plays the role of the final decision maker. Within the textile field and in all other areas, however, the fashion expert is a staff person, an advisor, who feeds information to line employees. A *stylist*, often a misused term, is the one who puts a line or collection into salable form, the way it will be shown to customers. The stylist eliminates extraneous, repetitive, or least-likely-to-win styles and concentrates on the ones that look best. The stylist of a manufacturer performs the same function, most commonly in concert with the designer and/or fashion director (in some cases the stylist is also the fashion director).

What a firm produces depends on management's decision: the nature of the business, the kind of merchandise, how and where it will be made, the customers to be served, and the business channels. Creating a line's styles is a designer duty. Coordinating a line's colors and styles; its proper accessorization; and its presentation to employees, customers, and the media are the fashion director's responsibilities. The fashion director researches the direction in which fashion is headed, puts the results into practical terms, and advises appropriate personnel—all important staff functions.

FASHION MANUFACTURING

The average manufacturing firm is a small business, and employees or owners often wear several hats. To say that fashion coordinators or fashion directors exist widely in this sector would be a gross exaggeration. By and large, styling for the manufacturer is a filter-down process; one of the owners or a designer simply selects what is to be made. In larger firms, the line-development responsibility is often in the hands of the stylist, who works with the designer. The stylist's other duties could include shopping the textile market as a scout for upcoming trends, visiting retail stores to review competitors' lines and give advice to store personnel, writing to the firm's salespeople to explain the importance of the line, and participating in seasonal sales meetings. In other words, the manufacturer's stylist takes on duties of a fashion director but concentrates most on the development of the line. The formal position may not even exist in many companies. Indeed, it is not rare for a showroom salesperson to be called upon to evaluate a line before it is offered to customers. Drawing on showroom experience, that person may be solicited for ideas about styling a new line and even assigned to shop the stores for possible new ideas. Smallness of firm makes for generality of duties.

Among the benefits accruing to large firms that employ a fashion expert is the trunk show, which often leads to early recognition of trends and also helps stores create departmental excitement. Another benefit is the publicity that can be generated, one that is most sought by firms whose stock is publicly traded.

RETAILING

Every type of retail operation of any important volume maintains a fashion office. The size and influence of the office varies with the organization, but the director or coordinator is a staff person who reports to the general merchandise manager as someone with an objective, researched fashion point of view.

Buyers are responsible for the selection of merchandise and "own" the budget; the fashion expert has no budget and cannot place an order. This is a fundamental distinction in the understanding of the role of the fashion advisor (or fashion coordinator or fashion director).

The position of retail fashion expert exists to ensure that the world is informed about what the organization is and stands for. This is an important task because imagery is a strong factor in influencing consumer patronage. The retailer selects merchandise for a selected audience, but the consumer builds a mental image of the store's ability to satisfy needs, and—even more—initiates the sales transaction by visiting the store to shop for a specific item. The fashion office is involved in forming organizational character through arranging and staging fashion shows; working with advertising and display to ensure presentations that are in line with consumer fashion expectations; and advising sales personnel about the fashion rightness of in-stock merchandise.

These activities amount to a communication process with consumers: directly in person at shows and indirectly through personnel, advertising, and interior and exterior displays.

A fashion office, which may consist of one or several people, is constantly engaged in updating information. Here are short descriptions of some of the main functions.

In order to formulate a view of the important trends of a new season, the market is surveyed prior to the buyers' market trip. The trends are assessed and put into concise form so they can be coordinated and passed on to the buyers. Research areas include both textiles and finished goods. Sometimes the trip will include obtaining editorial credits or tie-in promotions with magazines. The promotions can include a three-way effort: textile or fiber producer, manufacturer, and store. Naturally, trend information concerns new ideas and resources that embody them best, so the research effort often uncovers new resources, and they are given to the buyers for possible inclusion in their market trips.

One of the sensitive areas of communication in the modern retail world is between flagship store and branches, one that still needs additional channels and techniques. Information about branches, particularly fashion needs and customer attitudes, is often an important aspect of a coordinator's study.

The fashion expert in a large mail-order firm also acts in an advisory capacity, but with one significant difference. Mail-order commitments are made about one year in advance of publication, and merchandise is developed through the joint efforts of buyer and manufacturer. The stylist or fashion expert works in the market with the buyer and has strong input in helping the buyer come to style decisions. Although the responsibility is the buyer's, information is welcomed because it comes from an expert familiar with past, current, and future trends. The mail-order stylist usually comes from the merchandising ranks, having once been a buyer and therefore possessing full understanding of the relationship between inventory commitment and sales responsibility.

SUMMARY

A fashion director has considerable importance for the marketing strategy of firms in all parts of the fashion industry. A fashion director leads an organization's efforts to communicate its fashion know-how to its employees and customers. In this effort the fashion director advises personnel about trends, translates them into promotable themes, and identifies the importance of particular styles, colors, fabrics, and details so they can be highlighted for maximum selling results.

A fashion director's job often includes the responsibility to plan and supervise fashion shows and other fashion presentations. These activities require the dramatic presentation of new fashion, selection of models, organization of merchandise into proper groupings, and supervision of sundry details that make for an effective production.

A fashion expert, whether staff employee or outside consultant, helps unite fashion styles and ideas to show their importance, to make them understood by employees and customers, and most of all, to promote their salability.

QUESTIONS FOR DISCUSSION

1. What is the relationship between a retail buyer and a fashion director?
2. Why are fashion experts needed in industries that are not part of the apparel business?
3. What is the role of a fashion consultant?
4. What are the reasons for the entry of men into the profession of fashion expert?
5. What are the fashion-apparel research arenas in which a fashion administrator (director or coordinator) works? Explain.

16
CAREER OPPORTUNITIES IN FASHION COMMUNICATION

Job opportunities in the communication area of the fashion industry are many, and an applicant must examine job specifications and job descriptions. The former relate to the employee's necessary skills and training, the latter to activities and responsibilities of the jobs. Careful examination can lead to realistic understanding of both what the job entails and your qualifications for it. A frequent applicant misinterpretation is based solely on an incorrect impression gained from a job title.

This chapter discusses the "what" and the recommended "where" and "how" to research for a fashion communication entry job.

THE RESIDENT BUYING OFFICE

A resident buying office is a service organization staffed by market specialists who communicate with member stores on a constant basis. Their market activities are communicated through letters, bulletins, and special reports, by telephone and in person. Job specifications therefore include training or interest in an activity that is largely market research, analysis of facts, and the relation of them to retail clients.

A well-thought-out decision would include several considerations. A service job rarely pays as well as one directly concerned with profit-making. A buyer or salesperson, for example, is a line person who is measured and rewarded for contribution to the profit-and-loss statement of a firm. On the other hand, a service person is a staff member who has neither decision-making responsibility nor direct contribution to what a business is all about—making a profit. Hence the starting salary is modest, and the career person is paid somewhat below the scale of a store buyer. It is true, however, that some key executives of resident offices are paid on the same salary scale as executives of many other industries.

As a market specialist communicator, the resident representative must have three essential attributes: the ability to get along with people—manufacturers, clients, and employers—and to gain their respect by reason of personality and analytical ability; the skill to express researched information clearly, tersely, and correctly; enough self-restraint and poise to withstand the pressures of client demands and those of market weeks when offices are jammed with visiting store buyers who want immediate attention and are sometimes anxious to challenge the representative's information.

Resident buyer is an industry position that demands a high degree of sociability and constant interpersonal relations with people: in the morning with office personnel, salespeople, and clients; in the afternoons with manufacturers, sometimes accompanied by client store buyers; and before closing time back at the office with organization personnel and store buyers again. The job is totally people-related, and for a people-oriented person is an excellent profession.

Another benefit is the working hours, which are nine to five, with some exceptions during market weeks or when special events take place. Many buyers find the opportunity to travel in this day of the global market since resident buyers are often part of an office program that pools the orders of client stores and places them in foreign markets. The buyer is entrusted with responsibility in such arrangements by working with commissionaires and foreign producers.

The resident office offers career viability and satisfaction for those who have studied the purpose of an office and its working conditions and who have the necessary personal attributes.

The location of resident buying offices is the major markets. Since New York City and Los Angeles have the greatest number of manufacturers, offices are most numerous in these cities, with the greatest number in New York. The major offices also have branches or affiliations with other offices in other cities and countries—another job opportunity, usually a second step.

Offices can be located easily in trade books, including *Sheldon's Retail Directory* and the *Directory of Buying Offices and Accounts* published by The Salesman's Guide, 1140 Broadway, New York, NY 10001. This guide shows the address of each buying office, names of the executive personnel, the buyers and their classifications of responsibility, and the stores the office services. From this an applicant can make a qualitative analysis and determine the size of the office and the sizes and locations of the stores serviced.

Once having determined that the locale of offices is in line with your decision about where you want to live, the next step is to decide which organizations you should contact.

The next steps are familiar: the properly prepared resume and covering letter and the interviews that follow. As an interviewee you should give evidence of knowledge of the activities of an office and its importance, and your desire to be a communicator. Although interviewers vary in their predispositions and role expectancies, on the average, they seek well-dressed applicants who can articulate with conviction. Personality plays an important part in resident buying success, and one of the looked-for applicant characteristics is the ability to relate well to others.

It should be understood that in practically all cases, a trainee's first assignment after employment is that of a follow-up person or assistant buyer who checks deliveries of orders placed by stores and sometimes places orders written by or for stores. Formal training programs are rare, with training almost universally on-the-job.

MAGAZINES, TRADE PUBLICATIONS, ADVERTISING

We are in a world of instant and constant communication, and the apparel industry's message is about fashion, a response to life style. Even though current communication sometimes falls short of ideal, the effort of industry to relate is all-pervasive, and jobs in communication are numerous. However, the average applicant may be confused about how to go about getting that first job. A reasonable approach is to accept the idea that the main objective is to become a professional communicator, to be able to learn and sharpen the tools of the trade, and later specialize in a particular area. This may be seen as a compromise, but it is a pragmatic approach followed by many who have risen to the top of the profession.

The approach should therefore be broad, the goal obtaining a communicator position, regardless of type. The first step is to select a number of organizations from a variety of companies that staff writers:

- Magazines
- Trade publications
- Advertising agencies
- Resident buying offices
- Public relations firms
- Consumer magazines
- Department stores
- Newspapers
- Television stations
- Mail-order firms

Information about magazines and trade publications can be found in a library. All maintain a magazine section, although the trade publications may not be universally stocked. If they are not on hand, the alternatives are to visit a school library or file, or firms that produce or sell fashion products. General fashion magazines are available at most newsstands.

A job on a fashion magazine is rather difficult to get since it is a glamor position, the applications run into the thousands, and the number of jobs is limited. Trade publications, on the other hand, are numerous but most are not concerned with fashion (see page 231 for trade publications related to fashion).

Once the list is compiled, a resume must be prepared and mailed with an appropriate covering letter. Remember that as a communicator you will be judged on your writing ability before you can obtain an interview. The resume should be concise, factual, and applicable, and the letter should avoid the banal. A recipient is most often impressed with an approach that conveys creativity and, in this case, good communication skills. (See Appendix B.)

If you receive a favorable response you will be required to prove your writing ability, which can only be evidenced by a portfolio. The applicant who has documented all published or sample writings is in the most fortuitous position. Those who must garner past efforts at random will find the experience daunting. The portfolio should be neat, professional in appearance, and documented—names of publications, dates, and evaluations if available. School projects can be exhibited, particularly those that earned an instructor's accolade.

One of the advantages of selecting a career in advertising is that there is minimal restraint of location. Advertising is utilized in some form by most firms, and advertising agencies are located in most cities. An excellent source for information about advertising firms is the *Roster and Organization of the American Association of Advertising Agencies* (the AAAA is located at 200 Park Avenue, New York, NY 10017).

Obtaining a position with an advertising agency or on the staff of a firm that employs personnel for advertising may require a modification of your resume, particularly the career objective. You should not say, for example, that your goal is to write feature articles when applying for a place either in a firm that produces fabric or in an advertising firm. Employers seek people who have a way with words and are able to translate product and consumer research data into copy that will have an influence in motivating readers to react favorably to those messages. It may therefore be wise to have more than one set of resumes so that you can specifically target the type of firm to which you send them.

In culling a range of potential employers, the information in other chapters can be reviewed. For those who seek a job in a resident buying office as a copywriter, *Sheldon's* can be a most informative source; textile-area applicants can use *Davison's;* and as an additional example, retail stores can be located in the trade books listed previously. The initial goal is to pursue a variety of possibilities and thus open a range of opportunities.

When interviews are scheduled, in addition to putting the final touches on your portfolio, you should do some spadework about the company and learn how it operates and for whom. In addition to being able to write creatively, you should understand that the total thrust of business communication is sales promotion and includes the preparation of booklets, mailers of all kinds, signs, window displays, catalogue sheets, and salesmen's portfolios as typical promotional material. All or some of these activities are part of the commercial endeavors of firms and agencies, who employ people to create them with professional expertise.

The range of fashion or fashion-related positions is large, with one possible exception. Few advertising agencies concentrate on fashion accounts, so you must understand that being hired for a position with an agency does not assure even a future fashion-apparel relationship.

FASHION EXPERTS

There are two usual tracks to eventually becoming a fashion director or fashion consultant. One is to become a trainee; the other is to become a buyer and then specialize as a fashion expert. Which course of action is more productive is hard to say, and particular types of firms set up their own requirements. Major mail-order firms, for example, employ fashion experts to guide buyers in the choice of merchandise, and there is certainly good reason for such staff people to have a backlog of buying experience.

In any case, there are unique personal requirements that go far beyond "loving clothes." From the outset, the number of positions in a given firm are few, sometimes one, but not more on the average than three in a giant department store. And to use another case in point, how many are there in a large advertising agency? Perhaps one with an assistant or trainee. The configuration of opportunity is like a pyramid, many jobs in the line operation but perhaps two or three in the fashion office—and the demands of employment can be more rigorous than generally realized.

Certainly a fashion expert must have a certain degree of professionalism. This includes the ability to speak well, with authority, and in good English in front of small as well as large groups. Other attributes include a sense of curiosity, the ability to move quickly, and analytical ability to describe witnessed events and places, and the courage of conviction.

This is a long list of not so common characteristics, but the number of positions is also limited in any given firm. The main point is that a fashion expert is a specialist who gives advice, and advice is accepted to the degree of respect that is earned by the giver.

The list of fertile areas for possible employment is included in the preceding chapter. The best-known area is probably retailing. Where to apply is incorporated in the sources recommended for those interested in other fashion positions.

The how of obtaining a fashion-expert position is essentially the same: resume, covering letter, and interview. The uniqueness of the interview here is the role-playing and role expectancies of the players. How should an applicant look and speak? What educational background is required? What evidence can an applicant use to prove possession of skill, taste, ability, and a sense of fashion awareness?

The average candidate will bring a school record, showing involvement in fashion training, perhaps; instructor recommendations; and a statement of motivation. The evaluation is subjective. Realistically, in addition to formal college training, the applicant must have the primary requisites of being able to speak well, relate well, and give an impression of someone highly motivated to communicate fashion.

SUMMARY

Fashion communication travels through many channels: resident buying offices, fashion magazines and trade publications, advertising agencies, and fashion experts. The fashion business demands more than making styles and selling them.

The marketing system of the fashion industry, if it were likened to an automobile, would consider the line people the fuel that feeds the engine and the communicators the oil that ensures smooth running. Each needs the other; clothing without the messages to tell stores where it can be obtained, manufacturers without an education about the importance of textile developments, and consumers not educated to what is proper to wear would lead to a hit-and-miss industry of limited ability to produce and sell.

The fashion director, in the most glamorous of fashion positions, is a hard-working professional who advises in-house personnel as well as customers and other related individuals. The growth of the profession will continue. Fashion and fashion apparel have become phenomena of international interest. Effective fashion apparel selling is necessary for all retailers in order to achieve sufficient mark-up for business viability. And ironically, the newest form of broad communication, television, is still in its infancy so far as fashion use is concerned. Large-scale retailers, for example, are using closed-circuit television for in-house fashion shows as an educational tool for employees. Someday fashion retailers of every size will be using the medium in one form or another. And experts will be needed to put the show together.

QUESTIONS FOR DISCUSSION

1. Discuss the decision-making responsibilities of a fashion director of a retail organization.
2. What is the role of a stylist in an apparel manufacturing firm?
3. Resident representatives are market specialists and report on fashion trends. Why do resident buying offices employ a fashion director?
4. Explain the importance of location to job opportunities in resident buying, advertising, and retail fashion offices.
5. Assume you have job offers from both a major retail organization and a major resident buying office. In detail, explain the reasons for choosing either.

APPENDIX A

APPENDIX A

CAREER OPPORTUNITIES

Following is a summary of selected career opportunities in the three main branches of the fashion industry—textile, manufacturing, retail—and in the auxiliary fashion industries—the specialized service and advisory enterprises that play an important part in the marketing of fashion apparel. There are many other positions whose highly specialized activities elude classification but whose functions are vital to the industry.

The following includes:

1. Entry job titles; duties, specifications, attributes employers seek in candidates
2. Advanced career job titles; job descriptions

To trace the progression from entry jobs to advanced career jobs, refer to the charts of organization in the appropriate chapters.

TEXTILE INDUSTRY

Textile Industry Entry Jobs

DESIGN AREA

- Textile artist
- Colorist
- Assistant to stylist
- Embroidery designer
- Handweaver
- Silk-screen artist
- Assistant stylist

Jobs for textile design graduates may be found in textile mills, textile converting houses, textile design studios.

Personal qualities required: The personal qualities required for all listed jobs in design are similar. On jobs other than those of a strictly technical nature a high degree of creativity is a must, as well as an excellent color sense and eye for fashion trends. Other requirements include neatness, ability to follow through on a job from start to finish, ability to follow instructions, and ability to work at a fast pace. Interpersonal skills are required in those jobs involving public contact. Other requirements are specifically noted.

Skills/preparation required: For all listed jobs in design, the requirements are: excellent portfolio of textile designs, degree in Textile Design, precise drawing skills. Other requirements are specifically noted.

Textile Artist Does original textile designs; may also do color combinations and repeats.

Colorist Does various color combinations of existing designs.

Assistant to Stylist Sets up appointments for stylist, acts as a liaison with mills, works with clients and salespeople in stylist's absence, keeps clerical records.

Embroidery Designer Does detailed technical drawings on graph paper of designs for lace and embroidery; limited use of color.

Handweaver Executes designer's ideas on hand loom.

Silk-Screen Artist Executes designer's ideas through silk screen process; makes screens as well as doing the printing; may be given opportunity to create own designs.

Assistant Stylist Works with nonprint knit or fabric stylist or yarn stylist; duties include fabric analysis, color research, and possibly graphing for knits; may maintain yarn and fabric swatch books, prepare presentation boards.

Personal qualities required: Must have good color sense, be well organized, good at details.

Skills/preparation required: Textile Technology degree; excellent technical knowledge of fabric structure.

TECHNICAL/PRODUCTION AREAS

- Assistant converter/converting clerk
- Fabric technician
- Production assistant (see job description in Engineering/Production Management Area)
- Knit grapher
- Quality control trainee

Assistant Converter/Converting Clerk Assists the converter in overseeing the various processes involved in the transition of greige goods to finished fabric (all dyeing, printing, finishing processes); keeps production and inventory records; acts as liaison between mills and clients, expedites shipments and work flow, does follow-up work, has heavy phone contact, may do some costing.

Personal qualities required: Good at details and figures, well organized, good communication skills, ability to work under pressure, assertiveness.

Skills/preparation required: Textile Technology, Fashion Buying and Merchandising, or Management Engineering Technology degree; excellent math skills.

Fabric Technician Performs various lab tests on fabrics, yarns, fibers, and garments to determine durability, color fastness, shrinkage, etc.

Personal qualities required: Good at details, well organized, able to follow instructions and work alone; some writing ability for reports of findings.

Skills/preparation required: Textile Technology degree.

Knit Grapher Graphs instructions for knit fabric designs.

Personal qualities required: Analytical ability; ability to translate designer's ideas into precise instructions for factory production.

Skills/preparation required: Textile Technology degree or other degree with sufficient courses in knit technology; knowledge of knit-machine capabilities.

Quality Control Trainee Checks fiber, yarn, fabric, apparel to see that production specifications are met; identifies problems and works with production staff to correct them; may write reports based on findings.

Personal qualities required: Analytical skills, be good at details and follow-up.

Skills/preparation required: Textile Technology, Management Engineering, or Patternmaking degree, or technical school training.

ADMINISTRATION/SALES AREAS

Administration: Job titles, duties, skills, and training are the same as required by other industries.

Sales Trainees: Job opportunities are in fiber, yarn producer, and textile firms. Applicants train to sell to spinners, textile companies, and manufacturers of finished apparel (depending on firm's product). Training programs are in the form of formal classes or rotating on-the-job programs, or a combination of both. On-the-job duties include, for example: checking the details of orders placed by customers; checking delivery of orders; preparing swatch material for customers; returning samples to appropriate places in the showroom after sales presentations. After the training program, successful candidates are assigned territories (customer lists or specific areas of the industry).

Personal qualities required: Must be assertive, well-groomed, poised, mature, articulate, self-confident, competitive, self-starting, energetic, and have interpersonal skills.

Skills/preparation required: College degree, some selling experience desirable.

Textile Industry Advanced Career Jobs

Employment in advanced career jobs is obtained after industrial experience. Therefore, the information that follows is concentrated on job titles and job descriptions.

DESIGN AREA

Repeat Artist Given a **croquis** (sketch), improvises the design structure in order to put into repeat for printing purposes.

Print Designer Originates designs for use in industry.

Print Stylist Organizes and supervises studio work for maximum efficiency; works with clients and merchandising department in planning ahead for new designs; chooses patterns from other sources for future production; assumes responsibility for success of new line; often alternates between studio and print plant when new patterns are put into production.

Screen Print Designer Designs acetates; puts into repeat croquis; adjusts existing design for size and taste requirements.

Fashion Director Researches, analyzes, and advises on fashion trends; produces fashion shows; prepares and distributes fashion information to company personnel and to company customers.

Weaver Dresses loom; weaves complex samples; initiates colors and patterns; tests new fiber on hand loom.

Assistant Weaving Designer Oversees studio and work in progress; has responsibility for layouts and weavers.

Weaving Designer Designs and originates patterns and colors of sample blankets to be woven at the mill, in coordination with merchandising supervisor.

Weaving Stylist Designs the line; originates patterns; makes color decisions; works with customers and salesmen; supervises mill operations.

Freelance Designer Designs, originates, and develops designs for purchase by mills and/or independent design studios.

Studio Head Has design, management, and administrative responsibilities; designs to client's specifications and/or originates and develops designs for sale to textile firms.

Assistant Knit Designer Oversees work in progress; graphs designers ideas; maintains liaison with mills; designs original patterns.

Knit Designer Designs and originates patterns; maintains customer contacts; has total mill responsibility; plans color combinations.

Knit Stylist Styles lines; coordinates colors; advises on trends; works with customers.

Strike-off Artist Puts designs into production; changes designs if necessary to conform to capability of machinery.

TECHNICAL PRODUCTION AREA

Fixer Mechanic   Supervises junior mechanics; performs major repairs; changes equipment to new styles; establishes maintenance schedules for equipment.

Head Mechanic   Supervises mechanics; schedules mechanical work; hires and trains mechanics; advises management on purchasing new equipment.

Instructor   Instructs and trains new employees in their job functions and in general company policies.

Shift Supervisor   Supervises production employees on a shift; hires and trains new workers.

Purchasing Agent   Purchases raw material, equipment, and supplies.

ADMINISTRATION/SALES AREAS

Administration   Jobs similar to those of other industries.

Salesperson   Prospects, qualifies, and then sells and services customer needs in the sector of the market assigned by employer.

Sales Manager   Directs and controls sales personnel, including recruiting, selecting, training, allocating, motivating, compensating, and evaluating sales personnel.

MANUFACTURING INDUSTRY

Manufacturing Industry Entry Jobs

DESIGN AREA

- Assistant designer
- Cutting assistant
- Sketching assistant
- Sketcher (assistant to designer)
- Sketcher/stylist
- Junior designer

The personal qualities needed for all of the following jobs in the design area are similar. Applicants must be well-organized, flexible, fast workers with the ability to work under pressure in often cramped working conditions. Most jobs require creativity and a good eye for trends in silhouette, color, and fabric.

Assistant Designer   Executes designers' ideas by creating a first pattern from slopers or draping; instructs and supervises the work of samplehands; often keeps records, orders fabrics and trim, does follow-up, clerical work. Although job is primarily technical in nature, may be asked to shop stores for trends, sketch, possibly consult with designer about fabric choices and designs.

Personal qualities required: See above

Skills/preparation required: Fashion Design degree, good knowledge of garment construction (sewing), strong technical skills (making first patterns, draping, and sketching). Beginners must have a portfolio.

Cutting Assistant   Beginning assistant position in companies where there are several assistant designers. Cuts samples, alters patterns, generally assists in design room; may later have opportunity to assist patternmaker or do draping.

Personal qualities required: See above

Skills/preparation required: Fashion Design degree or technical school training, good patternmaking skills, some draping skills, knowledge of garment construction.

Sketching Assistant   Sketches principally for designers' records—precise technical sketches of constructed garment swatched with fabric and trim; may sketch freehand or with croquis; may sketch and prepare art work for presentations; writes specification sheets on how garments are constructed; usually orders fabric, handles a variety of clerical and follow-up duties; may do market research.

Personal qualities required: See above
Skills/preparation required: Fashion Design degree, ability to do precise technical sketches rapidly. Beginners must have a portfolio.

Sketcher (Assistant to Designer) Does freehand illustration-quality sketches of designers' ideas; may be asked to contribute own design ideas; may deal with buyers, do promotional work; runs errands; generally assists the designer. Hours are often long and irregular.

Personal qualities required: Extremely high taste level as evidenced by personal appearance and portfolio, awareness of new fashion trends both in the United States and in Europe, must be articulate, poised, and able to deal with high-level executives.
Skills/preparation required: Fashion Design degree, ability to do freehand illustration-quality sketches at a fast pace. Beginner must have portfolio.

Sketcher/Stylist Works directly with principals of firm; shops stores for current trends, sketches ideas, works with patternmaker in developing these ideas (may not do technical work of draping and patternmaking); participates in fabric selection, coordination of the line; may work with buyers in merchandising the line.

Personal qualities required: See above
Skills/preparation required: Fashion Design degree, portfolio, good eye for trends in silhouette, color, and fabric.

Junior Designer Sketches original designs, executes own first pattern, frequently sews sample; does market research in fabrics and trends; provides new design ideas and makes accurate predictions on what will be salable in coming season; designs garments within company's price range. Job is fast-paced and a high-risk position since continuation of employment may be based on success of line.

Personal qualities required: See above.
Skills/preparation required: Fashion Design degree, strong creative ability, excellent technical skills (draping, patternmaking, sewing), good eye for trends (silhouette, color, fabric). Portfolio must show evidence of strong creative ability in designing coordinated line of apparel.

PATTERNMAKING AREA

- Assistant patternmaker
- Cutting assistant
- Grader trainee
- Marker trainee

Personal qualities required All jobs in the patternmaking area demand the ability to work in a fast-paced environment under pressure as well as extreme neatness, accuracy, and precision.

Assistant Patternmaker Works under supervision of production patternmaker; assists in making perfect patterns; often assists in cutting, grading, and marking.

Skills/preparation required: Patternmaking Technology degree or completion of a substantial number of technical courses.

Cutting Assistant Cuts samples and duplicates by hand or machine; alters and balances patterns; may work under designer or patternmaker.

Skills/preparation required: Patternmaking Technology degree or completion of sufficient number of technical courses.

Grader Trainee Prepares production patterns in various size ranges. (May be combined with job of marker; see description below.)

Skills/preparation required: Patternmaking degree or completion of most technical courses and *all* grading courses.

Marker Trainee Works under production patternmaker; lays out production patterns onto fabric for maximum use of goods.

Skills/preparation required: Patternmaking degree or completion of most technical courses, good knowledge of fabrics.

ENGINEERING/PRODUCTION MANAGEMENT AREA

- Junior engineer
- Costing engineer
- Assistant plant manager
- Production assistant/assistant to production manager
- Quality control engineer

Graduates of a Management Engineering Technology program work in apparel manufacturing plants or offices. Those who wish to work in apparel plants should be aware that factories are widely spread geographically. Most businesses have multi-plant operations, and promotion frequently means relocation or traveling. The opportunities for a high-paying career in this field are greatly enhanced if applicants have geographic mobility.

Junior Engineer Sets piece rates; does plant layout time and motion studies; is involved in methods engineering projects.

Personal qualities required: Mature, well organized, good at details and follow through, strong analytical and math skills.

Skills/preparation required: Management Engineering Technology degree or completion of all major related courses; for nongraduates, significant work experience in the field.

Costing Engineer Determines costs of manufacturing apparel, taking into account such factors as piece rates, material costs, and all other production considerations; may travel to plants to explain production procedures.

Personal qualities required: Well organized, good at details and follow through, have good math skills.

Skills/preparation required: Strong analytical and math skills, Management Engineering Technology degree or completion of all major related courses; for nongraduates, significant work experience in the field.

Assistant Plant Manager Assists in staffing plant; assigns work loads; assists in supervising various plant operations, including cutting, pressing, warehousing, shipping, etc.

Personal qualities required: Self-starting; strong interpersonal, supervisory, and organizational skills; sense of priorities, high work-pressure tolerance, high energy level.

Skills/preparation required: Management Engineering Technology degree preferred.

Production Assistant Assists production manager in keeping records relating to production of merchandise—sales records, cutting records, inventory control, shipping records; keeps clients informed on progress of orders; expedites work flow and deliveries; is involved in heavy phone contact, details, and figure work.

Personal qualities required: Mathematical and organizational ability, accuracy, assertiveness, thoroughness, high stress tolerance, neat handwriting, ability to communicate well over the telephone.

Skills/preparation required: Management Engineering Technology or Merchandising degree preferred; prior work experience with a manufacturer may be substituted.

Quality Control Engineer Develops specifications for garments and fabrics; checks to see that specifications are being adhered to in fabric shipments and manufacturing processes; frequently must travel.

Personal qualities required: Detail-oriented, well organized, good at follow through, able to work under pressure and maintain high energy level.

Skills/preparation required: Excellent knowledge of garment construction and fabric technology; Management Engineering Technology, Patternmaking, or Textile Technology degree preferred.

ADMINISTRATION/SALES AREAS

Administration See Textile Industry Entry Jobs

Showroom Trainee Involves diversified duties depending on size and nature of the company. Job can include any or all of the following duties: reception; answering phones;

dealing with buyers on the phone and in person; writing up orders; follow-up work; filing; keeping records; learning to show and sell the line to clients; occasional modeling of garments. Can lead to showroom sales, merchandising, production, or piece-goods buying.

Personal qualities required: Excellent appearance and grooming, strong fashion sense, outgoing personality, poise; must be articulate, quick-thinking, socially at ease, and self-confident.

Skills/preparation required: Degree preferred but not always necessary; previous sales experience beneficial, course in salesmanship helpful.

Road Sales Trainee   Same duties as those that are described for showroom sales.

Personal qualities required: The same as those of Showroom Trainee but with the ability to be self-reliant, be able to cope with the demands of traveling alone and acting as an independent agent (working on commission).

Skills/Preparation Required: Same as Showroom Trainee.

Manufacturing Industry Advanced Career Jobs

DESIGN AREA

Embroidery Designer   Sketches ideas for embroidery or appliqué designs.
Sketcher   Sketches samples for production and showroom use; sketches samples for record-keeping purposes.
Designer   Creates new collection of garments every season; sketches ideas, selects fabric and trimmings; supervises the construction of first samples; often works with buyers and travels to stores across the country to promote sales; travels abroad for ideas.
Stylist   Puts the designer's styles into collection or line form, the way it will be shown to customers; suggests ideas or styles as part of new line.
Sample Maker (D)   Sews the first sample in fabric; works directly with the designer or assistant designer.

PATTERNMAKING AREA

Marker maker (P)   Makes a production cutting layout of all the paper pattern pieces for a style in an entire size range.
Duplicate Maker   Sews a duplicate of the first sample, conforming to standard sizes after patternmaker has made the stock pattern; tests stock pattern for production purposes.
Grader   Proportionately expands and contracts the perfected sample-sized stock pattern into patterns for an entire size range.
Patternmaker   Develops a perfect garment from the first sample; may have to adjust proportions to fit stock sizes without changing style of garment; sometimes works from a sketch.

ENGINEERING/PRODUCTION MANAGEMENT AREA

Quality Controller   Inspects product during various stages of production to ascertain conformance with specifications; when irregularities are found, notifies appropriate supervisor or foreman or returns to operator for correction.
Production Supervisor   Coordinates all production activities of subordinate personnel; determines how job will be performed; trains workers and oversees performance.
Instructor Trainee   Indoctrinates and trains new workers; retrains experienced workers; oversees job performance.
Plant Manager   Supervises all operations of the mill.
Piece-Goods Buyer   Purchases all piece goods, trims, and notions.

ADMINISTRATION/SALES

Administration   Jobs similar to those of other industries.

Inside Salesperson   Waits on trade in the showroom.

Local Area Salesperson   Calls on prospective customers in the local area of the showroom. In New York, calls on stores, chains, and resident buying offices.

Road Salesperson   Essentially a sales agent, with the basis of earning a commission against goods delivered* by the firm; travels to stores within an assigned territory about 39 weeks a year.

RETAIL INDUSTRY

Retail Industry Entry Jobs

MERCHANDISING

- Executive trainee
- Assistant to fashion director (chain or specialty store)
- Assistant buyer (small or moderate-sized specialty store)
- Distributor/planner trainee (chain store)

Entry positions in merchandising vary with the type of organizations. The major department stores and large-scale chains offer one entry position—executive trainee. Upon completion of the training program, trainees are placed in various progressive assignments in merchandising and/or management. Major department-store jobs in merchandising and management require long hours which include nights and weekends.

Personal qualities required: Maturity, high energy level, flexibility, decisiveness, initiative and leadership ability, stress tolerance, risk-taking ability, and self-confidence; excellent fashion sense; must be goal-oriented, self-starting.

Skills/preparation required: Associate or bachelor's college degree (Some organizations require a four-year degree); good retail math skills.

Executive Trainee   Receives temporary assignments in various departments of all major divisions; attends part-time formal classes (major department stores) from 6 to 10 weeks.

Assistant to Fashion Director   Helps coordinate fashion shows; researches fashion; collects and cuts fabric swatches.

Assistant Buyer: Aids the buyer in his/her duties and takes charge of department in buyer's absence.

Distributor/Planner Trainee   Allocates merchandise to various branches; works with computer printouts and unit control records; has frequent contact with buyers, merchandise managers, and store personnel. This is an office job found in large central buying offices. Advancement can lead to position as head distributor/planner, controller, or buyer.

The particular personal qualities required for this job are the ability to communicate well both in person and on the phone, good memory, decisiveness, thoroughness.

Retail Industry Advanced Career Jobs

MERCHANDISING

Assistant Buyer   Aids the buyer in most duties and takes charge of department in the buyer's absence; writes orders for basic stock with buyer's approval; checks merchandise as it is delivered from receiving department; provides buyer with information about sales and stock.

Associate Buyer   Same as an assistant buyer with the added responsibility of buying, with its accompanying activities, for a classification of merchandise rather than an entire department.

*known as *net delivered goods:* total cost value of shipment less trade discount(s) and goods returned by customers

Buyer   Anticipates wants; selects merchandise; determines sources of supply and time of purchase; budgets quantities, prices merchandise; buys goods at a price which permits a profit; participates in selling; plans sales promotion activities; works with merchandise manager and fashion coordinator to maintain fashion image of store; cooperates with personnel in operations and controls to maximize profit; trains subordinates; provides information for sales personnel at main store and branches.
Special Note: A department-store buyer is a complete merchant who plans, buys, and sells. A central office (i.e., chain-store central office) buyer is a market specialist whose main function is to *select* merchandise.
Divisional Merchandise Manager   Controls the activities of several buyers; coordinates efforts to maintain store image and maximize profit.
General Merchandise Manager   Coordinates and supervises all planning, buying, and selling activities of the entire organization; interprets and executes the policies of management; advises and supervises divisional merchandise managers and buyers.

STAFF AND RELATED

Fashion Director   Researches, analyzes, and advises on fashion trends; produces fashion shows; prepares and distributes fashion information to company personnel.
Comparison Office Manager   Supervises the activities of the shoppers who check the competing stores; participates in sales promotion by checking responses to the advertising of competing stores.
Copywriter   Creates the text, headlines, and slogans of ads.
Advertising Manager   Directs a company's advertising program by setting policies concerning type of advertising, amount of advertising budget; supervises preparation of promotional material.
Display Manager   Plans and directs the execution of window and interior displays.
Section Manager, Service Manager   In retail stores, maintains satisfactory standards of customer service throughout an assigned part of store; supervises sales personnel; handles emergencies arising in selling areas.
Floor Superintendent   Supervises a group of section managers within a selling area.

SELECTED CONTROL/OPERATIONS/MANAGEMENT JOBS

Receiving Manager   Supervises the receipt of merchandise, its marking, and its distribution to store departments.
Maintenance   Is responsible for keeping the building plant in operating order.
Warehouse Manager   Controls receipt of merchandise from producers and its delivery to customers (usually big-ticket items—appliances and furniture).
Credit Manager   Supervises the extension of credit facilities to store customers and the collection of accounts receivable against charge customers.
Store Controller   Supervises all figure work and expense control throughout the store.
Store Manager   Top executive of a store unit of a chain or a branch of a department store.

AUXILIARY FASHION INDUSTRIES

Entry Jobs in the Auxiliary Fashion Industries
- Resident buying
- Advertising
- Communications
- Fashion magazines

RESIDENT BUYING OFFICE

Assistant Buyer Trainee   Assists buyer in all duties, accompanying the buyer to manufacturers to shop the market, placing orders and re-orders for merchandise, following up on shipments, keeping accurate clerical records, maintaining phone and personal contact with manufacturers and stores. Training is on-the-job and advancement can ultimately lead to position as buyer or market representative. This job is found in central and resident buying offices.

Personal qualities required: Good memory, good handwriting, outgoing personality, fashionable appearance, physical stamina, good communication and interpersonal skill.

Skills/preparation required: College degree (associate or bachelor's); ability to work with figures and deal firmly with suppliers; previous work experience either in a retail store or of a clerical nature.

Assistant Fashion Director   See Retail Industry-Entry Jobs

Assistant Copywriter   See Advertising and Related Areas Entry Jobs: Junior Copywriter

ADVERTISING DESIGN

- Paste-up and mechanical artist
- Layout artist
- Assistant art director

Jobs for design candidates can be in either advertising or graphic design.

Advertising artists may work on trade or consumer accounts in advertising agencies, in-house advertising departments, or printing firms. They may work in print (magazine or newspaper) or television advertising.

Graphic designers develop "collateral material" which may consist of brochures, annual reports, packaging, logos and trademarks, corporate image projects, and the like. They may also work in publishing, doing editorial layout for books and magazines.

Boardpersons prepare the finished art for the printer. They may work in either advertising or graphic design.

Paste-up and Mechanical Artist   Prepares art for printer by pasting together elements of layout (type, illustration, photography); does color separations using T-square and ruling pen. May work for advertising agency, graphic design studio, service studio, printer, publication, or in-house corporate art department.

Personal qualities required: Ability to work quickly under pressure and meet deadlines; neatness, accuracy, precision, thoroughness, ability to follow instructions, care for details.

Skills/preparation required: Advertising Design or Illustration degree, course in paste-ups and mechanicals, portfolio demonstrating precision and accuracy in executing mechanicals and color separations.

Layout Artist   Designs layout for ads, usually under the supervision of the art director; specifies type face, does "comp" (comprehensive) rendering to indicate what finished ad will look like when printed; may do own mechanicals.

Personal qualities required: Ability to work quickly under pressure, meet deadlines, take direction and criticism.

Skills/preparation required: Design degree, portfolio demonstrating advertising layouts, thorough knowledge of type faces, skill at "comp" rendering and mechanicals.

Assistant Art Director   Works directly with art director. May perform any or all of the following duties, depending on the size and structure of the agency or firm: assist in developing concepts for advertising campaigns, rough and finished "comp" renderings, specifying type, mechanicals, paste-ups, layout, graphic design.

Personal qualities required: Poise, self-confidence, persuasiveness, thoroughness, ability to take criticism and direction, ability to communicate ideas.

Skills/preparation required: Advertising Design degree, strong portfolio indicating thorough development of creative concepts through fast, crisp, "comp" renderings.

Alternate Entry Jobs for Advertising Industry Candidates   Because of the highly competitive nature of most of the above jobs, candidates sometimes begin their careers by accepting such non-art positions in the field as guy/gal friday, advertising assistant, or advertising production/traffic assistant.

ADVERTISING AND RELATED AREAS

- Junior copywriter
- Public relations assistant/publicity assistant/special events assistant
- Editorial assistant/editorial trainee
- Media buyer trainee/media sales trainee

Junior Copywriter   Found in advertising agencies and in-house corporate advertising departments, this job is an entry-level position in copy-writing. Employee writes copy immediately, starting with small assignments; may also have some clerical duties.

Personal qualities required: Creativity, maturity, ability to translate ideas into words fluently, ability to work quickly and under pressure of deadlines.

Skills/preparation required: College degree (associate or bachelor's), excellent grades, good typing skills, excellent portfolio of copy including completed advertising campaigns. Portfolio must be approved by departmental advisor.

Public Relations Assistant/Publicity Assistant/Special Events Assistant   This job is found in public relations agencies and in-house publicity and special events departments. Involves answering phones, scheduling appointments, typing, clerical duties; very often making coffee, running errands, etc.; may include writing press releases, working on trade shows, and assisting in planning presentations, campaigns, and special events.

Personal qualities required: Maturity, poise, creativity, flexibility, excellent grooming and fashion sense, strong interpersonal skills, good speaking voice, responsiveness to clients' needs, ability to think quickly and work under constant pressure of deadlines, high degree of initiative; must be articulate.

Skills/preparation required: College degree (associate or bachelor's), good typing, strong creative writing skills evidenced in portfolio of publicity campaigns. Portfolio must be approved by departmental advisor.

Editorial Assistant/Editorial Trainee   These jobs are found in trade and consumer publications. Involves clerical and/or secretarial duties; may include working with photographers and models, writing editorial copy, researching the market for trends and news items.

Personal qualities required: Maturity, poise, flexibility, thoroughness, excellent grooming and fashion sense, ability to work under constant pressure of deadlines, ability to spot trends and identify resources, must be articulate.

Skills/preparation required: College degree (associate or bachelor's), portfolio approved by departmental advisor, good typing.

Media Buyer Trainee/Media Sales Trainee   These jobs are found in advertising agencies, marketing firms, publications, television and radio stations. Works at clerical or secretarial duties, working as an assistant to the media buying or sales staff; may answer phones, make appointments, contact clients, type contracts, etc.; may be trained either to sell or to buy print space or broadcast time.

Personal qualities required: Self-confidence, self-motivation, outgoing personality, strong interpersonal skills, good telephone manner, business sense, high stress tolerance, mathematical and organizational ability, orientation to detail.

Skills/preparation required: College degree (associate or bachelor's), good typing.

Alternate Advertising and Communications Entry Jobs   Because of the highly competitive nature of the advertising and communication field, some graduates accept such entry-level jobs as advertising production assistants, secretaries or guy/gal fridays in the advertising and communications field. Progress to the jobs described above depends on the candidate's qualifications and performance.

ILLUSTRATION AND RELATED

- Freelance illustrator
- Staff illustrator
- Photo stylist trainee or assistant photo stylist

Freelance Illustrator Jobs in illustration tend to be freelance rather than full-time. Freelance illustrators may work for advertising agencies, retail stores, manufacturers, textile and fiber houses, pattern companies, display houses and publications.

Personal qualities required: Ability to work rapidly under pressure of deadlines, good follow-through, creativity, aggressiveness, self-motivation.

Skills/preparation required: Illustration degree, excellent portfolio indicating distinctive illustration style and creativity; should be well organized and have ability to run own freelance business (negotiating contracts, setting rates, billing, keeping own records).

Staff Illustrator Staff illustrators may work for buying offices, retail stores, pattern companies, and some publications.

Personal qualities required: Ability to work rapidly under pressure of deadlines.

Skills/preparation required: Degree with emphasis on illustration, excellent portfolio.

Photo Stylist Trainee or Assistant Photo Stylist Job exists in photography studios and advertising agencies. While many of the jobs are freelance assignments, there are some staff photo stylists. Duties include booking models, accessorizing clothing, obtaining props, pinning up hems, ironing garments, running errands, picking up and returning merchandise. Long hours required during heavy work periods.

Personal qualities required: Enthusiasm, stamina, flexibility, resourcefulness, high stress tolerance, strong sense of style and color.

Skills/preparation required: Merchandising, Photography or Fashion Design degree; fashion coordination course helpful.

Advanced Career Jobs in the Auxiliary Fashion Industries

RESIDENT BUYING OFFICE

Representative (Buyer) Researches, buys with store buyer permission, and helps to promote goods; "eyes" and "ears" in the market of store buyers.

Divisional Merchandise Manager Controls the activities of several representatives (buyers) so that market information serves member stores best.

General Merchandise Manager Coordinates and supervises the activities of the line organization, representatives and D.M.M.s and ensures merchandising direction that serves clients best.

Art Director Supervises copywriters and artists involved in producing merchandise bulletins and reports.

ADVERTISING/COMMUNICATION/FASHION MAGAZINES

Graphic Artist Creates effective visual presentations of selected promotional themes; may design advertisements, posters, displays, etc.

Art Director Coordinates and supervises art work of promotional material.

Copywriter Creates the text of promotional messages.

Scriptwriter Develops the narration of a promotional event (fashion show, audiovisual presentation, etc.).

Fashion Editor Selects the fashion themes of a magazine as well as the supporting artwork, layout, and text.

Account Executive Advertising agency liaison between agency and client; works with agencies' creative personnel to develop promotional material.

Publicity Coordinator Creates messages, publicity, for dissemination in public media; published messages are free, considered as news.

APPENDIX B

APPENDIX B

APPLYING FOR A JOB: THE RESUME AND APPLICATION LETTER

One of the most critical steps of a job search is the submission of a well-prepared resume (also called a curriculum vitae or a vita), accompanied by a letter of application. The resume is a summary of an applicant's attributes and personal data. The individualized letter of application transmits the resume. To make the best possible impression, both should be typed on 8½-by-11-inch white paper, follow standard forms, and be correct in all details.

The following are brief suggestions. For more information, see the "Careers in Fashion" section of the Bibliography.

Since an employer is likely to receive many applications for a particular job or for entry into a training program, yours must be clear, correct, attention-getting. Your resume and letter are the means to an interview and the possibility of a job offer.

Here are some general suggestions for a resume:

1. Focus the resume on what employers want to know: your abilities, accomplishments, skills, education, other qualifications
2. Pre-research the needs of potential employers; visit their places of business when practical
3. Emphasize the benefits you can bring to an employer
4. Use action verbs such as "bought," "sold," "managed," "maintained"
5. Do not include a photograph of yourself and do not mention salary requirements

The following is a good example of a resume:

Mary Farrow
1950 Garden Place
Berwick, Illinois 61417

Home telephone: (309) 547-4754

CAREER ASPIRATIONS

Entry position: executive training program
Career: merchandising executive

PERSONAL INFORMATION

Birth date: September 26, 1961
Marital status: single   Dependents: none
Height: 5'3"   Weight: 112 lbs.
Health: excellent
Physical handicaps: none

EDUCATIONAL BACKGROUND

B.S., Northwestern University, June, 1983
  Major: Marketing
  Related studies: Mathematics (20 credits)
                   Advertising (20 credits)
                   English (18 credits)
                   Computer Science (6 credits)
Special abilities: speak, read, and write Spanish; type (60 words per minute);
                   write well (staff writer, *Northwestern Wildcat*, weekly university
                   periodical)

WORK EXPERIENCE

1981–present: part-time employment (full-time in summer)
  Marshall Field (Evanston Branch)
  Duties: Sell, manage sales floor, maintain department records

1980–1981: part-time employment
  The Casual Shop, Evanston, Illinois (men's and women's specialty store)
  Duties: Ticketed incoming merchandise, sold, managed store evening hours

1979–1980: part-time employment
  Smith, Greene & Barrow, CPAs, Evanston, Illinois
  Duties: Typed reports

1977–1980: summer employment
  The Wigwam, Berwick, Illinois (children's day camp)
  Duties: Arts and crafts counselor

REFERENCES

Dr. Clarence Mosely, Dean
School of Business
Northwestern University
Evanston, Illinois 60200

Professor Lawrence Belk
School of Business
Northwestern University
Evanston, Illinois 60200

Ms. Adele Forbes, Buyer
Women's Sportswear
Marshall Field
State Street
Chicago, Illinois 60600

Mr. John Campbell, Store Manager
Marshall Field
Fairfax Street
Evanston, Illinois 60200

Mr. Ralph Cherry, Owner
The Casual Shop
Park Place
Evanston, Illinois 60200

Note: Some personnel directors recommend that references be omitted, believing that they are of no value in influencing initial employer interest. Thus you should make your own decision about including them, depending on circumstances. When references are omitted, "References available on request" is usually typed at the end of the resume.
Here are some suggestions for a letter of application:

1. Be brief and to the point
2. State the purpose of the letter at the beginning
3. Assume a confident but polite tone
4. Be moderate; use moderate statements
5. Proofread to be sure grammar and spelling are correct
6. Be accurate in all details, particularly the name and title of the addressee and the name, address, and zip code of the firm

The following is a good example of a letter of application. It was sent with the resume above to major department stores in Los Angeles.

1950 Garden Place
Berwick, Illinois 61417

April 15, 1983

Mr. John Baker, Personnel Director
J. W. Robinson Company
Broadway and 7th Street
Los Angeles, California 90102

Dear Mr. Baker:

Please consider my application for your executive training program starting in September. I am enclosing a resume.

You will notice that I have already had retail experience.

The University placement office has a transcript of my record and letters of recommendation. If you wish, I will have copies forwarded to you.

My family and I are relocating permanently in California, with residence probably in the Encino area. We will be in California from June 15 to July 5. I will be available for a personal interview at any time during that period that is convenient for you.

My interest in retailing started when I was in high school. Now after four years of retail experience and college training in marketing, I can assure you of my genuine interest in pursuing the goal of becoming a retail executive.

Sincerely yours,

Mary Farrow

Mary Farrow

Additional Guidelines for a Resume and Application Letter

1. A resume consists of four parts: personal information, educational background, work experience, references. The order of the first three can be varied according to specific circumstances, but references (when included) are always placed at the end.

2. Work experience is usually listed beginning with the present or most recent employment and continuing in reverse chronological order.

3. Resumes and other business communications should be typed on 8½-by-11-inch white bond paper. A resume may be photocopied or printed, but each letter of application should be typed individually, with individualized wording when appropriate.

4. Some title should be used before the addressee's name in both inside address and salutation: Ms. Mary Brown, Personnel Director (address); Dear Ms. Brown.

5. When a letter is not addressed to a known person (for example, when replying to a box number), salutations like "Gentlemen" or "Dear Sir" were commonly used in the past. It is now considered more appropriate to use "To whom it may concern:" as a salutation to unknown people of both sexes.

6. The sender's address is not typed on stationery that already has a business or home address printed on it.

7. Even though "Street," "Avenue," etc., and the names of states are usually spelled out, abbreviations may be used, depending on the formality of the correspondence. The Postal Service's two-letter state abbreviations are increasingly used and accepted in all kinds of correspondence; both letters are capitalized and no periods are used between or after them (NY, PA, FL, TX, CA).

8. Letters should always be signed, even though the name is typed for purposes of clarity.

9. Type neatly and fold letter and resume straight in thirds. Use a business-size envelope.

10. Before mailing, make sure the resume and letter serve two purposes: the immediate purpose of getting an interview and the ultimate purpose of getting a job.

BIBLIOGRAPHY

BIBLIOGRAPHY

DYNAMICS OF FASHION

Allen, Edward L. *The Cotton Textile Industry*. New York: Holt, 1952.

American Textile Manufacturers Institute. *All About Textiles*. Charlotte, NC: the Institute, 1978.

American Textile Manufacturers Institute. *Textiles from Start to Finish*. Charlotte, NC: the Institute, 1978.

American Wool Council. *Fleece to Fabric*. New York: the Council, 1977.

Boucher, François. *20,000 Years of Fashion*. New York: Abrams, 1967.

Burke, John. *Advertising in the Marketplace*, 2nd ed. New York: McGraw-Hill, 1980.

Buskirk, Richard H. *Principles of Marketing*, 4th ed. Hinsdale, IL: Dryden, 1975.

Cobrin, Harry. *Men's Clothing Industry: Colonial Through Modern Times*. New York: Fairchild, 1970.

Collier, Ann M. *A Handbook of Textiles*. New York: Pergamon, 1970.

Contini, Mila. *Fashion: From Ancient Egypt to the Present Day*. New York: Odyssey, 1965.

Cooper, Grace Rogers. *The Sewing Machine: Its Invention and Development*. Washington: Smithsonian Institution, 1976.

Cummings, James. *Making Fashion and Textile Publicity Work*. New York: Fairchild, 1972.

D'Assailly, Gisèle. *Ages of Elegance: Five Thousand Years of Fashion and Frivolity*. London: MacDonald, 1968.

Daves, Jessica. *Ready-Made Miracle*. New York: Putnam, 1967.

Drew-Bea, Robert. *Mass Merchandising*. New York: Fairchild, 1970.

Dunn, S. Watson, and Arnold M. Barban. *Advertising: Its Role in Modern Marketing*, 3rd ed. Hinsdale, IL: Dryden, 1974.

Fayerweather, John. *International Marketing*, 2nd ed. Englewood Cliffs, NJ: Prentice-Hall, 1970.

Ferry, J. W. *History of the Department Store*. New York: Macmillan, 1960.

Frings, Gini Stephens. *Fashion: From Concept to Consumer*. Englewood Cliffs, NJ: Prentice-Hall, 1982.

Gorman, Walter. *Selling: Personality Persuasion Strategy*. New York: Random House, 1979.

274

Grace, Evelyn. *Introduction to Fashion Merchandising.* Englewood Cliffs, NJ: Prentice-Hall, 1978.

Greenwood, Kathryn Moore, and Mary Fox Murphy. *Fashion Innovation and Marketing.* New York: Macmillan, 1978.

Hill, Margot H., and Peter Bucknell. *The Evolution of Fashion.* New York: Reinhold, 1968.

Horn, Marilyn J. *The Second Skin.* Boston: Houghton Mifflin, 1968.

Jarnow, Jeannette A., Beatrice Judelle, and Miriam Guerreiro. *Inside the Fashion Business,* 3rd ed. New York: Wiley, 1981.

Kahler, Ruel, and Roland L. Kramer. *International Marketing.* Cincinnati: Southwestern, 1977.

Kelly, Katie. *The Wonderful World of Women's Wear Daily.* New York: Saturday Review, 1972.

Kenneally, James. *Women and Trade Unions.* St. Albans, VT: Eden Press Women's Publishers, 1981.

Kidwell, Claudia B., and Margaret C. Christman. *Suiting Everyone.* Washington: Smithsonian Institution, 1974.

Laver, James. *The Concise History of Costume and Fashion.* New York: Abrams, 1969.

Ley, Sandra. *Fashion for Everyone: The Story of Ready-to-Wear.* New York: Scribner, 1975.

Newman, Thelma R. *Leather as Art and Craft.* New York: Crown, 1973.

Packard, Sidney, and Abraham Raine. *Consumer Behavior and Fashion Marketing.* Dubuque, IA: William C. Brown, 1978.

Packard, Sidney, Arthur A. Winters, and Nathan Axelrod. *Fashion Buying and Merchandising.* New York: Fairchild, 1976.

Pickle, Hal B., and Royce L. Abrahamson. *Introduction to Business,* 2nd ed. Santa Monica, CA: Goodyear, 1974.

Poole, Michael. *Theories of Trade Unionism: A Sociology of Industrial Relations.* Boston: Routledge and Kegan Paul, 1981.

Richards, Florence. *The Ready-to-Wear Industry.* New York: Fairchild, 1951.

Robinson, P. O., and Norris B. Brisco. *Store Organization and Operation.* Englewood Cliffs, NJ: Prentice-Hall, 1949.

Rosenbloom, Bert. *Retail Marketing.* New York: Random House, 1981.

Roshko, Bernard. *The Rag Race.* New York: Funk & Wagnall, 1962.

Rubin, Leonard G. *The World of Fashion.* New York: Harper & Row, 1976.

Sampson, Harland E. *Advertising and Displaying Merchandise.* Cincinnati: Southwestern, 1967.

Seidel, Leon E. *Applied Textile Marketing.* Atlanta: W. R. C. Smith, 1971.

75 Years of Men's Wear Fashion. New York: Fairchild, 1965.

Shaffer, Vesta. "The Evolution of the Modern Resident Buying Office," *New York Retailer,* April, 1962.

Troxell, Mary D., and Elaine Stone. *Fashion Merchandising.* New York: Gregg Division, McGraw-Hill, 1981.

Walton, Frank L. *Tomahawks to Textiles.* New York: Appleton-Century-Crofts, 1953.

Walton, Perry. *The Story of Textiles.* New York: Tudor, 1937.

Watkins, Josephine. *Development of the Fashion Industry.* New York: Fashion Institute of Technology, 1977.

Wilcox, Donald J., and James Scott Manning. *Leather.* Chicago: Regnery, 1972.

Will, R. Ted, and Ronald W. Hasty. *Retailing,* 2nd ed. New York: Harper & Row, 1977.

Wilson, Ruth Ann. *Selling Men's Fashions.* New York: Fairchild, 1976.

Wingate, John W., and Joseph S. Friedlander. *The Management of Retail Buying.* Englewood Cliffs, NJ: Prentice-Hall, 1978.

Winters, Arthur A., and Stanley Goodman. *Fashion Advertising and Promotion,* 5th ed. New York: Fairchild, 1980.

CAREERS IN FASHION

Betancourt, Hal. *Advertising Basics*. New York: Condor, 1978.

Business Practices in Photography. New York: ASMP (Society of Photographers in Communications), 1973.

Cassiday, Doris, and Bruce Cassiday. *Fashion Industry Careers*. New York: Franklin Watts, 1977.

Changing Times Education Service. *Advertising Copy Writer/Real People at Work*. Cleveland: Educational Research Council of America, 1977.

Cochrane, Diane. *This Business of Art*. New York: Watson-Guptill, 1978.

Dean, Harvey R. *Manufacturing: Industry and Careers*. Englewood Cliffs, NJ: Prentice-Hall, 1976.

Dolber, Roslyn. *Opportunities in Fashion*. Skokie, IL: VGM Career Horizons, 1980.

Feingold, S. Norman, and Sol Swerdloff. *Occupations and Careers*. New York: Webster Division, McGraw-Hill, 1969.

Figler, Howard. *The Complete Job Search Handbook*. New York: Holt, Rinehart and Winston, 1979.

Folse, Nancy McCarthy, and Marilyn Henrion. *Careers in the Fashion Industry*. New York: Harper & Row, 1981.

Goodale, James G. *The Fine Art of Interviewing*. Englewood Cliffs, NJ: Prentice-Hall, 1981.

Groome, Harry C., Jr. *Opportunities in Advertising Careers*. Louisville: Vocational Guidance Manuals, 1976.

Haas, Kenneth B. *Opportunities in Sales and Marketing Careers*. Louisville, KY: Vocational Guidance Manuals (VGM), 1976.

Have You Considered Industrial Management? Opportunities for Women Are Expanding. New York: Catalyst, 1976.

Have You Considered Retail Management? Opportunities for Women Are Expanding. New York: Catalyst, 1976.

Have You Considered Sales? Opportunities for Women Are Expanding. New York: Catalyst, 1976.

Hawkins, James E. *The Uncle Sam Connection: An Insider's Guide to Federal Employment*, rev. ed. Chicago: Follett, 1978.

Holbert, Neil. *Careers in Marketing*. Chicago: American Marketing Association, 1976.

Hopke, William E., ed. *The Encyclopedia of Careers and Vocational Guidance*, 4th ed. Chicago: J. G. Ferguson/Doubleday, 1978. Vol 1: *Planning Your Career*. Vol. 2: *Careers and Occupations*.

Howe, Louise Kapp. *Pink Collar Workers: Inside the World of Women's Work*. New York: Avon, 1978.

Jabenis, Elaine. *The Fashion Director: What She Does and How to Be One*. New York: Wiley, 1972.

Jackson, Tom. *The Perfect Resume*. Garden City, NY: Doubleday, 1981.

Keppler, Victor. *Your Future in Photography*, 2nd ed. New York: Arco, 1977.

Krem, Viju. *How to Become a Successful Model*, 2nd ed. New York: Arco, 1978.

Lulow, Jo Ann. *Your Career in the Fashion Industry*. New York: Arco, 1979.

Manpower Research Associates. *Arco Handbook of Job and Career Opportunities*. New York: Arco, 1978.

Merrill, Martha, ed. *The Directory of Special Opportunities for Women*. Garrett Park, MD: Garrett Park Press, 1981.

National Research Council. *Work, Jobs, and Occupations*. Washington: National Academy Press, 1981.

New Jersey State Department of Education. *The Manufacturing Cluster, Exploring Manufacturing Occupations, Student's Manual*. Washington: U.S. Government Printing Office, 1975. Vol. 1 of 4.

School of Visual Arts. *Careers in the Visual Arts*, rev. ed. New York: Visual Arts, 1978.

Servian, Martha S. *Fashion and Textiles Careers*. Englewood Cliffs, NJ: Prentice-Hall, 1977.

Sherman, Jerry, and Eric Hertz. *Woman Power in Textile and Apparel Sales*. New York: Fairchild, 1979.

Solomon, Marc, and Norman Wiener. *Marketing and Advertising Careers*. New York: Franklin Watts, 1977.

U.S. Civil Service Commission. *Federal Career Directory, 1977–1979. A Guide for College Students*. Washington: U.S. Government Printing Office, 1977.

U.S. Department of Commerce/Industry and Trade Administration. *U.S. Industrial Outlook, with Projections to 1983 for 200 Industries*. Washington: U.S. Government Printing Office, 1979.

U.S. Department of Labor. *Dictionary of Occupational Titles*, 4th ed. Washington: U.S. Government Printing Office, 1977.

U.S. Department of Labor/Bureau of Labor Statistics. *Occupational Outlook for College Graduates*, 1978–1979 ed. Washington: U.S. Government Printing Office, 1978.

U.S. Department of Labor/Bureau of Labor Statistics. *Occupational Outlook Handbook*, 1978–1979 ed. Washington: U.S. Government Printing Office, 1978.

Wakin, Edward. *Jobs in Communications*. New York: Lothrop, Lee & Shepard, 1974.

Winefordner, David W. *Worker Trait Group Guide*. Bloomington, IL: McKnight, 1978.

CAREERS IN SMALL-STORE OWNERSHIP

Broom, Halsey N., and Justin G. Longenecker. *Small-Business Management*. Cincinnati: Southwestern Publishing, 1979.

MacFarlane, William N. *Principles of Small-Store Management*. New York: McGraw-Hill, 1977.

Packard, Sidney, and Alan J. Carron. *Start Your Own Store*. Englewood Cliffs, NJ: Prentice-Hall, 1982.

Shaffer, Harold, and Herbert Greenwald. *Independent Retailing*. Englewood Cliffs, NJ: Prentice-Hall, 1976.

GLOSSARY

GLOSSARY

AAAA (American Association of Advertising Agencies) The national association of advertising agencies.

A.B.O. (Association of Buying Offices) Organization of New York buying-office executives aiming to standardize and unify services available to stores; traditionally, the manager of the **N.R.M.A.** Merchandise Division is A.B.O. executive secretary.

accessories Articles worn or carried to complete a fashion apparel outfit, like jewelry, scarves, handbag, shoes.

ACTWU (Amalgamated Clothing and Textile Workers Union) Labor union of those engaged in the production of men's and boys' apparel and also textile products.

adaptation A copy of a design or style incorporating the outstanding features of the original, but not an exact duplicate. It is usually a **knock-off** with the features that have salability.

advertising Nonpersonal message in the media paid for by an identified sponsor. See **promotion; publicity.**

advertising agency commission Compensation by a medium to an advertising agency for its services in placement of advertising; usually a 15 percent discount on space and/or time cost. An agency also receives compensation from its clients in the form of charges for its services.

advertising allowance Money paid by a primary producer (textile manufacturer) to a manufacturer or retailer, or by a manufacturer to a retailer, for the purpose of advertising a brand or product, usually for the ultimate consumer.

Amalgamated Clothing and Textile Workers Union See **ACTWU.**

American Association of Advertising Agencies See **AAAA.**

apparel Men's, women's, and children's clothing.

Association of Buying Offices See **A.B.O.**

basic See **classic.**

boutique A small store or an area within a larger retail store featuring unique merchandise and ambience.

branch store Subsidiary store owned and operated by a parent or flagship store, generally in a suburban area.

brand An adopted name that identifies the goods of one producer or seller and distinguishes them from those of competitors.

caution French term for admission fee charged to trade customers for admission to haute couture houses.

chain store organization A group of stores selling essentially the same merchandise, all centrally owned and centrally merchandised from an office in a major market.

Chambre Syndicale de la Couture Parisienne The trade association of the haute couture (**high fashion**) houses of Paris.

check out A style that sells rapidly.

chop Go into production (women's apparel).

classic A fashion that remains popular over a long period of time; often referred to as a *basic.*

collection A higher-priced designer or manufacturer's group of garments for a specific season. Lower-priced groups are referred to as **lines.**

confined Merchandise that is sold by a manufacturer to a store on some exclusive basis in the store's trading area.

conglomerate A group of companies engaged in diverse businesses that are owned by a single parent organization.

consignment Selling goods to a retailer with a contract to take back unsold merchandise.

consumer demand The quantity of goods or service the consumer is willing to buy at varying prices.

consumer obsolescence The consumer's willingness to discard still-useful possessions in favor of something newer.

consumer orientation Knowing what ultimate users want, when they want it, at what price they can afford to pay for it, and in what quantities they can absorb it.

contractor A firm that does sewing or other operations for other producers. See **outside shop.**

converter A textile firm that buys **greige goods** from mills and applies print, color, or any form of finishing so that they are "ready for the needle."

cooperative advertising (co-op money) The amount of money contributed by a producer to help promote his goods. See **advertising allowance.**

cost price The price at which the manufacturer bills a store (showroom price) exclusive of trade discount or other buying arrangement that reduces the net cost of merchandise.

costume jewelry Relatively inexpensive jewelry, as opposed to jewelry of gold, silver, precious stones.

couture French for "needlework" or "sewing"; a synonym for **high fashion.**

couturier (couturière, feminine) French designer, usually one who owns a firm.

custom-made Apparel cut and finished to the specifications of an individual customer rather than mass-produced; opposite of **ready-to-wear.**

cutter The trade name for a manufacturer; also the person who cuts material in the manufacturing process.

cutting-up trade The manufacturing sector of the fashion industry.

cyclicality of fashion Return of a fashion of an earlier era with some difference in detailing.

department store A retail store employing at least 25 people and handling a wide variety of merchandise.

designer Person who chooses and arranges fabric, cut, and details to create a style.

direct advertising (direct mail) Printed advertising distributed directly to specific prospects, not through the media.

discount merchandising, discount store Low-margin retailing; selling merchandise below normal price levels and offering reduced services.

discretionary (supplementary) income Share of income not needed for essentials and therefore available for optional spending.

display Physical presentation of merchandise or ideas; for instance, in store windows.

exclusive merchandise See **confined.**

factor A private banker who buys accounts receivable.

fad A fashion briefly but intensely popular.

fashion That which is currently accepted by a substantial group of people at a given time and place. The broader interpretation goes beyond apparel and becomes synonymous with current culture.

fashion director The fashion expert of an organization who keeps it current with fashion developments and aids in presentation, merchandising, and other fashion and fashion-related activities.

fashion cycle The movement of a fashion from its rise to its abandonment. The configuration varies with the period of acceptance.

Fashion Group of Great Britain Association of English designers, founded in 1925.

fashion image Consumers' interpretation of a retailer's fashion importance, degree of leadership, and merchandising style.

flagship store The downtown or centrally located store of a group, the one where the executive, merchandising, and promotional staffs are located.

football selling Selling (retail) goods at discount prices.

Ford A style or design produced by many manufacturers at many different prices; "available from everyone."

franchised store An independently owned store that features the merchandise of a franchiser. The owner pays a percentage of the sales to the franchiser for the use of the name.

GATT (General Agreement on Tariffs and Trades) The 1947 codification of world trade rules.

general merchandise stores Retail organizations that include department stores, drygoods stores, most mail-order houses, and variety stores.

"going public" See **public ownership.**

greige goods Unbleached, unfinished fabrics as they come off the loom.

gross margin Difference between the cost of goods and sales.

hand The reaction of the sense of touch when a fabric is held in the hand.

haute couture The dressmaking houses in Paris that belong to the Chambre Syndicale and whose designers create original designs. By extension, the Paris houses and any others that create original designs that become **high fashion;** also the designs themselves.

high fashion, high style Those styles or designs whose acceptance is limited to fashion leaders; designs that are usually at the introductory stage of the fashion cycle.

hot item A style that is selling in quantity.

ILGWU (International Ladies' Garment Workers' Union) Labor union of those engaged in the production of women's and children's apparel.

impulse goods Merchandise susceptible to spur-of-the-moment consumer purchase decisions.

inseparables Coordinated apparel items designed to be sold together rather than as individual units.

inside shop An apparel producer with all production functions within his own facilities.

institutional advertising Paid messages used to create and maintain a company's reputation or image rather than to promote the sale of specific items.

integrated operation A mill or centrally owned group of mills that performs all processes of textile fabric production.

interior display Retail-store displays that feature merchandise on counters, in cases, on ledges, walls, and columns.

International Ladies' Garment Workers' Union See **ILGWU.**

inventory Noun: stock on hand; verb: to take a physical count of stock.

jobber A middleman between producer and commercial consumer.

job lot   Assorted or miscellaneous merchandise, a collection of leftovers available at a reduced price.

knock-off   A copy of a higher-priced style; see **adaptation.**

licensing   Giving a manufacturer permission to use a designer's name or designs; the licensor receives a percentage of wholesale sales.

line   A moderate- or popular-priced apparel manufacturer's group of styles for a season. See **collection.**

line-for-line copy   An exact copy of a foreign **high fashion** style.

main store   See **flagship store.**

markdown   Reduction in price of merchandise; difference between original and new lowered price.

market   1. Group of people within geographic boundaries who have the potential to purchase products. 2. Place where commercial consumers (retailers, for example) buy merchandise.

marketing   The business of planning, pricing, promoting, and distributing consumer-wanted goods or services.

marketing mix   The blending together into an integrated program of the four basic marketing elements: product, price, promotion, distribution.

markup (mark-on)   Difference between the cost price as billed (before cash discount) and the retail price.

mass production   Factory production of merchandise in quantity as opposed to hand or custom production.

merchandising   Planning, buying, and selling, not manufacturing.

national brands   Manufacturers' brands distributed nationwide.

National Retail Merchants Association   See **N.R.M.A.**

neighborhood shopping center   Usually a group of small shops, anchored by a supermarket or smaller food store, occupying 5 to 10 acres and including less than 100,000 square feet of selling space.

net profit   Gross margin less all business expenses.

N.R.M.A. (National Retail Merchants Association)   A nonprofit, voluntary trade group that specializes in the interests of department, chain, and specialty stores. Headquarters are in New York City; branch offices are in Washington, San Francisco, and Paris.

off price   A price lower than the original price, or below normal price; for example, the retail value established by a discount store.

open-to-buy   The amount of money a buyer can spend on merchandise within a given period.

opening   The first showing of a producer's seasonal **line** or **collection.**

outside shop   An apparel producer that uses **contractors** to sew garments or cut fabric.

"peacock revolution"   Increased interest in men's fashions in the 1970s.

piecework   Unit basis for paying workers.

prêt-à-porter   French for **ready-to-wear.**

price range   Price points from the lowest to highest levels in a merchandise classification.

primary market   Producers of the raw materials of fashion apparel, such as leather and fabric.

private brand   A brand owned by a middleman, wholesaler, or retailer in contrast to brands owned by a producer.

promotion   Activity designed to encourage the purchase of a particular product or group of products.

protectionism   Reduction, limitation, or exclusion of imported goods.

public ownership   Company shares (stock) are available to any purchaser.

public relations   The activities of an organization designed to enhance its image or the image of a client.

publicity   Media information about a company or goods that is carried free of charge because of its intrinsic interest.

readership   The number of people who read a publication, not necessarily the number of subscribers.

ready-to-wear   Mass-produced apparel.

regional shopping center   A shopping complex with 50 to 100 stores, including at least one major department store branch.

reorder number   A style that sells well to the ultimate consumer and is repurchased by store buyers.

resident buying office   Service organization located in a major market to represent member stores that have their own buyers.

resource   Term used by retailers for manufacturers, wholesalers, distributors.

retailing   The business of buying at wholesale and selling at retail to the ultimate consumer; all the activities of merchandising and the administrative functions of receiving merchandise and placing it in the hands of the consumer.

runner   A style that sells well over a period of time and is reordered frequently.

sales agent   Commission salesperson, usually for textile manufacturers.

secondary market   The producers of finished apparel.

section work   Production system in which each worker sews one segment of a garment.

self-service   Retail method whereby merchandise is arranged and displayed so that customers can select purchases without the aid of a salesperson.

showing   A fashion show.

specialty store   Retail establishment that handles a fairly narrow category of goods, like men's apparel, women's apparel, shoes, and the like.

stock turn   Number of times during a given period that inventory is sold out and replaced.

style   A garment with certain characteristics that distinguish it from other garments.

style piracy   The copying of the style of another manufacturer without permission.

trading area   The geographical area from which most of an organization's trade is drawn.

traffic   The number of people who enter a store and are exposed to its merchandise offerings.

ultimate consumer   The end user; one who purchases a product or service for personal purposes rather than for resale.

vendor   A seller, a resource for a retailer.

INDEX

Boldface numerals denote illustrations;
italic numerals denote charts or tables.